Keep your balance!

Joel F

THE
CEO
TIGHTROPE

HOW *to* MASTER *the* BALANCING ACT

of a SUCCESSFUL CEO

JOEL TRAMMELL

GREENLEAF
BOOK GROUP PRESS

Published by Greenleaf Book Group Press
Austin, Texas
www.gbgpress.com

Distributed by Greenleaf Book Group

For ordering information or special discounts for bulk purchases, please contact Greenleaf Book Group at PO Box 91869, Austin, TX 78709, 512.891.6100.

Design, cover design, and composition by Greenleaf Book Group
Cover image: 2jenn, 2014. Used under license from Shutterstock.com

For permission to reprint copyrighted material, grateful acknowledgment is made to the following:
The Copyright Clearance Center Inc. on behalf of John Wiley and Sons: From *The 2R Manager: When to Relate, When to Require, and How to Do Both Effectively* by Peter E. Friedes. Copyright © 2002 by John Wiley and Sons.

Cataloging-in-Publication data
Trammell, Joel.
    The CEO tightrope : how to master the balancing act of a successful CEO / Joel Trammell.—First edition.
        pages ; cm
    Issued also as an ebook.
    Includes bibliographical references and index.
    ISBN: 978-1-62634-106-7
    1. Chief executive officers. 2. Executive ability. 3. Leadership. 4. Success in business. I. Title.
HD38.2 .T73 2014
658.42   2014938278

Part of the Tree Neutral® program, which offsets the number of trees consumed in the production and printing of this book by taking proactive steps, such as planting trees in direct proportion to the number of trees used: www.treeneutral.com

TreeNeutral®

Printed in the United States of America on acid-free paper
14 15 16 17 18 19   10 9 8 7 6 5 4 3 2 1
First Edition

CONTENTS

Stepping Onto the Rope   1

Balancing the Five Responsibilities. 3

Responsibility vs. Control 15

Expertise vs. Need 31

Own the Vision   41

Planning vs. Action vs. Results 47

Leadership vs. Cheerleading 57

Flexibility vs. Focus 67

Provide the Proper Resources   75

Budgeting vs. Opportunistic Investment 83

Growth vs. Profitability 95

Recruiting vs. Hiring. 103

Talent vs. Experience/Knowledge 121

Saving vs. Trading Up 137

Build the Culture   149

Reward vs. Threat 153

Rules-Based vs. Values-Based 163

Requiring vs. Relating 175

Make Decisions   183

    Deciding vs. Building Consensus. 191

    Employees vs. Customers vs. Shareholders. 205

    Department vs. Department 217

Deliver Performance   225

    Trust vs. Verify 237

    Internal vs. External 247

    Personal Needs vs. Company Needs 257

How to Improve as CEO   265

Prepare Yourself for Tough, Rewarding Work   269

    Thanks 273

    Notes 275

    Index 279

    About the Author 292

STEPPING

ONTO

THE ROPE

BALANCING THE FIVE
RESPONSIBILITIES

I woke up in a cold sweat. My wife had given me a good shove to stop me from grinding my teeth and keeping her awake. I couldn't help it. The $13,000 check I had received for computers purchased by a guy in Maine had bounced like a rubber ball. When I had tried to contact the customer to see if there had been an honest mistake, I found that he had already skipped town. At this point in the life of my small business, $13,000 represented a third of the profits for the year. It was as if someone had kicked me in the gut and then laughed as they walked away. Welcome to my first real test as a CEO.

Why had I shipped such a relatively large order without verifying payment? Wasn't it obviously a risky bet? Well, the customer had placed a number of orders in the past, paying with a cashier's check, which was our policy at the time (this was long before PayPal or other instant payment options). When he requested that we accept a business check, I didn't think it was much of a risk. It seemed clear to me that he was building a solid business and being able to write checks would allow him to place more orders, allowing me to make more money. I was balancing the risk of a bad check with the reward of increased revenue.

That sleepless night happened more than twenty years ago. Since then, I have led several more companies, made deals worth hundreds of millions of dollars, and made more bad calls. But no decision has left me with a sicker feeling in my stomach than accepting that $13,000 check. Analyzing options and assessing risks and rewards are just two of the many things I have learned over the last two decades about the precarious tightrope balancing act required of a CEO.

Every CEO faces this challenge in his or her career: balancing the need for revenue, growth, and sustainability with the risks inherent in certain decisions. Some deals are tempting but could be too risky. Some customers offer growth but could damage your business. Some leaders seem sharp and driven but could diminish your culture. Some projects need funding and focus but may not deliver the same return as other projects competing for attention.

These are the decisions that make the CEO job so different from any other job in a business. They require us to take full responsibility for outcomes and events over which we have little control. We are responsible for the whole enterprise and must balance a massive array of needs, demands, interests, and perspectives if we want to be successful. We are asked to meet the needs of employees, customers, and shareholders. We are the arbiters of internal disputes between departments and divisions. We have to be on the lookout for leaders who can add the right ingredient to balance the executive team. Every day we have to fight to escape the draw of tactical activities that cause us to neglect strategic issues.

To take the tightrope analogy even further, not only are we weighed down by competing interests, needs, and demands for our time, we are also chased by the expectations of ever-increasing results. You can't find a point of balance and then stand still—on a tightrope, that's barely even possible. Whether you are a public CEO trying to make the quarterly number or a small business owner trying to provide for his family, the expectation is that the business must always grow and prosper.

And while all of these fires are burning, we are the only employees in the organization who have no day-to-day boss to provide guidance or to act as a sounding board when we are making tough decisions. As CEOs we are expected to self-diagnose our weaknesses, because rarely will subordinates directly point out our shortcomings. If we need guidance, we are expected to hire a coach or a consultant. But often the resources are not available, we worry that the outcomes won't justify the investment, and we aren't sure what kind of help we need anyway.

All of these challenges and many more point to the huge difference between the job of the CEO and any other executive in a company. And as the title of this book implies, the failure to keep the organization in a state of semi-balance and constantly moving forward often leads to serious consequences—you could fall to your death, and take the company with you.

Balance is the theme of this book, but on a tightrope balance is never actually achieved. Tightrope walkers avoid falling off by constantly making small adjustments as they move forward. The better the tightrope walker, the more natural the corrections appear. In contrast, we have all seen CEOs who make dramatic moves in one direction and then the other in a constant fight to solve the problem of the day. Eventually, they fall.

Like tightrope walkers, the best CEOs appear to be doing the least while moving the business forward—the better the CEO, the more subtle the adjustments, and the smoother the progress. And progress is critical. One of the enduring truths about running a business is that the situation is never static. Staying on the correct path requires constant movement toward one side and the other. How do we, as CEOs or aspiring CEOs, achieve this? By developing a better understanding of the critical roles the CEO plays; by learning how to balance competing needs, interests, and priorities in order to succeed in those roles; and by learning to ask reflective questions that will push us to learn and improve.

The goal of this book is to help make your CEO journey look as smooth as a Sunday stroll. Because the better you are as CEO, the less you will *have* to do each day and the more you will be *able* to accomplish.

WE AREN'T WELL PREPARED

"Success is a lousy teacher.
It seduces smart people into thinking they can't lose."

—BILL GATES

The fact that special challenges exist for anyone who sits in the CEO chair is not news. Most people accept that it is a difficult job that requires a wide range of skills. What is surprising is how little new CEOs understand about the job before they take it on, how little time they spend studying and preparing. Where are the courses that teach a person how to be a CEO? There's little content among the vast quantity of business books and research published every year—even by the leadership and management gurus—to address the unique challenges of the CEO job. If you want to learn more about marketing, sales, accounting, or any other major area of business specialization, opportunities are plentiful. The problem is a business cannot be viewed only as a combination of individual parts. Running a good business requires interweaving unique specialties in just the right way to maximize productivity and profit. It's big-picture balancing.

Many people think that the CEO job is just the next progression after being a senior executive in a business. Only occasionally are people groomed for the CEO position, though, and moved around the company to gain a breadth of knowledge and experience. How many times have those people seen all the pieces that came together for a CEO to make a decision? Instead, people find themselves in the CEO chair either because they started a business and became CEO or were selected for the position after demonstrating significant expertise in a particular functional area of a business.

Entrepreneurs are often better at—or at least more interested in—starting companies than running them long term. And when they first start out, they typically have little experience to draw on. I started my first company when I was twenty-five. What did I know about being a CEO? Only what I learned day by day.

And as for the second path, I would argue that the CEO job is actually not all that similar to other executive roles. Let's look at the typical career progression of a sales executive. She starts out in a bag-carrying role, selling a product. With success in that role she is promoted to be the manager of a group of salespeople. After many years of climbing the corporate ladder, this former salesperson might reach the pinnacle of her sales career by being named vice president of worldwide sales. At each step along the way she has developed more and more expertise in the area of sales and sales management. As VP, the problems that reach her desk almost always involve an issue that she has experienced at some point during her career. Her significant experience means that she is often the expert in the room and while she may face tough decisions, she doesn't necessarily have to depend on someone else to explain the issue. Her success will often depend on her ability to pass along her experience to her team and to train them to do the same things that made her successful.

Now imagine what happens when that person is one day made CEO. Most of the issues that come to her desk now will be issues with which she does not have the relevant expertise and experience. She will be asked to make decisions in areas as diverse as human resources, information technology, real estate, legal, technology, and many others. Her success will depend not on passing her experience along but in leveraging the expertise of others both inside and outside the organization. It will require her to think about the implications of her decisions beyond just a single group in the company to all shareholders, employees, and customers.

Before Carly Fiorina became CEO of Hewlett Packard, in July 1999, she had cut her teeth in marketing. It was no surprise, given her background, that she focused externally in the CEO role. She introduced numerous new strategies, including the contentious acquisition of Compaq. She spent much of her time in the public eye building her personal brand as well as the HP name. All of this might have been great if HP's biggest challenge had been a lack of awareness in the market. Unfortunately for Ms. Fiorina, the problems at HP were internal and operational in nature, as the actions of the next CEO, Mark Hurd, clearly demonstrated. By focusing on reducing costs and increasing efficiencies, Hurd was able to deliver exceptional performance. The company's profits increased for twenty-two straight quarters under Hurd and its stock price doubled.

When you consider the tremendously successful careers of most people who get a shot at the CEO position, it's amazing how many fail, by being fired or pushed out. In today's high-speed business environment, shareholders have little patience for long-term plans if performance in the short term isn't strong. The average life span of an "elite" CEO—the leader of one of the world's largest companies—is about five years, but a high percentage of CEOs are out in less than two years.[1] The numbers vary from study to study, but none of them allow for much learning on the job.

Lack of training for the role is one of the key factors in the rise of the executive coaching industry. Several studies have shown that it takes about 10,000 hours of practice at an activity to perform at a world-class level. Even Michael Jordan was cut from his high school basketball team before he mastered the skills necessary to be a star player. Unfortunately for the newly minted CEO, his practice occurs in a very public forum and his success can dramatically affect the lives of all the employees as well as shareholders and customers.

Obviously the CEO role varies depending on the size and characteristics of the organization. In the smallest of organizations the CEO wears many hats—from individual contributor, to manager, to one-man board. At somewhere between twenty and fifty employees, a company begins to require a systematic approach to management and a full-time CEO role emerges. Growth is also a key factor in the approach to the CEO role. A one-hundred-person company doubling in revenue every year will present very different demands from a one-thousand-person company that is stagnant. With every new CEO position, even experienced CEOs have to shift their perspective.

Yet the challenge all CEOs face is that to build and grow a world-class company, we must be strong in every area of the business—not experts, but well informed—and fulfill the responsibilities that only we can perform. The CEO is responsible for making sure that every group is delivering at the highest possible level. Each company is only as strong as its weakest link. Understanding how to balance performance across all departments requires a CEO with broad experience, big-picture vision, and an understanding of what the job requires.

THE JOB VS. THE JOB VS. THE JOB . . .

Many new CEOs struggle because they do not have a clear picture of what they should do in the job, the key responsibilities they should prioritize. Before taking the position for the first time, they have observed only a small fraction of the things a CEO does and can be overwhelmed by all the demands on their time once they are in the fray. It's dangerously easy to fall into a tactical routine, confronting each problem as it comes your way. But being reactive rather than proactive is not the path to building a great company. Instead, successful CEOs spend the majority of their time proactively fulfilling five key responsibilities related to the company vision, resources, culture, decision making, and performance—responsibilities that are owned primarily by the CEO.

Own the Vision

The CEO must be able to communicate the strategy, mission, and vision of the company—where it's going and why—to all constituents. She must be able to communicate it at the appropriate level for employees, customers, and shareholders, and ensure that everyone within the organization is clear on how the direction impacts his or her job and daily responsibilities. Other people may help create the strategic vision, but the CEO must tell the story of that vision in a way that is clear, engaging, and exciting. And everything the CEO does must support the vision.

Provide the Proper Resources

The CEO is responsible for determining resource needs and allocating those resources within the company. The two most important resources for the typical business are capital and people. The CEO must make both available in the proper quantities and at the right time for the company to be successful.

All executives have experience dealing with budgets and allocating resources. However, the CEO job requires balancing resources between groups and initiatives that are not necessarily comparable in terms of how they influence the company's progress toward goals. Being good at making these decisions requires a deep understanding of all aspects of the business, combined with a clear vision.

While balancing capital is hard, building the best team is even harder. Each person in your organization is a unique individual with different strengths, weaknesses, and expectations. Success as CEO will depend more on your ability to acquire and maximize human talent than any other skill.

Balancing resources is hard work and will often leave you comparing apples and oranges, but it is a key role that only the CEO can perform.

Build the Culture

Culture is the set of shared attitudes, goals, behaviors, and values that characterize a group. It is how things get done in the company, and it influences the entirety of the employee experience—and therefore the customer experience. Every organized group of individuals develops a culture—whether explicitly recognized or not—and the CEO must constantly observe and manage for the culture he wants. Just like the parents in a family, the CEO sets the tone, and what he rewards and allows will drive the culture. Culture is a popular topic in the business press, but articles often focus on perks such as free food or generous vacation policies. A company can have lots of neat perks and still have a lousy culture that increases turnover rates and delivers poor performance. In my opinion the most critical word in the definition of culture is *values*. It is the CEO's job to ensure that a company's values are applied consistently from top to bottom, across all departments. No person or group can be exempt.

Make Good Decisions

The new CEO is often surprised by the breadth of the issues she is forced to deal with—one minute discussing a new product, the next a building lease, and the next a legal issue. It is impossible for anyone to be an expert in all aspects of a business. However, the one thing the CEO *is* responsible for is *making a decision*. The buck stops at the CEO's desk. That is the job. If you don't like making decisions when you aren't sure of the correct answer, don't take a CEO job, because this might just be the biggest part of it. Many problems require a solution that impacts multiple departments and only the CEO can make decisions across the organization. Everyone else in the organization can pass the buck from time to time, but the CEO must make the final decision when no one else will or can.

Deliver Performance

Everyone agrees that the CEO is ultimately responsible for the performance of the company, and so the CEO must take an active role in driving that performance. He has to be in touch enough with the core business functions to ensure proper execution. He is the interface between internal operations and external stakeholders, which means that he has to ascertain the expectations for performance from different stakeholders (shareholders may be concerned about stock price while the community is concerned about job creation), interpret those expectations for internal teams, and then drive and refine metrics that reflect the true performance of the business—because you get what you measure. Combined with those demands is the need to maintain awareness of the industry and market. Performance in a competitive business environment is relative. If your company is growing at 10 percent while the market is growing at 25 percent, you are clearly underperforming; the same 10 percent growth in a declining market might be exceptional. Regardless of the circumstances, the stakeholders, or the size or type of business, the CEO sets the bar for the level of performance the business achieves.

—

The CEO's job sounds almost easy with just five things to worry about. Of course, I haven't mentioned emails, meetings, public appearances, or the many other ways that CEOs are asked to spend their time. It can be easy to sit back and let the job come to you; there will always be tactical things that can be done. Successful CEOs plan how they will spend their time in order to focus on the important responsibilities, not just the urgent to-dos. To successfully grow a company, the CEO must have a clear picture of how to fulfill the responsibilities that only he can fulfill, how to prioritize them, and how to find balance when dealing with the onslaught of issues that arise in each of these areas.

SUCCESSFULLY BALANCING
THE RESPONSIBILITIES OF THE CEO

In a recent survey, seventy-five members of the Stanford Graduate School of Business's Advisory Council rated self-awareness as the most important capability for leaders to develop.[2] Self-awareness gives you the ability to observe the secondary effects of your actions, to understand and mitigate your areas of weakness, and to leverage your strengths appropriately. This capability is more important for CEOs than for any other leader. We have the only job in a company without a direct feedback mechanism, without someone assigned to provide guidance on how well we are doing the job. And we cannot expect that kind of feedback to come from other leaders or employees in the organization. There's a great scene in my favorite business movie, *Barbarians at the Gate* (from the book of the same name), in which the CEO asks if people have heard a joke and his right-hand man begins to laugh at the joke before the CEO even tells it. As CEO, your jokes will be funnier, your ideas will be better, you will be smarter—at least according to the people you work with every day. Even people who aren't consciously currying favor will measure their comments in your presence. They may not praise you constantly, but they won't likely tell you where you're falling down, either.

This book is written from my experience in the CEO chair at one company or another for most of the last twenty-plus years. I wanted to do well, and so I studied business literature and research and I worked hard to be that self-aware leader. In recent years, I have begun teaching a course for CEOs and writing about the challenges, pairing theory with real-world observations. My goal is to help you become more self-aware as you navigate the challenges of the five primary responsibilities, section by section.

For each section, I lay a foundation for fulfilling each of the responsibilities, from communicating to engage different stakeholders, to assessing your human resources, to using what we know about neuropsychology to build a high-performance culture, to identifying the four villains of decision making, to setting goals to build alignment. Then, in each chapter I explore issues that can pull you off balance when you're trying to meet your responsibilities, and offer an approach for making the minor adjustments that will keep you moving forward. In the rest of this section, I'll tackle the universal struggles between responsibility versus control and expertise versus need. Influence and using our time to fill the right roles are the keys to finding balance in these areas and to successfully meeting the demands of all of our responsibilities.

Throughout the book, I use "failure modes" I have observed—when we lean too far in one direction or another and fall off the wire—to help you envision what it looks like to be pulled off balance. While these failure modes are exaggerated, I also include stories of CEOs who have exhibited some of these traits, including myself, and questions listed under the "Finding Your Balance" heading to help you consider whether *you* are in danger. Try to get your direct reports to anonymously answer the same questions and examine whether your answers are consistent with theirs. Be honest when answering the questions and you may find areas you need to work on, or a missing element at the top of your organization that you can look for in a new leader. While we are ultimately responsible in these five areas, and focusing on our own growth will improve our chances of success, we can also surround ourselves with smart, engaged people who balance our strengths and weaknesses.

Over the years I have developed some definite opinions on how to think about the job of CEO. I have had both home runs and strikeouts along the way. Yet I still often feel like I don't know the right answer in a given situation; I do think I have learned to ask the right questions, though. And I believe that asking the right questions is the key to improving.

I hope this book can make a small contribution to your education and success by helping you ask the right questions.

RESPONSIBILITY VS. CONTROL

*"Few things help an individual more than to place responsibility upon
them and to let them know that you trust them."*

—BOOKER T. WASHINGTON

I spent my first four years after college in the U.S. Navy teaching at Naval
Nuclear Power School. The military has an advantage from a leadership
perspective in that what members of the armed forces do *is* a matter of life
and death. Because of that, everybody understands the importance of performance, especially from commanding officers. The commanding officer
of a naval vessel at sea is in many ways similar to a CEO—held to a high
standard of responsibility for the performance of the ship, with nowhere to
turn if things go wrong.

One of the senior officers I met was given command of a submarine
group, responsible for not just one submarine but eight. Two weeks after this
officer was put in charge, a submarine from his group ran aground in the
Pacific. The whole purpose of a submarine depends on its operating quietly
and out of sight. When a submarine runs aground, it becomes a sitting duck
for an enemy attack. Grounding a submarine is one of the worst mistakes a
commander can make and is a huge black mark on his record.

It was no surprise, then, when the commander of the submarine was
relieved of command and forced to retire. What might surprise you, though,
was the black mark on the group commander's record. He was not on the

submarine, he had taken command only two weeks before the incident, and he had never even met the sub's commander. Despite all of this, he was still responsible for the performance of the group. After the incident, he received no other promotions and retired a few years later.

As CEO you are responsible for every aspect of the performance of your company, whether you are there to witness it or not. The stress of living with this level of responsibility while having little control can bring out the best and worst in us. Yet there is a way forward that allows us to deal with the tension, if we can overcome our natural tendencies.

THE TOTAL-CONTROL CEO
AND THE MASTER STRATEGIST

When faced with the intense burden of responsibility and the lack of control, we have a natural human tendency to seek control in order to mitigate the risk. The desire for total control by a CEO can cause a whole host of unhealthy behaviors and lead to a highly dysfunctional company. The term micromanagement was coined in the late '70s to describe this general approach to management. While it can happen at any level in the organization, it takes its most harmful form at the CEO level. The micromanaging CEO commits the sin of hubris. He believes that he can do any job in the company better than the person performing it and if people would just follow his instructions correctly everything would go well. He seeks control because he is trying to protect himself from repercussions when performance doesn't meet expectations. So whenever a problem arises, the total-control CEO must find a scapegoat to maintain his air of infallibility. His first instinct is to whip and berate people over any mistake.

The mental image I always have when I see this behavior is of a mule pulling a plow with a farmer in tow. The mule is assumed to be dumb and the job of the mule is assumed to be easy, so if the mule doesn't behave properly, you whip the mule. Mule going too slow, whip the mule. Mule going too fast, whip the mule. In 1960, Douglas McGregor presented the Theory X and Theory Y management styles in his book *The Human Side of Enterprise*. Today these styles still hold, although Theory X has been losing ground in recent decades. The total-control CEO tends to be in the Theory X camp: authoritarian, believing that his job is to "counteract an inherent human tendency to avoid work." Employees will certainly sabotage his performance through sheer laziness, so he must whip them to get anything done.

It is often easy to identify total-control CEOs just by observing what decisions require their approval. No decision is too small to be left to others. The color of the walls, the look of the business cards, and almost any expense must all flow through the top office. Because this behavior is rooted in their fear of making a mistake, the approval process will often become drawn out as they carefully weigh the pros and cons on even the simplest issue. CEOs who have come up the ranks by building on a particular area of expertise may exhibit these symptoms of total control in just that one area.

This type of behavior stifles the organization. First, good people want to be able to own their area and take responsibility for what they do. When the CEO is constantly dropping in and taking charge, it causes even the best employees to disengage. And the entire organization wastes valuable time waiting for decisions that should have been made quickly and at a much lower level. The best CEOs understand that leaders must be allowed to take ownership and be given the autonomy to make decisions that might be different from what the CEO would decide. Later in the book I explore how to balance the right amount of freedom with the proper level of supervision.

While no one likes the total-control CEO, it's also possible to lean too far in the other direction. Because micromanagement became a popular topic in business books and MBA programs, many executives believe they must avoid it at all cost. For these CEOs, the lack of control, the high level of responsibility, and the fear of being labeled a micromanager cause them to totally disengage from the day-to-day activities and results of the organization. They figure, "If I can't control everything, I shouldn't worry about any of the details." This type of CEO often evolves into the master strategist, believing that coming up with a winning strategy is all that matters. After they have revealed the grand strategy, they can sit back and watch. They are so removed from the day-to-day flow of the organization that they don't see a problem developing until it is too late. Then, like the total-control CEO, they blame the employee for failing to do the simple things necessary to execute their brilliant strategy.

The image that comes to mind whenever I encounter a master strategist at work is one that has been passed around the Internet. A donkey is connected to a cart that has been so overloaded that it tipped backward, leaving the donkey stranded six feet in the air. Master strategists put all their focus on loading the cart. When the donkey is left stranded—when employees are unable to execute the strategy because the CEO has abandoned other responsibilities—the CEO's first reaction is to blame the donkey!

SEEK TO GROW YOUR INFLUENCE

Clearly I have painted two extremes. The question is how we balance the inherent tension between having total responsibility with having very limited control. The key word that comes to mind for me is influence, which is defined as the act or power of producing an effect without apparent exertion of force or direct exercise of command. To be great, the modern CEO must have tremendous influence over his organization while in some sense seeming to do very little. This is a far cry from the very active and commanding CEO who is often portrayed in movies and the press. Recall the image of the tightrope walker I presented in the introduction, whose constant adjustments are often invisible to the audience. Another way to think of this subtle but active influence is by picturing a jockey riding a thoroughbred racehorse. The jockey and horse must work together in a consistent rhythm. While the thoroughbred is running at forty miles per hour, no one would say the jockey is in total control of the horse. But he does have influence. The best jockeys know how to move the horse around the track and subtly position it for victory. While they carry a whip, they will only deploy it as a last resort. Modern CEOs should think of themselves as jockeys trying to position their teams for maximum performance.

The influence approach to leadership is related to McGregor's Theory Y management style. Rather than being autocratic, the Theory Y leader works on the assumption that people work in order to satisfy their need for achievement, and she "assumes that people will exercise self-direction and self-control in the achievement of organizational objectives to the degree they are committed to those objectives." The purpose of the influence we exert is to build commitment to the objectives that will move the organization forward.

When you recognize that influence is the main method of action for the modern CEO, the logical question is "How do I maximize my influence?" I believe that CEOs have three major tools—the 3C's—that they wield in trying to influence the people and teams in their organization: credibility, competence, and caring. Exhibiting the 3C's consistently is the key to effectively fulfilling our responsibilities.

Credibility

"If you once forfeit the confidence of your fellow citizens, you can never regain their respect and esteem. You may fool all of the people some of the time; you can even fool some of the people all the time; but you cannot fool all of the people all of the time."

—ABRAHAM LINCOLN

When you communicate, do people believe that you are telling them the objective truth? If they do, then you have credibility. To maintain credibility you have to tell the truth 100 percent of the time. Telling the truth 90 percent of the time is not much better than telling the truth 10 percent of the time. It only takes a few instances of delivering non-credible statements to totally lose your credibility. And once you lose your credibility, it becomes almost impossible to lead effectively.

Many CEOs start out with the best of intentions, planning to shoot straight with everyone in the organization. When things are going well, it's easy to give everyone the good news about growing revenue and profits, the success of a new initiative, or a new client that could change the trajectory of the company. But when things turn south, CEOs often are reticent to share the negatives. They cannot face the responsibility of leading people through tough times, or the realization that they may have no control, so they try to pretend that it isn't happening, hoping that things will improve. When cutbacks and layoffs come after the CEO has claimed that everything is okay, all credibility with employees is lost. Regaining credibility becomes almost impossible in this situation, and a change of leadership may be the only answer.

Because credibility is attached to the person and not the job, CEOs can also lose credibility by their actions outside of the company. While being CEO doesn't mean that you give up all of your privacy, it does mean that you can't do things in your private life that call into question your ethics or honesty. People tend to believe that a person who is dishonest in her private life will likely be dishonest in her professional life. Because credibility is such an important tool for the CEO, anything that calls into question her honesty will be highly detrimental to her ability to lead. This doesn't mean that CEOs can't make mistakes. Employees understand that everyone is human and prone to human issues; but the CEO can't hide behind that excuse when it comes to integrity. If he makes a mistake, he must quickly come forward and take responsibility by being absolutely honest about the problem.

While the media might have us believing that it's difficult to find a CEO whose behavior is guided by ethics, integrity, and honesty, that isn't the case. In fact, I believe respected leaders are more common than those on the other side of the scale. Unfortunately, they are often just less interesting to read about—with some obvious exceptions. Leaders like Tony Hsieh of Zappos and Howard Schultz of Starbucks are commonly highlighted. But consider Dan Amos, CEO of Aflac since 1990. Aflac often appears on "best places to work" lists because of Amos's focus on ethical and socially responsible business practices. For examples from smaller companies, take a look at the WorldBlu List of Most Democratic

Workplaces and what people have to say about the leaders of those companies, particularly regarding transparency.

However, it is also deceptively easy for any leader to make one "small misstep" that becomes a major credibility killer.

BEWARE OF BECOMING PINOCCHIO

In January 2012 Yahoo hired Scott Thompson as CEO. Thompson came from PayPal, where he had worked since 2005 in several roles, including CTO. To many outside observers, the hire made sense—it brought an experienced executive to a company that had lost its edge. The company needed a CEO who would stabilize the organization and make it a relevant Internet property. The market was valuing the company at less than the sum of its parts, despite the fact that it possessed numerous valuable assets.

Dan Loeb, an activist investor, had taken an interest in the company and had been campaigning for the board to sell off some of the key assets to bring higher value to shareholders. He wasn't happy about Thompson's hire. Unfortunately for the new CEO, Loeb quickly went from being a minor nuisance to a major headache. In May 2012 he sent a letter to the board indicating that he had reason to believe that Thompson did not have the computer science degree that his official Yahoo biography and SEC filings indicated he possessed. The board quickly determined that Loeb was correct, although it was unclear how the information had made its way into the bio.

Thompson suddenly had a credibility problem. The media and online communities pounced. Somebody found an interview in which Thompson responded to a question that cited the computer science degree in a way that clearly implied he had the degree.

While the board initially tried to defend their hiring decision, it was obvious that the CEO's days were numbered and he resigned a few days later. No person or media outlet showed proof that Scott Thompson had ever specifically claimed to have the degree, but it didn't matter. Credibility is binary; you either have it or you don't.

I have seen situations like Thompson's happen again and again, and I have almost fallen into a similar trap. As CEO I have often had people write short bios to go along with a speaking engagement or to put on a web page. The people writing the blurb always want to make the person sound as important and qualified as possible, so they tend to embellish past jobs. During my career I worked at AMD as an IT manager for about a year and a half. One day when reviewing my bio for a speaking event I noticed a line that said I had "served in executive positions at AMD." I was about as far away from an executive at AMD as I could be, but someone felt the need to spruce up my resume. I could have ignored it, but I made sure it was corrected. It would have been easy for that line to become a standard part of my bio. I wouldn't be surprised if the same thing happened to Scott Thompson. Someone added a sentence along the way and he just never called it out.

While it may seem unfair to lose a job over such a small mistake, successful leaders require and demand absolute credibility in all their dealings.

FINDING YOUR BALANCE

1. Is there any discoverable fact about you personally that would cause your team to question your credibility?

2. Have others ever exaggerated your accomplishments? How did you respond?

3. Has there ever been a time, in your communications as CEO, when you shaded the facts in order to provide a more positive spin on performance?

4. Is the message you communicate to your stakeholders ever different from the message you send to your closest team members?

5. Have employees ever heard you skirt the truth with external stakeholders or customers?

Competence

People respect leaders who are knowledgeable and proficient in their chosen area of business, so competence is a necessary part of influence. And without it, it's possible to be credible—people believe what you say—and yet not to be seen as competent—people believe that you are wrong, ill-informed, or make poor judgments. If people don't trust your judgment, you will have little influence over their behavior. "Yeah, yeah," they'll think as you talk—and then they'll go right back to doing what they were doing, the way they were doing it. The CEO may be sitting in the Captain's chair, but every time he shouts an order, people will ignore it.

To be seen as competent, CEOs need to show a deep understanding of the company's business model—how the product is bought and sold—as well as how the product is made or how the service is constructed and delivered. They need to show a willingness to learn and adapt. And they need to prove that they understand the responsibilities of the job.

I often talk to people about their jobs—I'm curious that way—and I always like to ask specifically about their view of their CEO. I almost never hear that the CEO is incompetent, because to make that judgment employees would have to have a clear understanding of the CEO's job. But just because they can't name the five responsibilities I'm exploring in this book doesn't mean they don't expect a CEO to do those things. I often hear, "He's a nice guy, but he just can't make a decision." Or "He doesn't really understand what my team and I do." Or "He keeps setting goals but nothing seems to happen when we fail to meet them." Or "I just wish I knew where we're headed." Comments like these and many others I've heard relate directly to the CEO's ability to do the core functions of the job. People understand innately that if you are put in charge of an organization, you are responsible for owning and communicating the vision, providing the proper resources, building the culture, making decisions, and delivering performance by executing the plan. They feel the vacuum when these things aren't happening—if the CEO doesn't do them, nobody else will. And they feel the squeeze when these responsibilities are handled with an iron grip. While people may not keep a checklist, they will quickly recognize when a CEO is failing to effectively live up to these responsibilities.

Throughout the book, I'll provide approaches and tools that can help you build and exhibit your competence as CEO. New CEOs—new to the role or to the company—face a special challenge, though. Despite what I wrote in the introduction about the dangers of arriving as CEO with expertise in only one area of business, I believe a CEO can demonstrate competence, especially when first taking over, by leveraging a particular expertise. You might be skilled at closing large customers, recruiting new employees, building strategic partnerships, or raising money. CEOs shouldn't get bogged down in tactical roles in the business. However, picking one area where your experience and expertise, or even just your title, can be of value is helpful in building trust in your competence with a new team. If you have really good senior relationships with potential customers and can pick up the phone and get your sales team a meeting with key decision makers, you will begin to build a reputation for contributing value. These little helping hands also foster a sense of teamwork that is valuable to the CEO. I'll talk more about playing the contributor role later in this chapter.

NOBODY WANTS TO FOLLOW COLONEL KLINK

On September 30, 2010, the Board of Directors of Hewlett-Packard named Léo Apotheker as CEO and President. I was surprised and confused by the appointment. HP is one of the largest companies in the world, with a comprehensive set of offerings across hardware, software, and services—hardware being the largest division. Apotheker had been with SAP, a company that generates the majority of its revenue in enterprise software and has no significant hardware or consumer business, for more than twenty years. He had been forced out of the CEO chair after less than two years. In addition to his mismatch in market focus and possible poor performance in his only CEO role, Apotheker was unfamiliar with the Silicon Valley engineering culture that HP personified. With these disadvantages, he was going to find it difficult to build trust in his competence among the HP employees.

Unfortunately for Apotheker, things went poorly right from the start. HP made a big announcement that it was taking on Apple in the tablet market with the HP TouchPad. After only seven weeks—seven weeks of poor sales—Apotheker quickly reversed course and killed the product. The quick change in direction caused employees to doubt his competence and even to question his credibility. His inability to communicate a clear, strategic vision caused doubts about his market expertise. After more missteps and evidence of a clear lack of trust among the executive team, Apotheker was replaced less than a year after taking office.

Losing a single one of the 3C's is enough to sink a CEO, but losing more than one is almost certainly fatal.

FINDING YOUR BALANCE

1. Have you communicated a realistic plan for how the company will achieve success in the market?

2. How do you build your expertise in your company's industry and market week by week?

3. How do you learn about the operations of and people in different divisions and departments?

4. Do you consistently make projections that the company is unable to achieve?

Caring

"A good leader takes a little more than his
share of the blame, a little less than his share of the credit."

—ARNOLD H. GLASGOW

A CEO is expected to do what is right for everyone, not just for herself. Like credibility, it can take time to build this trust and a moment to destroy it. We reveal how highly we prioritize the success of the company, our teams, and individuals through our everyday actions. When we violate the trust of those we lead by placing our own interests above all others, by showing a lack of commitment to the organization's goals and vision, we lose the ability to ask anyone on the team to commit to or sacrifice for the greater good.

The most common trust killer for CEOs is the belief that they do not have to follow the same rules or be held to the same standards of performance as the rest of the employees of the company. People understand that the CEO's time is valuable, but we have all seen situations that reach the absurd—CEOs who take private jets on worldwide tours while everyone else in the company is on a travel ban; CEOs who spend millions decorating magnificent office suites while everyone else is warehoused in small cubes; CEOs who push for golden parachutes while the businesses they ran head for bankruptcy. All of these things and many other smaller "violations" instantly destroy trust and leave the CEO with little real influence or power to direct the organization.

I have a few simple rules that I think go a long way toward convincing people that you care first about the company and then about yourself. The first rule is "the troops eat first." This old military saying from the days of the cavalry emerged from the commonsense logic of feeding the horses first, then the foot soldiers, and only then the officers. This is still a good axiom for anyone in leadership. The second rule is that, if you want the upside that comes from being the CEO of a successful company, you should be willing to accept more of the downside if things go badly. For example, if cash is tight and you have to cut people and salaries, you should take a bigger pay cut than anyone else. Finally, as Harry Truman famously remarked, "It is amazing what you can accomplish if you do not care who gets the credit." At every opportunity you should look for ways to give your team the credit for the successes while owning the failures as your own.

ROMAN EMPERORS FELL
OUT OF POWER FOR A REASON

I only know of one time that a CEO lost his job over a birthday party, but *my*, what a party it was! The total bill for the party for Dennis Kozlowski's second wife, Karen, was $2 million, of which Tyco, the company that employed Kozlowski as CEO, paid only $1 million. What a deal! The birthday party was disguised as a shareholder meeting in order to justify billing the company. Of course, justifying billing the company for any party held on an Italian island and featuring a massive fireworks show, a golden chariot, and an ice sculpture of Michelangelo's David urinating Stolichnaya vodka is hard to imagine. It didn't help that in a video shot at the party Kozlowski said that the party would bring out a Tyco core competency: the ability to party hard. It is easy to watch the video and wonder what could ever possess a CEO to think that this kind of company-funded extravagance was okay.

Unlike many examples of CEO failure, the company was actually performing quite well under Kozlowski, and even after he was removed as CEO, the company's successes continued. The problem for Kozlowski was that no matter how well a company is doing, the CEO cannot justify treating the company as his personal bank account. When expenditures are made that don't have a clearly definable business purpose, the CEO crosses the boundary from CEO to Emperor. Today, emperors of industry are not above the law, and Kozlowski was convicted of fraud and grand larceny, among other charges.

Whether a CEO's actions are criminal, wasteful, or simply unfair, she sends a message to the employees that her wants and desires are more important than what happens to the business or what happens to them. People will only place their trust in leaders who they believe put the interests of the team ahead of their own personal interests.

By the way, the Tyco party came to be called the Tyco Roman Orgy. Probably not a good sign when your parties are named so suggestively.

FINDING YOUR BALANCE

1. Have you ever spent corporate money on something that did not have a justifiable business purpose? Have you ever looked the other way when a member of your executive team has done so?

2. What perks do you have that others in the company do not? What about your executive team?

3. Have you ever exempted yourself from otherwise all-encompassing policy changes?

4. When times are tough and cuts are made, what type of a hit do you take? How does it compare to the sacrifices other employees make?

No matter how great you are as an orator, or how much you look the part, or how smart you are, you won't be an effective leader if you cannot influence others—if you do not have credibility, competence, and caring. People are inspired by a great speech only if they believe in the message and the messenger. Credibility, competence, and caring are the most powerful tools you have to achieve top performance as a CEO.

Steve Jobs had an incredible run as the CEO of Apple. People often focus on his volcanic outbursts and miss why he had such a tremendous influence within the organization. While I am sure some people feared his temper, top talent will not perform for someone only out of fear. Most of the top Apple employees would have left Apple and had another job in a heartbeat if fear had been the primary method of influence. No, Steve Jobs had influence because he demonstrated the 3C's in spades.

Jobs had credibility with employees and the public. His product launches were legendary because it was obvious he believed deeply in the value of what Apple produced. What other CEO has been so personally identified with the products of the company? His competence in building the best possible computers, phones, and tablets was unmatched. Almost all of his recorded tirades were about making a product better in one way or another. His ability to push his team to innovate even more than they imagined possible showed him to be a master designer.

Jobs was fired by the Apple board in part because he was so totally focused on the Macintosh product that he was incredibly disruptive to the rest of the company. He was failing to care about the organization as a whole. Most people don't realize that Jobs had never served in the CEO role prior to leaving Apple. Though he cofounded the company, there had always been a CEO in place above him. I believe it was during his time as CEO of Next, the computer company he founded after leaving Apple, that Jobs began to understand the necessity of putting the company first. When he triumphantly returned to Apple, he returned *because* of his love of the company. He never even took a salary while CEO. Many people believe that his focus on what was good for the company even hastened his death by delaying him in seeking medical attention for his condition. Steve Jobs wielded more influence than almost any CEO in modern times, but it wasn't because of his strong personality. His influence came from strict adherence to the 3C's.

EXPERTISE VS. NEED

"Never become so much of an expert that you stop gaining expertise."
—DENIS WAITLEY

When I started NetQoS in June of 2000, I was thirty-five years old. I remember going to lunch with the mother of one of our employees where she commented on how young I was. While it wasn't my first time running a business, it was my first time running a business with other people's money. I felt a great deal of responsibility to do everything in my power not to lose it, and I knew that I had many things to learn if I wanted to be a good CEO.

I wanted to feel confident that I was spending my time on the right things, so I began to observe the CEOs I came in contact with to see how they spent their time. Two particular CEOs caught my attention. One was the CEO of the company from which we were subletting our space. Because we were on the same floor of the building, I would often run into him in the hall or lobby. I wanted to get to know him better and learn what I could. The problem was that every time I saw him he was on his cell phone, involved in some seemingly animated conversation. I don't mean some of the time or most of the time but *every* time. I was always curious to know whom he was talking to and what was so important. In almost a year of being in the same building on the same floor, I never got past a short "Hi, how are you?" Maybe he was just maximizing his time by taking calls on the walk to and from his car, but it seemed odd to me how much time he spent on the phone. It made me wonder if he spent his time wisely or if he knew how to delegate. Needless to say, I didn't learn much from him.

The second CEO who stands out in my mind was one I intentionally sought out because his company was in the same general industry as mine. We would often run into each other at events around town or at the industry trade shows that were almost a must for companies in those days. Whenever I ran into him, he would launch into a description of the big deal he was working on. The first time, I thought it was just a particularly big deal and that was why he was so involved. About the fourth time I heard about the next big deal, I realized that this CEO focused solely on sales. He had no interest in any other part of the business. He was the head salesperson for the company, not the CEO.

Both of these companies were eventually liquidated for pennies on the dollar. While neither of these CEOs was able to teach me a lot about how to be successful, watching them did help me think more clearly about how CEOs should spend their time.

As I eventually learned, we have six hats we might wear—roles we might need to play—as we attempt to fulfill our responsibilities and build our influence. Understanding these roles helps us develop the right level of influence in any given situation and find balance that makes our work sustainable. But first we have to get out of our own way.

THE FIREFIGHTER AND THE SUPER VP

Almost every kid growing up goes through that stage at which he or she wants to be a firefighter. It seems so exciting, constantly rushing through the flames to save the helpless child or animal from destruction. Unfortunately, the firefighter CEO sees his job from the same perspective—he must constantly rush in to save the day, no matter how small the fire. In some cases, if he doesn't see a fire he creates one, just so he has something to do. This type of CEO believes that he is the only one in the company who can really make things happen. He often laments the fact that he is the only one who can make a decision, but of course if anyone else tries, he will likely rush in to overrule. No issue is too small for his input and wisdom. The fonts on the business cards, the color of a wall in the break room, or the right vendor for office supplies. Many start-up CEOs begin as firefighters before there is a real need for a CEO. Getting a new company off the ground requires many decisions to be made quickly, and often a founding CEO can make these best. If these CEOs have success and the company grows, they will need to transition out of the firefighter role and into a more balanced, proactive, strategic approach to spending their limited time and energy.

FINDING YOUR BALANCE

1. Do you require almost all decisions in the company to come across your desk?
2. How often are others allowed to make decisions without your input?

As I've described previously, the natural tendency of a many new CEOs is to focus on the area they understand the best. If their background is sales, they will spend most of their time with their sales executives, poring over the sales pipelines and trying to help on every deal. They will feel like they're making a difference and contributing to the company, although they may be doing more harm than good. It's one thing for a CEO to pinch-hit in a particular area that needs help or spend time training a new executive, but if the executive who leads a particular group is not allowed to make decisions and chart the path forward for her team, she'll leave. Acting as a super VP is a terrible way for a CEO to spend time. If the executive in place can't do the job, then she should be replaced; otherwise she needs to be allowed to accomplish her goals with minimum interference.

FINDING YOUR BALANCE

1. Do you spend the majority of your time focused on a single department or functional area?
2. Do people in any area come directly to you for decisions, bypassing the leader who is supposed to be in charge?

THE SIX HATS

In my search for experienced CEOs to learn from, I found and joined a peer group called the CEO Project. Led by Jim Schleckser, the group was particularly valuable in my thinking about how a CEO should spend his time. Jim is one of the best CEO coaches in the country; his experience working with fast-growth companies in many different industries provides him with a great perspective on the CEO job. Jim has written about the five hats a CEO should wear to maximize his impact and effectiveness: player, coach, architect, engineer, learner. I've added an additional hat—priest—that I think is also valuable. Being conscious about which hat you are wearing and how you allocate your time between the different roles is critical to fulfilling your responsibilities and appropriately leveraging and building your influence.

The Player Hat: Contributing

When the CEO is acting as a direct contributor in an area of the business, she is wearing the player hat. If your business is small you may feel that you constantly wear the player hat. I have known many CEOs whom I would describe as "CEO and blank," where the blank might be salesperson, engineer, admin, or accountant, depending upon the day of the week. This is often necessary in the early stages of a company, but as the company grows above fifty employees, it is almost always best for the CEO to take off the player hat the vast majority of the time. CEOs need to allow their executive teams or department heads to lead their teams and determine the best way to accomplish specific goals. Total-control CEOs wear this hat a lot, even when they don't have much to contribute, and it destroys morale.

There are three situations in which I think the player hat can be useful. The first I described previously: when you are a new CEO trying to build credibility with your team. The second situation is when some part of the team is overwhelmed with work and is having to put in long hours just to get the job done. I believe the CEO should be willing to jump in and help out wherever and whenever his skills allow. In one of my businesses we sent candy to each of our customers every year around the holidays. At first this wasn't that big a deal, but as our customer count grew it became a major production. I made sure to stop by when it was occurring and spend a few hours packing boxes. Some might say a CEO should have something better to do with his time, but I felt it proved to the team that we were all in it together. It helped me build a culture of teamwork and show people that I cared.

The third reason to put on the player hat is when your particular expertise is otherwise lacking in the company or is crucial to solving a problem or making progress. This requires an honest and accurate self-assessment of your talents and abilities. With the proper fit, this is an opportunity to improve the chances of achieving goals and to exhibit competence and commitment. Maybe you have a sales background and you can help close a really large customer, or you have particular technical knowledge that can be applied to a specific process. If you have real expertise that could add value, don't let it go to waste. Steve Jobs's expertise was being a product design perfectionist. By pushing the limits of innovation for every product, he made a real difference while wearing the player hat.

The Coach Hat: Talent Development

The CEO wears the coach hat when he focuses on team members and how they are performing. The role of a coach is to get the maximum performance from everyone on the team, to attract and develop top talent, and to identify areas where he does not have the right talent on board. If you don't wear the coach hat often—and I would argue for wearing this hat more than any of the others—you will find it difficult to provide the proper resources, build a high-performance culture, or deliver performance.

For a CEO, coaching begins with spending time with his direct reports, showing that he is interested in their challenges and cares about their success. A short weekly session with every one of your direct reports is an important time to gather information and provide insight and direction that should lead to increased performance. CEOs who follow the "hire top talent and ignore" approach rarely retain top talent or achieve sustained growth.

Another critical task, particularly in fast-growing organizations, is working with your executive team to identify areas of the business that need additional talent. You should also spend time identifying and discussing the top talent at lower levels in the organization, those valuable team members who can be groomed for future leadership positions. Assigning a mentor for these future leaders can pay off as the business grows and positions of greater responsibility open up.

Coaching is critical to building a great company, and you should constantly be on the lookout for opportunities to improve your team's performance. The upcoming "Provide the Proper Resources" section is the longest section of this book for good reason.

The Architect Hat: Strategy

When wearing the architect hat, you are working on the strategy of your business—owning the vision by determining how you will achieve it. You are focused on your product and market, and on critical questions about your business: Who is the customer? What problem are we solving? How do we make money? In the early stages of a business, when introducing a new product, or when taking a company down a new strategic path, you'll need to spend a lot of time in the architect role.

The nature of the work of strategic thinking requires us to set aside large blocks of time to focus on and discuss the business. You must make time for this function on a regular basis. Even in a business with a well-established strategy, I would reserve at least one full day every quarter to review and think about strategy, and some time every week to review how the quarter is progressing. At other times, when things in the business or market are changing rapidly, the right answer may be to spend several days focused on this role.

If you make good decisions in this area—proving your competence to your team—everything else becomes a little easier.

The Engineer Hat: Operations

Engineers use analytical approaches to solve problems, and that's just what you will do when wearing the engineer hat. The engineering process involves defining a goal, creating metrics related to the goal, analyzing those metrics, and improving the process. This continuous cycle of improvement is critical to building a high-performance business and culture.

When wearing the engineer hat, you'll work closely with your management team to identify the key processes in each area of the business and then undertake a systematic approach to improving each one. Some companies will have a chief operations officer who may take primary responsibility for this work. Whether you have a COO or not, you should spend time on a regular basis reviewing metrics and focusing on the processes that make the biggest difference to the business. If you leave this role entirely up to the members of your executive team, you often won't have the knowledge you need to make effective decisions when issues escalate and land on your desk. You may be seen as disconnected from the company, and that could limit people's trust in your competence.

The Learner Hat: Continuous Improvement

The French author François de La Rochefoucauld observed, "The only thing constant in life is change." The great CEO understands this truth and so constantly works to improve and expand her knowledge. We should focus on learning both inside and outside of the business. Inside, we should learn about our products, our customers, and our competitors in order to draw a path from our current reality to our vision. It is easy to lose sight of these critical aspects of the business if we don't force ourselves to pay attention. Scheduling at least one extended series of customer interactions per quarter and attending industry trade shows every year are good ways to improve your knowledge.

Outside the business, we can focus on learning more about a wide array of topics, from other related industries, to economics, to basic research on markets similar to ours. Areas tangentially related or similar to your own business can yield valuable insights. Using CEO peer groups to add to your knowledge can also be valuable. The two keys to any peer group are the quality of the leader and the individual members.

Devoting a few days every quarter to wearing the learner hat will pay major dividends for your success.

The Priest Hat: Morale

The one hat I would add to Jim's collection is the priest hat. I was reared Catholic so I use the term *priest*, but feel free to substitute your own term for spiritual advisor. While wearing the priest hat, you are concerned with the morale of the organization, with how people feel, with helping others resolve personal or interpersonal struggles. Any time you have people on a team who are passionate about what they do, you will see tempers flare or personalities clash. This is a natural part of human interaction, but the CEO can often play a particularly powerful role in smoothing the waters and maintaining strong morale.

In smaller companies, employees will want to tell the CEO about their problems or frustrations. As a young CEO I would often react to these conversations by immediately jumping into action and trying to solve the issue. Usually this would cause problems and undermine the leader who was responsible for that particular team. I may have proved to the employee that I cared, but not to the leader. I have learned that often the best thing to do is to listen, and to ask questions to make sure I understand the issue. Once I think I understand, I may coach the employee on how to work within the organizational structure to achieve the results he desires. Because employees usually complain about their managers (studies have proven time and again that the biggest cause of employee disengagement and turnover is management), I have to be careful about how I handle the information I've gathered. Like a priest who hears confession, I don't use it directly. Instead, I keep it in the back of my mind. I may address it tangentially in a coaching session while protecting my source.

Building trusted relationships with frontline employees is an invaluable skill for a CEO and can help you prevent bigger problems from developing. For example, I am proud to say I have never had to deal with legal problems of harassment or discrimination in any of my businesses. I believe that while wearing the priest hat, I have learned of many small problems before they escalated. I am a big proponent of management by walking around, and when I am walking around, I am often wearing the priest hat.

A SYSTEM FOR HAT SWITCHING

Think it sounds almost impossible to play all of these roles? Take a page out of Jack Dorsey's book. Dorsey, who is currently leading two companies, Square and Twitter, has what he calls a "disciplined" approach. In an interview with *Fast Company*, he described how he meets the needs of both companies by following a thematic schedule for the week: "'Monday is management. At Square we have a directional meeting, at Twitter we have our opcomm [operating committee] meeting. Tuesday is product, engineering, and design. Wednesday is marketing, growth, and communications. Thursday is partnership and developers. Friday is company and culture . . . On days beginning with T, I start at Twitter in the morning . . . Sundays are for strategy, and I do a lot of job interviews.'"[3] It might sound rigid, but for a guy facing a lot of demands on his time, a system approach makes sense.

One of the most critical acts of balance for any CEO is walking the line between total responsibility and lack of control. If we cannot find that line, it will be difficult to fulfill our responsibilities. It can be overwhelming, but if we focus our efforts on building our influence internally and externally and playing the six critical roles, we'll find our footing as we face big and small challenges.

FINDING YOUR BALANCE

1. Considering the six hats, what role consumes the majority of your time?

2. Based on your company's current market position, growth, or culture, what role or roles should receive your greatest attention?

3. When you wear the player hat, are you pushing somebody else out of position or are you contributing unique value?

4. Do you wear the priest hat effectively—to build trust and a sense of caring?

OWN

THE

VISION

*"The very essence of leadership is that you have
to have vision. You can't blow an uncertain trumpet."*

—THEODORE M. HESBURGH

WHEN MY WIFE, CATHY FULTON, AND I STARTED NETQOS IN 1999, WE saw a clear strategic market opportunity to be identified as the network performance experts. At the time, no other company was competing for this title, and so it became our mission. Our vision developed from there: "Become the premier provider of services to optimize the performance of the world's most demanding networks." Not quite as simple as Walmart's "Always low prices," but it did the job. To communicate this mission and vision to employees, I showed them the movie *Hellfighters*, made in 1968 and starring John Wayne. *Hellfighters* was loosely based on the life of Red Adair, who built a company of the world's leading experts on oil-well fires. If you had an oil-well fire and you wanted the best, you called Red Adair. I wanted the same for NetQoS— for network performance management, not oil-well fires. I would often refer to the movie in company presentations to remind people of the mission and vision. Employees and customers connected with our mission and vision; it answered the question of what they should expect from NetQoS.

As a venture-funded company we also needed a clear way to communicate our vision for shareholders. After receiving our first round of funding, I asked one of the venture partners what he hoped to achieve with NetQoS. He said, "Hit a home run."

Being an engineer, I was never satisfied with vague answers. "Can you quantify that?" I asked.

He wanted the company to be valued at $200 million, which would deliver a 10 times return on their investment. In order to get to this kind of valuation in a reasonable amount of time (most venture funds only run for ten years), we would have to grow very fast. In our industry, companies growing 50 percent or more annually could expect to achieve exit multiples of about 4 to 5 times revenue, which meant we had to grow to $40 or $50 million in revenue to reach the valuation goal. The marching orders for the company became pretty clear and could be summed up in one sentence: grow as fast as we can—without running out of money—by becoming the network performance experts. This one sentence clarified our vision and made decision making much easier.

In these two facets of our vision, we connected with people's hearts and heads. Employees aspired to making us the network performance experts, and they were clear-eyed about our financial goals. Customers understood what we would deliver. And shareholders trusted that we took their interests seriously. When we sold nine years later for $200 million we had accomplished our goal and achieved our vision for NetQoS. It is important to have something for all three major stakeholders (employees, customers, and shareholders) in your vision.

The first thing to do before any long journey is to figure out where you are going; and the first step for any CEO is to determine and communicate the strategic direction of the organization. Until you know where you are going, it is hard to make decisions about anything else in the business. Without this clearly communicated direction, a company is merely a collection of people pursuing their individual goals, guided by their own values. Too many CEOs have allowed these core elements of a business to become slogans on a piece of paper rather than tenets that inform all key decisions.

The CEO must take ownership of the mission, vision, and values to drive the company forward. I use the phrase "owning the vision" to indicate the personal relationship the CEO has to have to the mission, vision, and values of the company. Whether or not the CEO created the vision, she must embrace it at every turn. The responsibility for making sure everyone in the company is clear on the direction rests solely with the CEO and is the first item that should be addressed when she takes over.

The vision describes the idealized view of the world the company hopes to create. A properly structured and communicated vision turns a group of people into a team with a clear purpose. Some visions are so simple they can almost fit in a tagline. For example, Walmart's longtime tagline of "Always low prices" combined with a set of values that defined how the company would accomplish the vision enabled Walmart CEOs to continue to drive the business forward long after the retirement of Sam Walton, the founder.

In addition to leading the development of the mission, vision, and values, your job as CEO is to rally all the stakeholders of your company—especially employees, customers, and shareholders. The vision must be ingrained deeply in the culture of the company. All major decisions should be considered in light of it, to ensure they move the company in the proper direction. As CEO you may get tired of repeating this message, but for the vision to take hold in the company, it must be front and center for employees, and for all other stakeholders.

To help stakeholders engage with the vision, you have to answer the question, "What's in it for me if the vision is realized?" The answer for each group may be different. This can be easy for shareholders: they'll receive a financial reward. Yet I often find that CEOs spend too much of their time focused on shareholders and forget that there are other critical stakeholders. If the vision doesn't provide value for employees and customers in the long term, it will be impossible for shareholders to profit. An engaged workforce is critical for maximizing company performance. I have always operated businesses that were focused on rapid growth. Being part of a growing organization provides employees the opportunity for increased responsibility, continuous learning, career progression, and more. Sheryl Sandberg, COO of Facebook, related the advice she received from Eric Schmidt, executive chairman and former CEO of Google, when interviewing for a job: "If you get a chance to get on a rocket ship, don't worry about what seat, just get on." Customers benefit from growth, too, because more resources can be devoted to improving products as well as hiring great employees who, in turn, deliver superior service. Understanding that each group and even every person may be motivated by slightly different rewards is important to tailoring the message appropriately. You aren't changing the vision for each group; you're merely focusing on the value that each group uniquely receives from accomplishing the vision.

Everyone knows that for a CEO, being a good communicator is vital, but knowing it and doing it well are two different things. In a cover article in *CIO Magazine*, CIOs who have broken into the CEO role described discovering gaps in their skills and experience, which—not surprisingly—had nothing to do with hard skills. One revelation was the "relentless storytelling that's required to get and keep employees supporting a common vision."[4] A good communicator knows his or her audience and how to appeal to each group within it. Certainly having emotional intelligence helps make you a better communicator (and I'll address this more in the "Build the Culture" section), but exhibiting the 3C's—credibility, competence, and caring—through storytelling can also make all the difference.

Creating the mission and vision is a challenging part of driving the strategic direction of the company. However, executing to achieve them can be much more challenging. While the mission and vision provide a clear destination for the journey, there are many decisions that will have to be made along the way. To help make these decisions, employees need guidance from the executive team and specifically the CEO on what trade-offs the organization should make. Guidance for these daily decisions comes from the values established within the organization. While values are on par with vision, I will address them in the "Build the Culture" section because I believe that a values-driven culture is key to high performance.

Once you have clearly established the mission, vision, and values of your organization, then the challenge becomes communicating these in a balanced way. How do you communicate more than the destination, but also the intent behind the vision in order to foster a sense of purpose and to improve decisions at all levels? How can you be positive without losing credibility? How do you develop a strategic plan but not become a slave to that plan?

PLANNING VS.
ACTION VS. RESULTS

"Great leaders are almost always great simplifiers,
who can cut through argument, debate, and doubt
to offer a solution everybody can understand."
—**GENERAL COLIN POWELL**

What is the plan? Four simple words that make up one of the toughest questions a CEO has to answer. People look to their leaders to help them understand exactly what they should do and when they should do it. Unfortunately, most modern businesses don't lend themselves to being planned out step-by-step in intricate detail. Much of the work done in modern corporations requires creativity and adaptability from employees to adjust to different customers and ever-changing business conditions.

Here is a perfect example. People have one of two reactions to Vegas: "Yuck" or "When can we go?" I've always fallen into the latter camp and look for any opportunity to make the trip. It's the trade show capital of the world, so I often have a good excuse. Trade shows have been an important part of several of my businesses. But while they often provided a lot of value, the costs could be significant, especially because hotels are notorious for raising their rates when a convention is in town. One year, in an attempt to cut down on our lodging costs, we made a deal with a small, off-strip hotel to house our entire group for a per-room rate well below their normal rack rate. We booked more than thirty rooms for an average of three-plus nights and booked the conference rooms to meet and entertain customers.

I had planned to stay three nights, but at the last minute my plans changed and I made the "sacrifice" to go a day early. Because it was a last-minute decision, I forgot to call the hotel ahead of time. I arrived at the hotel in the afternoon with the rest of our advance team, waited for them to check in, and then asked if the hotel had any open rooms for the night. I wasn't worried; this was a Tuesday night in Vegas and I knew that if they didn't have a room, I could easily find one. The desk clerk happily informed me that they did have open rooms and began to check me in. As she reached for my credit card she said the rate for the night would be $199, which was the full-price rate. I explained that I was with the previous group and that we had negotiated a rate of $129 per night. She said that because I hadn't reserved the room early I would have to pay the full price. Thinking that maybe her tune would change if she knew who I was, I explained that not only was I with the group that had just checked in, I was also the CEO and the one who had specifically chosen this hotel. She was not impressed. She repeated her policy-driven mantra that because I hadn't reserved the room ahead of time, I had to pay the full rate. I decided to give it one more try. I explained that we were unlikely to use this hotel in the future if she couldn't change my rate to the negotiated price, and then asked if there was a manager I might talk to. This approach didn't help my cause. She was the manager on duty. At this point I knew I wouldn't win the argument, so I resigned myself to finding another hotel for the night.

Now some of you are probably thinking that this is what I get for going to a small, mid-tier hotel, or that the problem here was just a bad employee or low customer service standards. I don't think that was the problem. This employee actually impressed me as being quite capable. She was patient and courteous with me. She was efficient as she checked people in. She greeted everyone with a welcoming smile. She just made a bad decision. And she made a bad decision because of a lack of alignment between the goals of the company as a whole and the goals of the employee and her direct workgroup. I bet the hotel manager's number-one goal was to increase the revenue the hotel was generating. An obvious and worthy goal. After analyzing the situation, someone probably decided that their average price per room was lower than their competitors' and that they should focus on increasing their average. This was translated down to the next level as a policy of no discounts for walk-in customers. Voilà! In three easy steps you go from a perfectly appropriate goal to a policy that can actually work against the higher goal. Each step in the process involved a reasonable decision, but it led to a bad outcome. Because the employee I dealt with didn't understand the reason for the policy and the higher-level goals, she was unable to see that her actions were probably not in the best interest of the hotel or moving the hotel toward its vision, if she even knew what that vision was.

My hotel problem was easily solved. Later in the evening I received a call from one of my employees. The hotel manager had come by one of our meeting rooms to check on things. When my employee explained the problem his CEO had at check-in, the manager was horrified. He asked the employee to call me and tell me that a free suite would be ready for me by the time I got back to the hotel. When I arrived, the manager apologized profusely and the rest of the stay was uneventful.

Unfortunately not all such problems are so easily solved. When perfectly competent and productive employees behave in ways that they believe are totally correct but that actually work against the broader interests of the business, their goals are not aligned with the high-level goals of the company. Over time, as the number of layers in an organization increases, groups can become so disconnected from the goals of the larger organization that they create their own independent vision within the company and eventually become totally removed from the purpose of the business. Understanding that these problems are alignment problems and not employee problems is critical to making your company maximize productivity.

So how do you build alignment? Through highly detailed plans? Can Tim Cook, CEO of Apple, write an exacting plan for creating the next revolutionary device? Did Alan Mulally save Ford by creating a detailed plan describing every car they would build, how many they would sell, the exact nature of every agreement with every vendor, and so on? Of course not. Most businesses operate in a highly competitive environment with constantly changing conditions that make most detailed strategic plans out-of-date before the planning process is complete. Some CEOs react to this by trying to gather more data and do even more analysis. This approach can spiral into a continuous process of planning and replanning without any action ever being initiated. It's like a line from the now famous *Fortune* article by Ram Charan and Geoffrey Colvin, "Why CEOs Fail": "It's bad execution. As simple as that: not getting things done, being indecisive, not delivering on commitments."[5] Obviously this doesn't lead to strong operating results.

While most businesses have struggled with this problem of operating in a highly competitive and dynamic environment only for the last few decades, one organization in society has been dealing with this problem for centuries. From a management perspective, military operations have a great deal of similarity to business operations. The battlefield is a complex place where everyone is highly motivated to succeed and conditions change rapidly and in ways that are unpredictable. In his book, *On War*, Prussian General Carl von Clausewitz sought to explain the inherent issues in managing large-scale engagements. He introduced two key concepts that are applicable to any organization looking to maximize performance. The first concept is *internal friction*, which describes the gap observed between planned actions and actual actions. No matter how well communicated, a given order will never match the action the leader imagines. The second concept is *external friction*, which describes the gap between desired outcomes and actual outcomes. When competing against an intelligent and dynamic opponent, the actual outcomes will never be as successful and clean as those in the plan. Clausewitz wrote, "Everything in war is very simple, but the simplest thing is difficult. The difficulties accumulate and end by producing a kind of friction that is inconceivable unless one has experienced war . . . Friction is the only concept that more or less corresponds to the factors that distinguish real war from war on paper."[6]

Change the word *war* to *business* and any CEO will recognize this friction as part of their daily battle. Clausewitz is often quoted as saying that no plan survives first contact with the enemy—because of these frictions.

So what's a CEO to do? Should we throw out the entire planning process and just wing it? That certainly doesn't seem like a professional approach to management. The answer to overcoming the friction that will keep you from achieving your vision is not better or more detailed plans. No human planning can anticipate every internal and external source of friction. The answer lies in communicating intent and communicating reality.

THE SECRET AGENT AND THE AMATEUR

When I taught at Naval Nuclear Power School, the information we taught, including details about the operation of the reactors that powered the U.S. Navy submarines, was quite sensitive. But instead of marking a few specific documents secret, the navy considered almost every document secret, including things that could have been found in any high school or college textbook on the subject. Taking the control of information one step further, the navy (and all branches of the military) operates on the principle of "need to know": even if you have the clearance level necessary to know something, you would not be given the information unless it was necessary for you to know it to perform your job.

Unfortunately too many CEOs operate in the same way; they seem to believe they're in charge of an espionage operation rather than running a company. They keep their employees in the dark about even the most basic facts regarding the operation of the business. And even though they don't tell people much about the goals of the company, they expect employees to be able to perform their jobs well. For most workers, this "need to know" type of operation is terribly demoralizing. As Daniel Pink discusses in his book *Drive*, to achieve true employee engagement and motivation, you have to instill a sense of autonomy, mastery, and purpose. It's impossible for employees to act autonomously when they don't know enough of the big picture to understand what it is they should do, and they can't feel a part of some bigger purpose if the boss doesn't tell them what that purpose is.

FINDING YOUR BALANCE

1. What information about the performance of the business do you share with employees?

2. Before sharing information with an employee or group of employees, what factors do you consider? Is one of the factors whether the employee or group needs to know the information?

3. Are you afraid that if basic information about your business leaked out, it could significantly harm your business?

All businesses must perform basic "housekeeping" functions, such as accounting and maintaining employee and customer records. You would expect as a company gets bigger, it would develop more sophisticated and efficient systems to collect, analyze, and disseminate information and data. Yet I have been shocked at the inability of some large businesses to answer even basic questions about their business due to a lack of proper systems and processes. This can occur when a business experiences rapid growth and the systems and procedures couldn't keep up. Or it may be the result of a business that acquired many different companies with different systems, none of which were ever integrated into one universal system. Unless the CEO leads a concerted effort to build or integrate these systems, a company can find itself without access to critical information. Without that information, leaders don't understand the reality of the company. Only amateur CEOs allow their companies to move forward without basic information or well-run housekeeping functions needed to support the business. None of these areas require rocket science to understand; they just require focus from the CEO to make sure consistent processes and procedures are in place.

FINDING YOUR BALANCE

1. Are there fundamental questions about the factual operation of your business that can't be answered easily by you or your leadership team?

2. What are your current sources of data or information about customers, employees, or finance? Do they ever provide conflicting information?

3. How quickly do you receive information about the financial performance of the business?

ALIGNMENT THROUGH INTENT AND REALITY

The first question in the Gallup Employee Survey—presented in *First, Break All the Rules*, by Marcus Buckingham and Curt Coffman—is "Do I know what is expected of me at work?" The problem is that in far too many organizations, lower-level employees have only a vague idea of how their daily job is tied to the success of the company. When they encounter friction, they behave in ways that seem to solve the problem, but often a different path would better support the company's overall success.

Obviously each employee can't know everything the CEO knows about the business. So what is the core essence that gives employees the tools they need to take smart action? This essence flows directly from the mission, vision, and values of the company. It is the responsibility of the CEO to make sure that the mission, vision, and values have been taught to and are observed by every group within the organization. When I wear the priest hat discussed in the chapter "Expertise vs. Need," I walk around the organization and try to observe whether every group seems to have internalized the mission, vision, and values. I spend most of my time listening—listening to see if people understand the *why* of their actions. If they are struggling to make low-level decisions, it is often because they don't understand the higher-level *why* that flows from the core of the company. If a Walmart employee isn't sure whether he should match a competitor's lower price or make the company a few extra dollars, it's because he either doesn't understand or doesn't agree with the core essence of the company. It is no different in your organization.

While the bigger *why* is crucial for smart action, employees should also be acting to support a specific set of strategic priorities. And instead of trying to execute a detailed plan that prepares for every contingency, you should work to build proper alignment within these priorities. Proper alignment empowers all employees with an understanding of not only the big-picture *why* but also the more immediate *why* behind current strategic initiatives. These employees make better decisions, achieve better outcomes, and move the company toward its vision faster.

To achieve this type of alignment, you have to communicate the strategy from the top to the bottom of the organization. Help every employee answer the question, *Why are we doing this?* Stephen Bungay, in his enlightening book *The Art of Action*, calls this approach "directed opportunism." With directed opportunism, the top level of an organization creates and communicates a clear intent through goals for the company. The vision provides the direction, while the goals express the top priorities of the organization as a whole in a given time frame. Well-formed goals also reflect measurable outcomes, such as "Generate $50 million in revenue in the quarter." This is a statement of intent, not a detailed plan. The translation into specific actions takes place at each level in the organization—employees working with leaders to determine the best way to achieve the goal. They develop related goals (something I'll address much more in the last section of the book), and each individual is given the autonomy to determine how best to achieve his or her goals, responding to the different circumstances and situations they encounter as they perform the duties of their jobs. By allowing each level of the organization to refine and adjust actions, you increase your chances of reaching good outcomes whenever the inevitable internal or external friction is encountered. Additionally, the freedom given at each level allows workers to feel autonomous while still working as part of a team.

Of course, your strategies must also be aligned with the realities of the business. And so alignment also requires feedback from employees about the likelihood of accomplishing their goals. As challenges arise, they must have a mechanism for communicating back up through the organization, prompting assistance to meet the objectives, improvements in alignment, and adaptation to changing conditions. I'll describe a good system for this in the last section of the book.

—

Execution is possibly the biggest challenge CEOs face. Great execution starts by building a deep understanding of the mission, vision, and values and the intent behind every goal and initiative. Help your employees understand the connection between their actions and the broader goals for the success of the company.

FINDING YOUR BALANCE

1. If you surveyed your employees as to the key goals of the organization, would their answers agree with yours?

2. What information do you currently share with all employees about the company's strategies?

3. How do you help your leadership team communicate the intent of the company's goals and initiatives to their teams?

LEADERSHIP VS. CHEERLEADING

"A leader is best when people barely know he exists; when his work is done, his aim fulfilled, they will say: we did it ourselves."

—LAO TZU

One night I was out at a local gathering of technology company executives when I ran into the CEO of one of the early-stage companies in town. I had visited with him a few times before, but we weren't close friends and had never worked together. He quickly launched into a detailed and passionate monologue about how great business was and how his company was going to be the next billion-dollar company. He seemed to be trying hard to convince me of how well things were going. The whole conversation struck me as a little odd, but I'm all for entrepreneurs being passionate about their businesses so I didn't give it much thought.

The next day I happened to have lunch with a former employee of mine who was now working for this CEO. I mentioned that I had visited with his CEO and that things seemed to be going well. To my surprise, he grimaced and said that they had missed revenue in the most recent quarter by 30 percent! Now a 30 percent miss is not something most CEOs would refer to as a great quarter. Why had this CEO gone out of his way to tell me how well things were going when that wasn't really the case? He could have just said business was fine and left it at that. Instead he essentially lied. It doesn't matter that this CEO lost credibility with me. I wasn't a key stakeholder in his company. But I wondered: if he was spinning the news for me, had he done the same thing with employees, and might he do the same thing if he had public shareholders? This CEO was later replaced when he lost credibility with his board.

How many times have you seen public company CEOs stand in front of the camera and say everything is fine only to announce a massive layoff a few weeks later? Once they lose credibility with their teams, I have never seen any CEOs fully recover.

An obvious challenge for the CEO is how to balance the required enthusiasm for the business while maintaining the credibility necessary to lead. Many CEOs shoot themselves in the foot when they talk about where the business is headed by over-promising and under-delivering or by overreacting to every negative bit of news about the economy or the market. Balancing the perspective on and messaging about the company's progress is critical to success as a CEO, but it is probably the most common mistake I see CEOs make. The best CEOs set up a communication infrastructure within their companies that promotes transparent information flow both from the CEO and to the CEO, and this transparency helps keep the company on course toward its vision.

CHEERLEADER AND EEYORE

I have always had a fascination with the presidency of the United States. I watch shows like *The West Wing* and read biographies of the presidents and memoirs of cabinet officials. One thing that I find myself unable to do, though, is listen to the speeches of the recent presidents. I haven't been able to listen to a speech from a sitting president for more than twenty years. Neither Republican nor Democratic presidents have had any credibility by the time they completed the campaign season and reached office.

If you think about it, cheerleading is an important function of a presidential candidate. Slogging through the primaries and general election requires a leader to be constantly upbeat so as to convince her followers that she is likely to win. No one wants to volunteer to work for a candidate who has doubts about getting elected. Because the election is of a finite duration, it doesn't matter if the candidate loses credibility at the end by not being elected. Only if she is elected does she continue to lead her followers. Unfortunately, this cheerleading approach is not very successful once the candidate becomes president. As president, credibility is critically important if she wants to have the popular approval necessary to accomplish things politically. It is almost impossible to switch overnight from the campaign mode of unbounded optimism to the leadership mode of maintaining credibility. No surprise that George W. Bush was head cheerleader at his boarding school or that Barack Obama found his greatest success as a community organizer. The attitude of optimism regardless of the situation that is necessary for each of these jobs is great for getting elected, but not so good for leading after winning the position.

For CEOs who fall into this trap, like the one in the previous story, everything that happens is met by a cheer. Meetings are often started with rousing emotional appeals. I believe this behavior is often driven simply by the fear of failure. Most people who reach the level of CEO have not had much experience with failure and may be almost paralyzed when faced with the potential of a very public misstep. It is a natural human emotion to want to delay facing a negative event as long as possible. Some CEOs ignore negative news because they don't want to confront the fact that the poor performance is their responsibility, so they convince themselves that things are fine—or will be soon. The longer the CEO goes without acknowledging anything is wrong, the worse the problem gets and the more embarrassment he faces when he is eventually forced to address it. And of course, employees almost always know that things are not going well.

I often hear CEOs justifying this cheerleading behavior by claiming that morale could suffer, their employees might worry too much and become distracted, or employees might leave the company because they cannot handle the uncertainty that bad times bring. I think this is a rationalization. In fact, uncertainty and distraction are more commonly caused by a lack of clear information. Imagine being on a football team and, while playing four hard quarters, not being allowed to see the score. To most people this would be even worse than losing and would quickly lead to players not putting in much of an effort. It's the same in a company. Employees want to win, but if they are told they are always winning they quickly realize that they are not getting the honest truth and begin to disengage.

FINDING YOUR BALANCE

1. Are there material facts about the health of the business that you have withheld from the board or your executive team in the last six months?

2. Would employees be surprised if they knew what you know about the company?

3. How often do you talk about metrics or news that isn't positive? How do you approach the conversation?

The opposite of the cheerleader as CEO is not any better. If a salesperson told me about a great prospect, I would say, "Show me the order." If a salesperson showed me a great order, I would say, "Let's not celebrate until we get the check." When a check came in, I would say, "We knew that was coming. What does the pipeline for next month look like?" Yes, when I started my career I was an Eeyore. No matter what happened, I had trouble celebrating the victories as I quickly moved on to the next potential problem. I can trace my glass-half-empty outlook to my father. He was a very smart university professor and he expected his children to perform to very high standards. First was the only acceptable finish and all A's were the only acceptable grades.

If you identify with these views, you too may be an Eeyore. While cheerleaders destroy their own credibility, no one is excited to work for or inspired by Eeyore as CEO. If the CEO constantly insists the sky is falling, employees will soon reflect the CEO's pessimistic outlook. Eeyore is a less common failure mode for CEOs than the cheerleader mode; you don't often get to be a CEO without being an optimist at heart. But the pressures of the job can cause some CEOs to wear down over time and adopt a consistently negative or overly paranoid attitude. For these CEOs, everything an employee does well could have been done better, every win is temporary, and every sign of growth in the economy or market is not to be believed. Because of this constant negativity, employees learn to avoid the CEO whenever possible. This creates a culture of fear or avoidance in which good outcomes are not communicated up the chain and bad outcomes are buried. This kind of culture can easily lead to real problems, because the various groups within the company operate in secrecy. When you see a major scandal break out in the lower levels of an organization and the CEO had no idea what was going on, it can often be traced to a culture of fear that developed because of an Eeyore CEO.

FINDING YOUR BALANCE

1. Do you feel the need to always be the voice of "reason" or to set "realistic" expectations? In other words, do you respond to every positive event with a negative comment?

2. How often are you the first to learn of good news in your company? How often are you the last to learn of it?

3. When you compliment an employee, do you also mention an area in which they can improve?

PARANOID OPTIMISM

So how do you maintain your credibility with employees while maintaining good morale and effective communication within the organization?

I started to change my attitude when I noticed how excited our sales team would be at the end of a good quarter. I could see how the positive energy gave them a boost going into the next quarter. I began to understand that while I needed to continue to be slightly paranoid about any potential problems, I shouldn't weigh my team down with those burdens. Over time I was able to balance my "Yeah, great, but we still haven't ..." perspective with the optimism needed to inspire a team. I like to describe the balanced CEO attitude as paranoid optimism.

In *The Power of Negative Thinking*, famed coach Bob Knight communicated a similar idea. In either good or bad situations, you should always be preparing your team to win rather than standing back and hoping they will win:

> I am not arguing for being a strict negativist, for walking around with a sour look, for always seeing the dark side, always expecting failure. That's not my intent at all. Quite the opposite. I'm saying that being alert to the possible negatives in any situation is the very best way to bring about positive results. And the reverse is true, too—ignoring or failing to spot potential hazards in advance makes failure all the more likely ... Don't be caught thinking something is going to work just because you think it's going to work. Planning beats repairing ... Stop and think: That's what I'm saying is always the best approach before rushing forward with carried-away zeal.[7]

I like to think of the CEO role as that of a shock absorber for the inevitable highs and lows that a business will face. When things are going well and the team is winning, that is the time to celebrate but also to challenge the team to continue to improve and not become complacent. One of the most public examples of this approach was when the coach of the Los Angeles Lakers, Pat Riley, "guaranteed" a repeat championship at the victory celebration for their 1987 NBA championship. This feat had not been accomplished by any team in the previous eighteen seasons. Riley understood that his team was on top of the world and needed a challenge to keep them from becoming complacent, as previous teams had. "Guaranteeing a championship was the best thing Pat ever did," said Lakers guard Byron Scott. "It set the stage in our minds. Work harder, be better. That's the only way we could repeat."[8]

Conversely, when things are not going well, it's the CEO's job to provide the positive energy the team needs. While being realistic about the situation the company faces, the CEO should look for every opportunity to pat someone on the back. Richard Branson, founder of the Virgin Group, calls it "Finding people doing something right every day," an often-heard phrase from modern leaders. I have found that the most talented employees will be harder on themselves than they should and a little positive feedback goes a long way.

I had the unique situation at NetQoS of being CEO while my wife, Dr. Cathy Fulton, was the chief technical officer. We were still a very small company with an uncertain future when the events of September 11 caused a dramatic slowdown in business activity. Things were so bad that I had a customer actually say to me that he thought we had the best new product he had ever seen, but if it cost more than the dollar in his pocket he couldn't buy it. Given the economic realities, no one was blaming my wife for not having built a great product, but she was blaming herself. As her husband, my encouragement didn't have much of an effect. At one board meeting, she explained that the lack of success the company was experiencing must be due to her failure to build the right product for the market. I could see the shocked look on our lead investor's face after hearing these comments. He said, "In all my years, I've never heard an executive take so much personal responsibility for a failure that is so clearly not theirs. We're very happy to have our money invested with you." That simple vote of confidence instantly energized my wife and built tremendous rapport between her and the board member. She would have done anything to validate the trust he placed in her. Supporting your employees when things are not going well can build tremendous loyalty and drive exceptional performance.

No company wins all the time. It's not realistic to think a CEO won't face problems during her tenure. I managed NetQoS through thirty-one consecutive quarters of double-digit growth, but that winning streak was bookended by the recession after 9/11 and the great recession beginning in 2008. Things were incredibly tough in both recessions and were a test of my credibility and competence. We reexamined our mission, vision, and values to make sure we hadn't missed responding to a fundamental change in the market. And I told employees that, while I couldn't promise that we would never have a downturn and have to lay people off, I could promise that I would be honest with them about our results and how the business was performing. When we did have to do a small layoff, no one was shocked because we had consistently communicated the struggles in the business and the need to cut expenses.

Transparency is key to credibility and to inspiring people to push forward. One of the ways you maintain balance in your approach as CEO is to use a set of consistent measurements to communicate to employees and the board how the company is performing, something I will talk about much more in the "Deliver Performance" section of the book. Cheerleader CEOs tend to change the metrics at each board meeting to focus on whatever positive news they can find. If they can't find a positive metric, they just talk about the big deal that is going to jump-start everything. Using a consistent set of metrics that are tracked over time to judge progress will discipline the cheerleader and all the employees to pay attention to what is important, regardless of whether the company is doing great or hitting a rough patch. Revenue, cash flow, growth rate, margin, and other metrics that track progress on the business fundamentals must be constantly reviewed to create an objective view of the company.

—

The well-balanced CEO is a paranoid optimist, focusing on reality and adjusting his attitude to counterbalance the natural ups and downs in a business. When you can do this successfully, you'll keep your teams focused on the vision and mission and what they need to do to keep the company moving forward.

FINDING YOUR BALANCE

1. Consider the last time your company went through a rough patch. How did you communicate with your team about it? What did you do to support and encourage them?

2. When a team achieves a big win or when the company is doing well, how do you maintain their focus on continually improving?

3. What information do you share every month and quarter with your employees and your board? How does that information align with your mission and vision?

FLEXIBILITY VS. FOCUS

"No battle plan survives first contact with the enemy."

—FIELD MARSHALL HELMUTH VON MOLTKE

Over my career, most of my companies have served as vendors to larger companies. When interacting with them, I always found it interesting to ask the employees about their company. I wanted to hear their opinions of the CEO and the culture. Because most of the people I interacted with were several levels removed from the executive team, it was a good indication of how much influence the CEO really had in those organizations. As you can imagine, in many of the large companies it was clear that there was a pretty big disconnect between the C-suite and the lower-level employees. However, I also saw situations in which the employees were so totally aligned with the CEOs that it seemed unhealthy. How could that be? Well, everyone in the company was so convinced of the superiority of the company, its products, and its plans for the future that disagreement was not allowed and conflicting data were ignored. When I visited with these employees, their belief in their companies was so strong that it reminded me more of a religious conviction than a corporate attitude.

The question for the CEO is, How do you communicate a vision and path for the company while also being flexible enough to change rapidly if business conditions change? If the CEO is doing a great job communicating the mission, vision, and values internally, it's possible that no one will challenge her view. That means that a CEO *must* constantly check her view with external sources that are not biased by connection to the company or loyalty to the CEO. However, if you become too focused on external information, you'll find yourself shifting focus with the shifting winds of the market. And a company with a constantly changing direction never gets anywhere.

The value of a business model is that it provides a framework to constantly test and refine your assumptions as new data is presented. Spending your time adapting to reality is far more useful than trying to plan for what you can't possibly know. Trust your instincts, but verify them with valid information, and you'll maintain your forward momentum.

THE CULT LEADER AND MR. MAYHEM

As I was sitting in church listening to the pastor one day, I realized that pastors have an advantage over CEOs. For example, if they are Christian they profess a belief in Jesus Christ, and trying to follow his teachings is their strategy. They don't have the constant need to watch what other religions are doing to see if they need to make a change. They have a set of beliefs, a vision, that is unchanging, and only their interpretation, or strategy, may change over time as the world progresses and the nature of our lives change. For instance, the new Pope Francis has some views that will likely shift the focus of the Catholic Church.

Next I considered the even greater advantage of cult leaders. They have no need to consider adjusting their vision or strategy because they have surrounded themselves with people who believe in the absolute righteousness of it. Cult leaders have developed such an intense level of belief in their vision among their followers that no cult member questions any of their decisions, regardless of how bizarre, dangerous, or even fatal they may be.

The cult leader as CEO indoctrinates his employees in a vision that is almost spiritual in nature. He convinces them that questioning the vision is like questioning the king—not allowed. Any doubts are treated as disloyalty and failure to get with the program. Companies run by the cult leader CEO can be quite successful, until they encounter an issue where their fundamental assumptions need to be challenged. Then they often fail spectacularly because no one in the organization has ever considered any other possibilities. Employees are frozen because they have been trained to never question the vision or strategy, even when the company desperately needs to adapt. As a CEO you can't be so dogmatic. One of my favorite statistics is that over half the companies that were listed in the Fortune 500 in 1995 were not on the list in 2007. After a mere twelve years, half the list had turned over. No CEO can ever be confident that his strategic vision today is permanent.

A CEO WITH BLINDERS

One company with an unfailing and unhealthy belief in its own prowess was Research in Motion, better known as the maker of the BlackBerry smartphone (and now called BlackBerry). While the company certainly had much to be proud of, growing from $300 million in 2003 to almost $20 billion in revenue by 2011, the faith placed in the two CEOs, Mike Lazaridis and Jim Balsillie, proved to be unhealthy. A quick Internet search will reveal many "great" quotes from each that illustrate how completely they missed the threat posed by the iPhone and other smartphone platforms. In February 2007 Balsillie said this about the iPhone: "It's kind of one more entrant into an already very busy space with lots of choice for consumers . . . But in terms of a sort of a sea-change for BlackBerry, I would think that's overstating it."[9] Unfortunately for Balsillie and RIM, it was not an overstatement.

FINDING YOUR BALANCE

1. When was the last time you solicited feedback on the vision, mission, or strategy of your company?

2. Do employees bring issues or information to your attention that potentially conflict with the current course of the company?

Dean Winters plays the character "Mayhem" in a series of funny Allstate Insurance commercials that show how mayhem can turn any situation into a disaster. The purpose is to convince people of the need for insurance. Unfortunately, if you work for Mr. Mayhem as CEO, you can't buy insurance that will solve the problem.

Mr. Mayhem CEOs inject new projects and redirect resources constantly, creating an environment of chaos. These CEOs are always high-energy individuals who have often been successful in their career because of their willingness to change rapidly and take on new initiatives. While this skill can be valuable in certain types of employees, when deployed at the management level it leads to a lack of focus and to high stress among most employees. Managers with this characteristic drive exceptional employees crazy with their "idea of the day" approach. Most people aren't that fond of change and won't be able to adapt to a new direction every day or even every week or month. Some CEOs cause this chaos without realizing it by merely thinking out loud and having their thoughts translated into action by eager-to-please employees. CEOs must be careful to distinguish between directions and musings.

FINDING YOUR BALANCE

1. Do you often redirect the priorities of employees within your organization outside the formal planning process?

2. Do you regularly start new initiatives with employees working outside the existing organizational structure?

3. Do employees seem confused as to what your top priority is at any given time?

PROVING YOURSELF WRONG INSTEAD OF RIGHT

Trust, but verify. I have a chapter on this concept in the "Deliver Performance" section. There, I address it as a method for managing performance. Here, I want to discuss it as a method for managing yourself.

You must trust your instincts. There's a reason you are CEO. Whether you started your company or grew into the position, you have likely earned it by making smart decisions over time. You have to trust that you know what's best for the organization, because it's your job to know. If you don't, there are bigger problems than focus or inflexibility.

However, you have to temper your confidence with a clear-eyed analysis of what you're hearing in the market. NetQoS originally started as a services company leveraging our technology, but over time we became predominantly a software company selling licenses. The vision changed to include software and not just services.

How do you know when you might need to adjust? You have to seek out intel. It's critical to have objective data that comes unfiltered from outside the organization when reviewing your strategy. I always looked to competitors for outside intelligence first. Obviously they had a bunch of smart people working hard to defeat us, so I wanted to pay attention to what they were doing and what they had to say. By going to trade shows and being active in the industry, I closely followed our key competitors. While many times I thought we had a better approach, I was always looking for objective data that might indicate I was wrong. Was our win rate in competitive deals going down? Were their growth rates increasing faster than ours? Whenever possible, I would interview their employees or ex-employees for positions with our company, hoping to learn how they really viewed our company.

The second place I looked for intel was with customers. What were they saying about our competitors and us? We consistently surveyed our customers to understand how they felt about the solutions we were providing, and we were particularly interested in understanding what it would take to get the incremental customer, which requires figuring out what customer problems are big enough and painful enough for them to justify a major purchase. If you ask customers what product they want to buy from you, they will often not have an answer. The correct questions get them to reveal their biggest problems, and then it is up to you and your team to figure out the best product to solve that problem. Customers didn't tell Lee Iacocca they wanted a minivan. They told him they wanted the doors of their station wagons to be easier to open because they were often trying to hold a baby and load bags of groceries at the same time. The engineers at Chrysler took that problem and the minivan became the solution.

The third tactic that I found to be very successful was adding a new executive to our team every year or two. I found that after running NetQoS for several years, the number of new ideas I had about the business dwindled dramatically. I had implemented the key ideas I had and I needed input from other sources to see the warts in the business that I could not. Bringing in a new executive who had new ideas was a breath of fresh air for the team and often created growth in areas that we wouldn't have otherwise found. On most executive teams, a healthy level of turnover will bring you fresh ideas.

If you think your team needs a more immediate infusion of ideas, for example, to handle a sudden shift in the market or a perpetual slowing of your business, you might consider working with a strategy consultant. That said, you cannot solve leadership incompetence with strategy. The CEO has to own the vision, which means he has to understand it. Consultants can be highly valuable, but they can't take over this role. They can offer ideas, but the CEO has to be the one to choose the right path. The best consultants ask the right questions, they don't dictate the answers.

TRASHING A BUSINESS MODEL

John Legere calls T-Mobile the un-carrier. Uninterested in talking about the fact that T-Mobile's network is growing rapidly and is as fast as the networks of AT&T and Sprint, who control half the market share, Legere recognizes that basic elements of cell and data services are no longer a competitive advantage. Today, customers can get essentially the same service just about anywhere with just about any carrier. Instead, customers are tired of feeling bullied or restricted or robbed. They want freedom and lower prices without giving up the basics. So that's what Legere is giving them.

Legere has been gradually abandoning all the trappings of the standard telecomm business model: long-term contracts, free phones, increasing prices based on the idea that networks are growing and data is flowing. In July 2013, Legere announced that the company was giving up on long-term contracts entirely. It has been focusing on attracting customers with its lower prices and emphasizing that its network is big enough for almost anybody. It doesn't give away smartphones for free, but it often offers discounts, and you can buy an iPhone with a year-long, zero-interest installment plan (its only long-term contract). And the company recently began giving away a small amount of free data for life if you buy a tablet through them.

Legere's tactics are paying off. In the second quarter of 2013, T-Mobile gained 685,000 customers compared to Verizon's 472,000 and AT&T's 153,000. These kinds of successful strategic moves that only the CEO can make justify every dollar they are paid.

—

Once you develop a clear definition of success for your company, it's important that you not allow the vision or strategy to stagnate. Business conditions are constantly changing; and while the big picture vision should not often change, the details of the story must be constantly refined.

FINDING YOUR BALANCE

1. In the last eighteen months, how many strategic initiatives were abandoned? How many were begun?

2. How often do you do a competitive analysis of the market? What information do you gather and from where?

3. What do you learn from your customers and how do you use it to examine your strategy?

PROVIDE

THE

PROPER

RESOURCES

SEPTEMBER 15, 2008, IS ONE OF THOSE DAYS EVERYBODY IN THE BUSINESS and investment world will remember. The financial downturn had begun in 2007, but when Lehman Brothers declared bankruptcy early that Monday morning, we knew the world had changed.

I was CEO of NetQoS at the time, and we had been on a winning streak. We were about to complete our thirty-first consecutive quarter of double-digit, year-over-year growth. If things continued, we would be well positioned for an IPO in the next twenty-four months. But when Lehman failed all bets were off. We saw it in our metrics almost immediately. Everything we tracked—deals, revenue, etc.—began to move sideways instead of up and to the right. I had seen this movie before (during the dot-com bust) and knew almost immediately that I needed to take dramatic action.

At the next board meeting I presented the most likely scenario. The steady and rapid growth that we had seen in the business was going to end. The fourth quarter revenue was likely to fall below the previous year's number. It would take time to rebuild our growth track record and position the company for an IPO.

The one silver lining was that, while we were suffering, other companies were on life support. Companies that had been showing slow growth were now shrinking at an alarming rate. The public markets were crushing stock prices as the crisis deepened. I wasn't happy to watch other companies fail, but the situation presented an opportunity to acquire complementary assets at an attractive price. If we could find a good fit, we could significantly increase our revenue and look very attractive when the recovery eventually came.

We found the perfect target in a small, publicly traded French company. The CEO was trying to figure out how to survive and resurrect a stock price that had fallen to reflect little more than the cash on the balance sheet. Doing a French take-private transaction is not for the faint of heart, but plenty of investment banks were happy to have some work to do. We just needed to raise enough money to move forward with the transaction. Over the previous few years I had established relationships with numerous late-stage venture capital and private equity firms; some had almost begged me to let them put money into NetQoS. I thought it would be relatively simple to put together the financing for the deal. The numbers were pretty straightforward. We were doing about $50 million in revenue and needed to raise about $50 million to complete the transaction. The company we were acquiring was doing about $60 million in revenue. If I could raise money at a valuation of two times our revenue, then I could more than double our size and give up only a third of the company. The combined entity would have had over $100 million in revenue and been well positioned for an IPO when the markets recovered.

I began the process of talking to potential funding partners. What I thought would be an easy fund-raising process turned into a repetitive grind of talking to forty-six different firms without finding a single dance partner. Some of the conversations took on such a surreal quality that I could only laugh to keep from crying. One particularly memorable exchange occurred during a conference call with a big-name venture firm. Immediately after I went through our standard pitch deck showing our long history of rapid growth and efficient operations, the investors asked if I had any questions for them or wanted to hear more about their firm. I said, "Can you describe your investment time horizon and how you think about getting a return?" They answered by saying that they were long-term investors with a five- to seven-year holding period; that made them different, they claimed, from other investors who were focused on quick turns. I had heard this story before and I knew that, under the present circumstances, their reality was probably different from their marketing. So I immediately turned it back on them and asked if they had any questions for us. The only question from this "long-term" investor was, "How is the current quarter looking?" I almost threw something at the phone. Thirty-one consecutive quarters of double-digit growth, and all they cared about was how the current quarter looked during the worst recession in memory!

Six months later, we agreed to sell NetQoS for 3.7 times revenue, in case you thought my two-times valuation was too much to ask. Any of these firms could have picked up a huge return in the short term if they had funded the acquisition. Not to mention that the combined entity would have been worth more and would have had more potential acquirers as well as the possibility of a lucrative IPO.

In this situation, I was not able to provide the resources we needed to make the deal happen. And I'll be honest: my track record for providing capital is not great. Raising money is hard. Over my career of leading multiple companies, I have talked to more than a hundred institutional investors and have reached a deal exactly once. For this reason I advise companies to take the money when they can, because it often isn't there when you really need it. No company ever failed because they had too much cash on the balance sheet. Of course the biggest source of capital within a business should be organic capital—money generated from core operations or sales of products and services. A CEO who cannot grow a company organically will eventually drive it into the ground.

Fortunately my record in providing the right human resources has been much better than my efforts at raising capital. I have spent an incredible amount of time throughout my career seeking out and collecting top talent. More than anything else, my ability to place the right person in the right role has made me successful. I don't think I have any special skill; I have simply made it a consistent focus. Many CEOs seem to believe that talent acquisition, development, and retention are not areas on which they should spend significant time or resources. They often leave them to human resources or to department heads to handle, with little accountability for and few metrics to track the quality of the talent pursued or already within the organization. I hope to convince you in this section that focusing on talent acquisition and development is not only an appropriate role for the CEO, it may also be the role that provides the greatest return on investment.

To measure performance, you have to have a standard to measure against, right? This is just as true with people as it is with financials or other goals. In human resources, the standard should take into account the competitive marketplace in which your company operates. Charles Koch's book *The Science of Success: How Market-Based Management Built the World's Largest Private Company* convinced me of this idea. Through his belief in "laws that govern human well-being," Koch helped build Koch Industries, a refining business his father started, into the world's largest privately held company. Maybe his engineering background and systems approach to management are what made his ideas so attractive to me.

To illustrate Koch's premise, imagine you are the owner of an NBA basketball team. You have a point guard on your team who was a phenom as a kid, the best player ever from his small town. In high school he led his team to two state championships and was the most valuable in the state his senior year. In college he was an All-American twice and was the star player his senior year while winning the NCAA championship. He was a first-round draft pick and now he is on your team. Sounds like a star, right? Well, actually he is ranked twenty-fourth in the NBA. So do you want him starting every night for you? No! Because with thirty-two teams in the NBA, most nights he steps on the court he would put you at a competitive disadvantage. Every person in an organization must be evaluated compared to the competitive environment in which the company operates.

Koch's system is simple in that each employee is given a grade of A, B, or C based on the competitive advantage he or she offers the company.

A-level individuals perform in their current role in a way that provides significant advantage because it is better than those employees in similar roles at principal competitors. A's (whom I also sometimes call A players) are exceptional contributors to long-term profitability because they are among the top 15 percent of their peers throughout the industry. A's also contribute to competitive advantage by being aligned with and supporting the values of the organization, which influence the culture. And a strong culture is critical to the success of the teams that operate within it. Notice that someone cannot be an A player if he does not support the culture of the organization. It is a primary responsibility of management to ensure that these employees are retained and fully engaged. The company should *always* be in the market for A-level talent and must continually improve its ability to identify and recruit these exceptional individuals. Management policy decisions should be made based on how this group will react.

B-level individuals perform at least as well as their peers at principal competitors. These individuals are between the top 15 percent and 50 percent of performers throughout the industry in their current roles. B's are valuable contributors who consistently meet and may exceed expectations in many areas of performance. They are, collectively, critical to a company's success. They are not an afterthought living in the shadow of A performers. Management's responsibility is to facilitate and empower these individuals in order to grow them into A performers in their current roles or move them into roles that can best utilize their strengths.

Performance of **C-level individuals** in their current role puts the company at a competitive disadvantage by being below average relative to their peers at principal competitors. C's are not meeting expectations. Management's responsibility is to rapidly develop them in their current role or get them into a role where they can be an A performer. If this cannot be done in a timely manner, the individual should not be retained. Inability to create value at one organization does not mean the same will be true elsewhere in an organization with different values or culture.

When I discuss this rating system with other CEOs, they often worry about the sandbagging problem. What prevents managers from rating all their people as A's? they ask. Well, I tell my managers that if they rank all their employees high, they have no excuse for their groups not dramatically outperforming the competition. If they don't, I'll know where the problem is. That usually keeps managers from getting carried away. An important task of the CEO is to review these rankings every quarter.

How much time do you spend in the recruiting process? After employees are hired, do you have a way of knowing if the hire was successful? Have you studied your successful employees to find the common threads that might allow you and other leaders to find more of them? Once you have an employee in place, what do you do to make sure they continue to develop and perform? And if they do not perform well, how do you handle it? All of these are critical questions for a CEO.

Successful CEOs work hard to deliver whatever resources the company needs to prosper—capital and people are the two most important. In the "Deliver Performance" section of the book, I'll also address other resources, such as expertise in the form of advisors and critical relationships with vendors and the community. In this section, I'll explore ways to address budgeting and investment challenges and ways to build a team of A and B players who can ensure your company will succeed.

BUDGETING VS. OPPORTUNISTIC INVESTMENT

"Adhering to budgeting rules shouldn't trump good decision making."

—EMILY OSTER

Even though I have spent most of my career in the CEO chair, I have also worked in several large organizations along the way. The one lesson that has stood out in those experiences is how often management action is driven by budgets and the budgeting process. This is not a positive.

In a large company, budgets are often the only tangible plans to which lower-level managers and employees are exposed. While the company may have a vision, it is rarely translated into actionable direction for employees. And so the budget often takes on the role of divine scripture when it comes to making business decisions.

In 1997, after selling a small computer business, I was looking for an interesting opportunity and I heard about one at Advanced Micro Devices (AMD). At the time AMD was trying to break Intel's monopoly in the business PC market. They had recently hired a new CIO who was shocked to learn that almost all the PCs used by AMD employees had Intel chips inside. Because AMD had such a small presence in the PC market, none of the major business PC vendors offered machines with AMD chips. The new CIO made it known that he wanted to change this immediately, which meant they needed a vendor to custom-build PCs for their thousands of employees. My previous business had been a custom PC business, so I knew the market well. Through a friend of mine who worked there, I was able to get an introduction to the project manager and the IT director.

I knew that a large company like AMD would need a vendor to deal with the logistical issues associated with buying parts, assembling machines, and providing warranty service. Like most large companies, they wanted to pay on terms, and this would cause cash flow problems for many of the small local vendors that normally do this kind of work. I put together a presentation explaining the problems they would have dealing with many of these small vendors and concluding that if they dealt with me, I could solve them. During the presentation, I could tell that I had clearly hit a nerve by identifying some key issues they were already experiencing. However, I could also tell that one of the executives in the meeting was not buying everything I was selling. When the meeting ended I thanked them all for their time and waited for a phone call. When it came, I was surprised by the offer. Instead of agreeing to my vendor proposal, the executive wanted to hire me to manage all of their IT vendors. He said I was the first person they had talked to who understood their problems, and while the PC problem was important, they also needed to solve vendor issues across all of IT. I wasn't really looking for a job, but it was something I certainly knew how to do. This is how my first and only voluntary foray into corporate America was launched.

Part of my job was to manage relationships with the large number of vendors. Having owned an IT business, I understood how vendors operated and knew AMD was wasting a significant amount of money. A few weeks into the job, I began to regularly notice a group of IT providers in the halls, identifiable by their contractor badges. One day I stopped one of them to find out what they did. He told me they provided desktop support services for AMD and were employed by a local vendor. I went back to my desk and found the invoices for the vendor. I was shocked to see that AMD was being charged $75 per hour for all of these desktop technicians. I knew that they were probably making $20 per hour at most and that the vendor was pocketing the difference. These workers weren't temporary help hired to get us through a particularly busy period; they were the everyday support that AMD employees called on when they had IT issues. I felt like I had just found a gold mine. There were roughly twenty-five of these contractors, and

I figured we could save at least $50 per hour per person if we simply converted these contractors to employees. That equated to about $2.5 million in savings every year. Even for a company the size of AMD, that was a significant savings for such an easy change. I quickly made an appointment with the director in charge of the group so I could present my brilliant plan. After exchanging pleasantries, I immediately cut to the chase. "Do you know that we pay $75 per hour for the desktop support contractors?" I asked.

"Yes," he said somewhat proudly, "we used to pay $150 per hour."

Undeterred by that surprising piece of news, I plowed on. "Well, we could hire all of those people as employees and pay them $20 per hour. They would probably cost the company in total about $25 per hour. I've talked to a few them and they would rather work for us."

"But that wouldn't save us any money," the director countered.

At this point in my career, being young and stupid, I almost walked to his white board and did the simple math of $75 minus $25 times 2,000 hours, but I was so shocked by the answer that I just said, "What?"

Sensing my confusion, he began to explain the intricacies of corporate budgeting to me. Because the budget was already set for the current year, making this change would not "save" any money because money not spent from a given bucket would just disappear, rather than become available for other expenses. Also, my plan would require adding headcount that had not been planned for in the budget, so it would look like he was requesting more resources during the year. That would be perceived as bad planning on his part. He closed by saying, "We can look at making the change for next year's budget." I stumbled out of his office, dazed and confused.

Some people may dismiss this story as just a bad decision made by a weak employee, but I would argue differently. I believe it was a bad process that produced certain incentives that caused otherwise competent employees to act in a way that was bad for the company. The budget process had conditioned this director to avoid any changes during the year, regardless of the big-picture benefit for the company. This was a learned behavior. I am sure the CEO had no idea that people in the organization were making these kinds of decisions. Or maybe he did.

Budgeting is an important aspect of running your company, as is providing resources for the right investments at the right time. However, if your management system defaults to following the budget, you have a big problem. Instead, focus on inclusive planning, constant re-forecasting, and driving productivity.

BUDGET TYRANTS AND BUDGET BLOWERS

Some CEOs are budget tyrants. The budget tyrant acts like the budget was a divine creation passed down from an infallible god. This type of CEO will often have a financial background and believe that the key to a successful business is the financial planning process. Deviation is the enemy and following the yearly budget is the way to reduce variability in the business. Unfortunately for this executive, business is conducted in a constantly changing environment. The budget that was written six months ago under one set of business conditions often doesn't apply to today's environment. It is bad for the business, because opportunities that were not part of the plan are often missed or ignored. Also, when executives and managers are not asked to think about spending within the business, they stop behaving like leaders. The organization becomes a plane on autopilot, flying the same path regardless of the changing weather conditions. These types of businesses are ripe for disruption by competitors, who take advantage of their slow course corrections.

FINDING YOUR BALANCE

1. Do you focus on comparables to budget as your primary metric?

2. Is it possible for executives to rearrange their spending within budget without your approval?

3. If one of your executives found an acquisition or partnership that was great for the company but was unplanned, would it have any chance of making its way through your organization?

The budget-blower CEO can't seem to help himself. Every shiny object draws his attention. The biggest chunks of money usually go to acquisitions, with new corporate headquarters and a jet thrown in for good measure. Of course these kinds of shopping sprees cannot occur unless the company is throwing off a significant amount of cash. It may be because of this success that the CEO feels overconfident in his ability to generate returns from any asset. In a 2006 study on CEO confidence, Geoffrey Tate and Ulrike Malmendier found that overconfident CEOs were 65 percent more likely to make an acquisition—and the effect is even higher if the acquisition does not require external financing.[10] Unfortunately for these CEOs, the market reaction to an acquisition is usually significantly more negative when compared to the acquisitions of non-overconfident CEOs.

Sometimes the budget blower is driven by a feeling that the company is being left behind by some new technological wave. Of course every CEO should be concerned about disruptive forces in her industry, but the basic math has to make sense. I once had a Fortune 500 CFO try to justify her boss's buying spree by asking me how I liked the deal, ignoring the price. I wasn't sure how to answer, because inherent to any deal is a price that makes the deal work and a price that makes the deal stink. She followed up my quizzical look by stating that $350 million wasn't really very much money for a company their size. And at the time this conversation was occurring, the company was laying off people in order to meet budget numbers for the new year. In my opinion, $350 million is always a lot of money.

FINDING YOUR BALANCE

1. Do you often decide on major expenditures that are a surprise to your team?

2. In your company, is there a consistent set of guiding principles—from the top of the organization to the bottom—for how company money is spent?

Some CEOs are budget tyrants in one area and budget blowers in another, based on their own interests or ideas about what is best for the company. For instance, one area where budgets often seem to have no meaning is acquisitions. It is amazing to me that CEOs will pinch pennies and subject every expense report to the most detailed review and then decide to acquire a company for hundreds of millions or even billions of dollars. Often the price is justified after the executives have already decided to do the deal, even though it's obvious to the industry and the market that they paid too much or acquired when they should have passed.

ACQUISITIONS GONE WILD

I don't mean to pick on Léo Apotheker, but as I write this, Hewlett Packard has just written off $8.8 billion due to its acquisition of Autonomy. It paid over 11 times revenue for the company, which to almost every observer was a ridiculous price. Now HP is trying to claim it was somehow misled by some of the accounting details. There are no accounting details that explain paying 11 times revenue for Autonomy. It was a terrible waste of shareholder money by a CEO who felt pressure to do something, even if it was wrong. Of course Apotheker received a $25 million severance package for his mistake. I would love to see the analysis that showed how HP was going to get its $11 billion back from the deal. This failure to properly consider the interest of shareholders is to my mind almost criminal. A CEO must not allow the pressure to do something override his fundamental business sense of profit and loss.

PLANNING, FLEXIBILITY, AND PRODUCTIVITY

So what is a CEO to do? Am I advocating getting rid of budgets? Not at all. Every business I have run has had a yearly budget. But the budget-balancing act requires the CEO to consistently align decision making with the long-term success of the business. Here are some ways to plan well but remain flexible in order to make the best choices for the business.

Prioritize the Forecasting
Process Over the Budgeting Process

At NetQoS the number-one performance metric for the sales group was how accurately they forecasted revenue for each quarter (at the beginning of the quarter). Predicting the future is hard, but over time they developed a process that allowed them to predict new license revenue within a tolerance of less than 5 percent, more than 90 percent of the time. This is world-class in the software business, and their success was driven by their strict focus on accurate forecasting. As CEO, I had a one-quarter crystal ball from a revenue perspective, which allowed me to properly adjust resources to maximize growth without running out of cash. It also made for much less exciting board meetings!

The biggest source of capital is usually revenue generated from sales of core products and services, so it's critical that companies build a sales process that makes this capital source as predictable as possible. The value of a good sales process is that it converts anecdotal data to predictive data. Too many times sales forecasts are based on hopes and dreams and not the analysis of real data. CEOs shouldn't let this happen. Mastering the sales process is critical to prevent the company from being constantly expanded and contracted by the results of a given quarter. Providing the proper resources requires the ability to properly size the organization for the resources available without reacting to short-term issues.

DITCHING THE BUDGET

If you can handle the "uncertainty," some experts advocate doing away with budgets entirely and moving to a rolling forecast, which is exactly what

Northern Quest Resort and Casino did. Every year, they would spend almost half the year developing the annual budget for the next year—reviewing department projections, asking for verification, and on and on—and so the budget was out-of-date by the time it was finalized. According to an article in the *Journal of Accountancy*, Tim Quinn, CPA and vice president of finance, said, "'To go through that whole, long, arduous process to come up with a document that's essentially useless—I decided it was kind of a crazy idea.'"[11] So they moved to a fifteen-month outlook of revenue and expenses. Based on analytics and financial software, the outlook updates itself every quarter based on the results of the previous quarter. "'It's a living, breathing document,' Quinn said. 'It's more in tune with what reality is becoming.'" The results for the company? The finance staff spends more time on strategy and identifying ways for the company to adapt to changing business conditions, managers and employees have less of a use-it-or-lose-it or spend-to-the-max mindset, and the departments are less siloed (because they aren't in competition during the budgeting process and they have to collaborate to ensure the outlook is valid).

Sounds pretty good, right? All we have to do is buck tradition for the new age of flexibility.

Disperse Control

The final say on budget development and compliance must be placed in the hands of the operating executives or leaders in the business, not the CFO. Any significant spending decision has to be considered by whether it advances the goals of the department or division and the company as a whole, not just how it compares to a plan.

I tell managers who work with me that the budget is the maximum amount of money they are expected to spend to accomplish their goals. To exceed expectations they can spend less money and accomplish their goals, or exceed their goals while spending their full budget. The focus should be on achieving the goals of the organization for the least amount of money, not making sure that every budget category in every division or department is in balance or that every dollar available is used up. I touch base with the leaders frequently, but I also let them decide how to spend their budgets effectively. They should know better than I. Of course, this commonsense approach will prevent the kind of problems I experienced at AMD only if everyone understands the goals of the organization.

Develop Smart Goals and Metrics

One tool that will help you avoid slipping into total-control mode is good goals and metrics. I don't mean basic financials. A good CEO measures the performance of every group based on metrics that are aligned with the goals of the company. Managers need to be aware of those goals, quarter by quarter, and understand how their efforts support them. Otherwise, they will quickly begin to operate out of alignment, moving toward their own purposes.

Again, the real problem at AMD was a lack of direction. The budget was the only tangible guidance that leaders and employees had for making a decision. With no other guiding principles, the budget became the bible by which all actions were judged. The fundamentals of the business never entered into the conversation. The IT director at AMD should have had a clear goal of delivering high-quality desktop support at the lowest possible price, with a customer satisfaction metric (in addition to cost) attached to that goal. If he found a way during the year to improve those metrics significantly—reduce costs or increase satisfaction—he should have been commended, not penalized.

Budgets are static, but business changes on a daily basis. However, in many companies the only consistent feedback a manager receives is whether or not she is meeting budget—often a budget she had no opportunity to influence. If that is the situation in your company, your leadership team will quickly become conditioned to manage to the budget instead of managing to achieve or exceed the goals of the business.

I cover goals and metrics in much more detail in the "Deliver Performance" section of the book.

Plan for Change and Push the Limits

I have two favorite questions that I ask of managers who work for me: "What would you do if you had significantly more money to spend?" and "What would you do if you had significantly less money to spend?" These two questions force managers to consider the cost/benefit trade-offs necessary to dynamically adapt to an ever-changing business climate. And at the beginning of any given year, you may not know what resources will be available six months later, especially if you are a fast-growth company. I have seen managers suddenly receive a windfall and spend it poorly because they had no plan. I have also seen managers forced to get by on significantly less, yet deliver close to the same productivity. At the end of the day the company that delivers the most productivity for a given unit of capital will be the most successful company. The CEO must constantly force the organization to make spending decisions in this business context instead of basing them on numbers in a spreadsheet. Cheaper and better is often possible, but only if better is clearly defined.

It is easy to tell if a company is driven by budget rather than driven by growth and vision. Budget-driven companies tend to make dramatic policy changes, such as a hiring freeze, a travel ban, or eliminating pay increases, in order to improve their numbers on a short-term basis or when it looks like the business is not performing. While easy to enforce, these types of absolutist moves are rarely the best solutions because they often limit your ability to move toward your vision faster or grow out of your slump.

I believe that to be a great company you must have great people, and great people aren't necessarily available on your schedule. A hiring freeze can cause you to miss top performers when they come on the market. Great people are rarely available, and when they are available it's often because of some sudden disruptive event. When these top performers are available, grab them quickly because they don't stay on the market for long. If your company has a culture built around fidelity to the budget or tightening the belt without thinking clearly about the long term, it won't be possible to make these opportunistic hires. I tell managers to always look for great people they can add to the team. If the company can't afford the additional headcount, people who are not performing should be let go to make room. I have never seen a company that was so full of great people that they could afford to pass on a superstar.

The travel ban is another quick-fix method for improving the bottom line. If you think people are traveling excessively or extravagantly, address those issues but don't lay down a blanket policy. I know a senior manager at a large company who went eighteen months before he ever met his direct manager face-to-face because of a travel ban. Finally the ban was lifted and he traveled to headquarters to meet with his boss. One hour after meeting with him, an announcement came out reorganizing the senior manager to a different group. Needless to say he didn't feel very positive about the company and soon left for greener pastures. Also, the travel ban almost never applies to the CEO or other members of the executive team. I have seen travel bans put in place for the rank and file while the executive team continues to fly around solo on the corporate jets. This is the kind of behavior that gives CEOs a bad reputation.

Sometimes employees have to sacrifice a little to keep the company moving forward. However, you won't retain your top talent if you don't pay them what they're worth. Banning pay increases for more than a few months is a sure sign that the company doesn't have a plan to get out of its revenue or growth slump. I once met a woman who worked for a company that had eliminated pay increases, even cost-of-living adjustments, for more than two years. They were losing people at an ever-increasing rate, of course, particularly because they didn't pay very well to begin with. The company had a reputation as a cool place to work—great culture, great parties, great perks. At the end of the day, though, people need to feel that they will be more successful as a result of their commitment to the company. People aren't always or exclusively motivated by pay, but they will leave if they think they are not being compensated fairly.

When times are tough and you feel the need to reduce expenses, think about your mid-term and long-term goals first. Rather than implementing a knee-jerk policy, gather your team and let them know that the day has come for them to review their answers to the question, "What would you do if you had significantly less money to spend?" Smart leaders (that top talent you scooped up when it was available) and strong teams will find ways to weather the storm and come out whole on the other side.

—

How you manage your financials influences and is influenced by the culture of your organization. If you want to build a high-performing organization, you need to trust your managers to make smart decisions but also give them the tools and information they need to stay aligned with company goals. Sticking to a budget is not necessarily the best sign of a business's or a manager's success. Growth, profitability, and flexibility matter more.

FINDING YOUR BALANCE

1. Does your team do an objective cost-benefit analysis before a decision is made on any major expenditure?

2. How do you involve your leadership team and managers in the budgeting process?

3. What metrics do you have in place to keep spending decisions aligned with company goals?

4. Do all of your leaders have a backup plan for cutting expenses while maintaining productivity and progress toward long-term goals?

GROWTH VS. PROFITABILITY

"Growth is never by mere chance;
it is the result of forces working together."

—JAMES CASH PENNEY

I remember sitting in my office one Friday afternoon, catching up on email as the weekend quickly approached. My staff had learned that I usually stayed late on Fridays and if they wanted to run something by me it was a good time to get my uninterrupted attention. So it was no surprise when my software development director popped his head in and asked for a few minutes of my time. We were nearing the final stages of development on a new product, and when he appeared I immediately began to worry that the project might be behind schedule. Containing my fears, I asked casually, "So how's the schedule looking?" His concerned expression was a red flag.

"Well, the schedule is fine," he said, "but I'm just not feeling good about our ability to test the final product. With the limited equipment we have, I'm not sure we will know how the product will behave in a customer environment." I knew where this was heading—money and in such amounts that he felt it would be necessary to get me on board early.

"So what's it going to cost to properly test it?" I asked.

"I talked to our vendor, and they promised we can simulate a very large environment with their latest chassis." It was a non-answer.

"How much is it going to cost?" I repeated.

"I negotiated a great deal and we can have everything we need for $125,000," he finally admitted.

At the time of this request we were doing about $20 million per year in revenue, so the request, while significant, didn't break the bank. Because it hadn't been budgeted, though, it would require me to approve it and decide where the money would come from. I said, "Let me think about it over the weekend and we'll discuss it at the staff meeting on Monday."

No sooner had my development director left my office than in came my CFO. "Hey, boss," he said, "What's up?"

"Well," I said, "Jim was just in here and he says he needs to buy a new test system to properly qualify the new release."

Being a CFO, he quickly got to the point: "How much is that going to cost?"

"He says the best we can do is $125,000," I replied.

My CFO then got that pained expression on his face that CFOs get when any new expenses appear. He repeated the number and said, "That's interesting."

Interesting is not the word you typically expect to come out of a CFO's mouth when he hears about a large, unplanned expense. I was immediately on guard. "What's interesting about it?" I asked.

"You know I've been telling you that we need to upgrade our accounting and business systems. With the growth around here, my team can barely keep up, and we don't have quick access to the data you need. I think we need to bite the bullet and do the upgrade as soon as possible before we start falling behind," he concluded.

"And just how much is this upgrade going to cost?" I asked.

"I hate to say it, but with the cost of software, implementation, and training, it will be about $125,000." I couldn't help laughing. In the span of ten minutes I was being asked to approve two unplanned expenses of $125,000, and they were as different as apples and oranges.

CEOs face this type of dilemma every day. It's unique to the job. How do you provide the proper resources for everybody when your resources are finite? How do you compare competing expenses when they have almost no relation to each other? And how do you make the right choice for your particular goals? For most executives, allocating resources is simplified by the fact that the goal of their department is often, although not always, straightforward. If you are the VP of sales, you are trying to maximize revenue. When you have to decide between two expenses, you choose the one that you think will generate the most revenue. While making the correct decision may be difficult, framing the problem is easy. For the CEO, framing the problem is often not so easy. Even if we simplify things and say that the goal of any company is to achieve long-term shareholder value, it is often unclear how that is best achieved.

To simplify the complexity, some CEOs place all their focus on either growth or profitability. Sometimes it's a smart short-term strategy. Focusing only on growth may even be a fine mid-term strategy. As I write this, there's a lot of buzz about the Twitter IPO, which raised roughly $2 billion for a company that was in the red in the most recent quarter by $70 million. Investors believe in Twitter's longevity, despite the lack of profitability. Ignoring certain giants (Amazon for one), a company needs both long-term growth and profitability to avoid risking the chance of catastrophic failure.

GROWTH JUNKIES AND PENNY-PINCHERS

Every CEO should strive for growth, but it can be an incredibly powerful force. Companies with high growth rates are often valued dramatically higher than slower-growing companies in the same industry. Because of this valuation advantage, many CEOs will push growth at all costs. Pursuing unprofitable ventures just to drive top-line revenue can take a company out of balance. Selling dollars for seventy-five cents is often addictive. While it is not unusual for a company that is not profitable to go public, it is generally expected that as the company increases in size, economies of scale will take over and the company will move toward profitability. If, as revenue grows, profit margins become even more negative, the CEO may be driving the company toward a death-by-growth experience. Some CEOs become so enamored with short-term monthly and quarterly revenue that they take their eyes off the horizon and miss signs that the future of the company is in danger.

TOO BIG, TOO FAST

That's what the media said about Groupon as they reported on the various challenges the company faced during its IPO and the eventual ousting of founder and CEO, Andrew Mason. Mason, true to his quirky self, called the company a toddler in a grown man's body less than six months after the IPO. Certainly, the market revealed that the company's IPO came too soon or at least at the wrong time, with the stock plunging 75 percent from its IPO high. Problems with accounting and disclosures to the SEC, as well as reports from employees of a high-pressure, even abusive, work environment (leaders in Europe were accused of being slave drivers who used threats to drive employees to achieve unrealistic goals[12]), created a sense that Andrew Mason was a growth-and-valuation-at-all-costs—even ethical costs—CEO. It's hard to know whether that was a fair assessment without being inside the company. But it was clear from all the results that the company grew too fast for the systems that were in place.

Of course, nobody else involved in the IPO, even the underwriters, raised red flags about the $950 million round of funding before the IPO, $810 million of which was paid out to employees and investors. Nobody seemed concerned about the company's working capital deficit paired with unsustainable growth rates.[13] If it couldn't maintain its revenue growth, it could have trouble covering its old liabilities. Finally, other companies had already successfully eaten into Groupon's market share with similar business models. The attraction of the triple-digit growth blinded everybody to the realities. But eventually the market responded to those realities as Groupon began to founder. Right now, Groupon's stock price is hovering around $10, although some analysts believe even that is too high.

FINDING YOUR BALANCE

1. Will you do almost anything to close a deal? Have you instilled that mindset in your sales team?

2. Have you implemented controls to align spending with projected cash flow?

3. If you are focused on growth and are operating at a loss, do you have a clear plan and potential timeline for heading into the black?

The penny-pincher CEO cares about one thing: the bottom line. He acts like every expense is taking money directly out of the pockets of shareholders. This attitude is often seen in entrepreneur CEOs who have bootstrapped their businesses. No expense is too small to scrutinize, and they spend their "spare time" reviewing expense reports, looking for that unauthorized bottle of wine or an overly expensive airfare. Spending is controlled at the very top; every expenditure requires direct approval of the CEO or a similarly minded CFO. Often, one of them will take on the responsibility of ordering office supplies or other resources the company needs.

Like managers who are afraid to deviate from the budget, executives and managers who are scared to spend any money cannot act as leaders. They become passive, waiting for direction from above before acting. Many leadership decisions in business involve an expense in one way or another. This makes for an organization that is slow moving, risk averse, and likely to lose any competitive advantage it has. While this is a great way to maintain equity, it's also a great way to create a culture of ignoring opportunities and harming shareholder value in the long run.

FINDING YOUR BALANCE

1. Do your employees have the tools necessary to perform at their maximum level of productivity?

2. Compared to your competitors, are your workers more or less efficient?

3. Do you approve any significant expenditures in your organization? Do you approve less significant expenditures?

4. When past revenue projections are compared to actual results, is there a consistent correlation?

CLARIFY AND COMMUNICATE YOUR GOAL

What is the goal in your company? Maximize revenue or hit a certain level of profitability? Or a bit of both? CEOs of different companies will have different answers to this question. For privately held companies that are supporting their owners, maximizing cash flow may be the overwhelming goal. Public companies will be focused on maximizing the share price, which often means trying to positively position the company in either growth or profit against others in the same industry. Private companies that are investor backed are usually interested in seeking maximum return for those investors, which often means growing as fast as possible.

Regardless of the overall goal, it is the CEO's job to clarify the financial goals of the company and communicate them to every member of the team via quarterly plans, annual plans, and a three- to five-year plan. The purpose of these plans is to help the team understand the inevitable short- and long-term trade-offs between growth and profitability, and how making those trade-offs will move the company closer to its vision.

The most valuable, successful business would have a high level of profitability while also growing very rapidly. Of course, achieving this combination is almost impossible because high growth is a drag on profitability.

When you are growing rapidly you must make investments in people and equipment, providing resources to handle the future production of higher levels of goods and services. These expenses subtract from profitability. If you choose not to provide these resources, your growth will slow over time, but your profitability may rise. The question is, where do you want the company to fall on this spectrum?

THE RULE OF 45

An experienced Wall Street banker once told me about his "Rule of 45." He explained that for a company to achieve an exceptional valuation in the market, its annual growth rate plus its operating margin needed to exceed 45 percent. While this is just a rule of thumb, it is surprisingly valuable in thinking about balancing growth and profitability. At one extreme it means that if you grow at a rate north of 45 percent, you can break even or actually operate at a loss and still be rewarded in the market. Fast-growing companies often go through an IPO when they are still losing money because their growth rate is strong enough for people to believe in their ability to generate future profits. After the dot-com bust, though, when companies evaporated because they lacked sound strategies for sustainable growth and future profits, smart investors became more cautious about valuing growth over profitability.

On the other end of the spectrum, if a company is not growing or is growing slowly, it needs an operating margin north of 45 percent to achieve a high valuation. High operating margins are very tough to obtain and even tougher to maintain over time. This is just one supporting point for the idea that companies cannot stagnate for very long and remain valuable or relevant.

Use the Rule of 45 as a simple way to benchmark your business against the best in the world. If you are striving for a certain growth rate, consider how that might affect your operating margin. If you are striving for a certain level of profitability, consider how that might affect your ability to grow. Establish goals that are realistic, communicate them to your team, and provide appropriate resources. If you want growth, you cannot limit expenses. You have to invest in new ideas, new products, and new resources in order to maximize productivity. But you must balance those investments against the long-term plan for eventual profit. If you want profitability, you will still need to provide resources to maximize productivity and maintain enough growth to ensure that the company is moving forward and staying relevant by adapting to the changing market.

—

You may be wondering how I responded to the two leaders at NetQoS who asked me for $125,000 on the same day. Recall from the chapter on vision that our goal at the time was to grow as fast as possible without running out of money. I wasn't sure exactly how either would contribute to our growth (although I knew putting out a stable product would obviously help). So I decided to test for criticalness. I asked each of the managers to find the money in their own departments. When they both told me that they wouldn't pull money from other areas to fund these new expenses, I knew they weren't critical. So we delayed both investments until a better time.

Regardless of whether you are prioritizing growth or profitability in your business, you will need to provide the appropriate resources—but you also need to invest carefully and wisely.

FINDING YOUR BALANCE

1. How do you establish and communicate the financial goals of the company?

2. Are your goals realistic? Do they acknowledge potential trade-offs between growth and profitability?

3. Do you provide appropriate resources to achieve the goals? What questions do you ask of your leaders when you're making decisions about investments?

RECRUITING VS. HIRING

"At most companies, people spend 2 percent of their time
recruiting and 75 percent managing their recruiting mistakes."

—**RICHARD FAIRBANK, CEO, CAPITAL ONE**

I was on a flight one day with former Texas Tech football coach Spike Dykes. Spike is a legend in west Texas, where he transformed Texas Tech from an also-ran to a formidable football power, often beating his better-funded contemporaries at the University of Texas and Texas A&M. I mentioned to Spike how I thought the job of head football coach and the job of CEO were very similar. Both have a set of stakeholders that can be very powerful and demanding. If you win, you're the hero; but a few losses, and everyone thinks they could do the job better.

As we were discussing all the great coaches he had worked for and coached against, I asked him how much of a coach's success was due to actual coaching and how much was due to the talent level of the players he recruited. I said, "Is it 50-50?"

"No," he quickly said, "it's 75 percent the players and 25 percent coaching. You give me the best players and an average coach and we will beat the best coach with average players every time."

I thought to myself how much that resonated with my business experience. I have always felt that I should attribute the majority of my success to my efforts to get the right people in the right positions. For me, it has been the most important task, because I believe that all the strategy in the world cannot make up for a lack of capabilities.

If you agree that 75 percent of the success of an organization is driven by the abilities of the people in the organization, then logic tells you that you should spend 75 percent of your time on people issues. However, many CEOs spend very little time on recruiting, developing talent, and making sure that good employees stay put. Those tasks get left to lower-level leaders.

Here's what that often looks like: everything is running normally in Company X, until one day a key employee announces she is leaving the company. The manager, clearly stressed out, rushes into the CEO's office and says, "Sally, my best employee, just quit. She's going to the Acme Company. They offered her 20 percent more salary and some equity. I asked her if there was anything we could do, but she said her mind is made up and she is leaving in two weeks."

The CEO says, "This is sudden. I thought things in your group were going great. Did you know she was looking?"

"She says they found her; though I have noticed over the last couple of months that she hasn't seemed as engaged. I just thought she was stressed about the big project due at the end of the quarter. I don't know how we are going to finish it in time unless we can find someone quick."

Later in the "Saving vs. Trading Up" chapter I'll talk about how to retain your best employees. But for now, let's assume that the horse is out of the barn. What will most companies do to fill the open slot? If the company is big enough to have a dedicated human resources department, the manager will notify HR that he has an opening he needs to fill immediately. After some back-and-forth over the job description and the proper keywords, the HR group will provide a dump of the latest resumes they have seen that might possibly fit the opening. The manager will then have to sift through possibly hundreds of resumes to identify candidates who would need to be phone screened and then eventually brought in for interviews. Additionally, the manager may reach out to his network of friends and industry contacts to let them know that an opening exists and to solicit resumes through this channel. If the company is too small to have a recruiting function, the manager may draft a job description on his own, or even ask the employee who is leaving to help him, and then take out ads on one of the online sites emphasizing the key experience he is looking for in a candidate. This will produce a stream of candidates that the manager must sift through in hopes of finding someone who can fill the job. All the while, a big project is delayed more and more each day the job isn't filled.

Is this a recipe for finding the best possible candidate? Do the top performers in an industry send their resumes blindly into a company and patiently wait to hear something? Are top performers often looking for work on job sites? If such a candidate did send her resume in, would anyone looking at it be able to tell that this might be a high-quality candidate for this particular position?

Most organizations I have observed treat hiring as a tactical fire drill instead of as a core component of their strategic plan. If you are not regularly recruiting and encouraging every leader or manager in your company to do the same, you will be stuck when you lose a critical member of your team. And you may not have any A-level talent on your team to begin with. A's, even B's, aren't always right there when you need them. You must constantly recruit if you want a continuous stream of intellectual capital ready to take on new roles. Finding people with some basic keyword qualifications to fill a position is staffing, not recruiting. Staffing at best puts you even with the competition, and most times puts you at a serious competitive disadvantage. If your business needs the best intellectual capital to be successful—and it does, regardless of your industry—you must build a well-managed recruiting function.

BODY COUNTS AND BLACK SWANS

Many CEOs, especially in larger companies, are not involved in the hiring process. Even if a CEO cannot meet every interviewee, she should find a way to be involved in the hiring process to ensure that the standards she has established are being applied. But for body-count CEOs, hiring is a matter of numbers. Her main concern is whether the open positions are filled with warm bodies. Quality is not really a concern just as long as there are enough people on the bus to carry out her strategy. In this way, the body-count CEO is similar to the master strategist I described in the first chapter. While few CEOs would state this position publicly, it is the inevitable outcome when companies focus on filling positions and have no way to evaluate the quality of their hires. Often the entire recruiting and hiring process is outsourced to third-party firms whose compensation is based on the number of positions filled. With incentives like that, it's no wonder that the company gets mediocre employees and delivers mediocre performance.

FINDING YOUR BALANCE

1. Does the executive responsible for personnel report directly to the CEO?

2. Are executives and managers formally evaluated on their ability to recruit?

When the phrase "black swan" was coined in the English language, such a creature was presumed to be nonexistent. When a black swan was discovered, it deepened the meaning of the phrase, used to describe an item or event so rare it could not be planned for. Black swan CEOs are on the hunt for individuals who have such an unusual set of experiences and skills that it is very unlikely that they could ever be found or, if found, that they would work for the hiring company. Job postings guided by these CEOs are a laundry list of qualifications and experiences, degrees, and skills. And they rarely want to pay what an appropriate candidate, if one exists, would ask. Good candidates—people who could actually do the job well even if they don't meet every criterion—are scared away by the lengthy qualifications, while the people who overrate their own skills apply in droves. It is a lazy approach to recruiting, and it shows that the company has not spent time thinking about what they really need in a given position or what type of person would be successful in their company.

I often see CEOs fall into this trap when hiring executives. They expect to hire people with spectacular resumes who have worked at bigger companies and have been very successful. The problem is that every top performer I know wants to make a move up when changing jobs, not sideways or down. The only people typically willing to make a sideways or down move are people who don't have a choice because they were unsuccessful in their previous role. Occasionally, top performers will make a sideways move if they want to change industries or head in a different career direction, but the black swan CEO probably wouldn't want these candidates. If you put out a black swan job posting, don't be surprised when most of the candidates applying are ugly ducklings.

HOW TO GUARANTEE A HIRING FAILURE

I was asked by a small nonprofit to help them hire their next executive director. Because I didn't have great familiarity with the workings of the organization, I asked them to send over the job posting they were using to recruit candidates. When I read the job description, I was flabbergasted. They were looking for someone with years of experience in every different facet of operating a nonprofit—fundraising, grant writing, management, and more—with detailed requirements in each area. My first thought was, "Wow, if I work really hard I might be qualified to run this organization in another ten years!" My next thought was, "I wonder how much they're paying for this position, because someone with this experience will be very expensive." So I called the chairwoman. She told me they had engaged a consultant and he had advised that they should expect to pay about $65,000 per year, considering the size of their organization. Well, that was clearly a problem when compared with the job description. Anyone reading it would expect the position to pay well into six figures. Then the chairwoman told me that since fund-raising had been tight they could only afford $45,000 per year. With this information, the outcome to me was obvious. They were guaranteed to hire the worst person who had ever had an executive director title. With the job posting, they would scare off anyone who hadn't held the title and couldn't claim experience in multiple areas. And the only person who would accept the job for $45,000 would be someone who had been fired from other positions and didn't have a choice. When I pointed this out to the chairwoman, she posed that they might find someone who was willing to do the job out of the kindness of their heart because it was such a good cause.

She was looking for a black swan.

It was clear what had happened. They had looked on the Web for every executive director job description they could find and pieced together what they thought were the best of each. Excellence and experience in every minute aspect of a job is almost impossible to find. And it leaves no room for growth.

FINDING YOUR BALANCE

1. Are job postings in your company scrutinized carefully to ensure that they only include experience that is absolutely necessary?

2. Is it hard to find any candidate who meets the requirements of your job postings?

3. Does it take a long time to fill jobs in your company because you can't get enough candidates?

RULES FOR RECRUITING THE BEST

If one of your five critical responsibilities as CEO is to provide the proper resources, and people are one of those resources—the most important, in my opinion—you will need a rigorous system for maximizing those resources, just as you have an accounting and budgeting system for maximizing your financial resources. That system begins with recruiting. What follows is a list of ten rules for building a top-notch recruiting function.

1. Recruiting is a continuous process.

You can't wait until you have a position open to start the recruiting process. Good people are available when they need a job, and that is not necessarily tied to when you have an opening. Also, the best people will generally already have a job and may need to be wooed to consider making a switch. If you don't begin that process until you are in need, you will be left with an unfilled position for much longer than is good for the company. Instead, be constantly trolling in the market to seek out top performers.

As CEO, you must lead this charge. No good college football coach would ignore recruiting and leave it all to his assistants. In the same way, a CEO should have a recruiting process that is closely monitored and measured to ensure success on the people side of the equation. College football teams spend a lot of money and time scouting the country, looking for new talent that might give them a competitive advantage. How much time and money does your company spend in the same pursuit?

Sometimes, you'll have to engage with people months, even years, before you hire them. A players, particularly at the executive level, often have to be courted to make a move. These relationships will develop over time, and then one day the person will be ready to make a move. For this reason, it's critical for you to develop relationships with top executives in the industry—you'll have a bench to call on should the need arise. It is rarely a good thing for an executive team to remain static for years without any changes. As I mentioned before, you need new ideas to keep your strategy fresh.

2. Always hire A-level talent when it is available.

Unless your business is already filled with A's and you don't ever plan on growing, why would you turn down a top performer? In the nine years it took to build NetQoS from the ground up, I hired every A player who would take a job with us. Top performers usually come on the market because of some disruptive event—a business closing, major restructuring, or a change in family situation. You have to take them when you can get them. By definition, A-level individuals add more value to your business than they cost, so when I didn't have a job for an A, I created one.

Most companies don't take advantage when these talented individuals become available. I watched this type of recruiting failure happen to an exceptionally talented woman I know. She had a 4.0 GPA while obtaining her electrical engineering PhD from the University of Texas and is one of the world experts in computer network management. While she was perfectly happy at her job, the company announced they were closing the facility where she worked. They wanted her to relocate, but she wasn't interested in leaving Austin. I knew an executive at a local network management firm, so I passed her resume along to him. The company had recently gone public and was considered a high flyer at the time. The executive passed the resume to the appropriate department head. The department head gave the resume a cursory glance and tossed it aside. "Looks interesting," he remarked, "but I don't have a position available." He didn't even bother to contact her and have a conversation. She didn't fit in the box he had drawn for his positions. What happened to the PhD? She started her own business and was the creative force behind a company that sold for $200 million. The once high-flying network management company sold years later for a small fraction of that amount.

If your company stumbled across a game-changing talent, what is the chance you would hire the person?

3. Recruiting is a dual sales process.

Not only does the potential employee have to sell himself to the company, but the company also has to sell itself to the employee. Over and over again I have seen companies forget the second part of this equation and just assume that the employee will take the job if it is offered. While mediocre employees probably will, the best performers often have options and will have to be convinced that the opportunity with a particular company is their *best* option. They can usually afford to be picky.

I have spent a lot of time considering the key traits of A players so that I could spot them when recruiting. Unfortunately that's only half the challenge to hiring A talent. Too many managers spend all their time thinking about what they want in a candidate without considering how they can convince that ideal candidate to come work for them. Every company should identify the unique opportunities they offer that will help them attract the best candidates. Make a conscious effort to put together a list of the five to ten reasons your company is the best place to work. If putting that list together is hard, you probably haven't spent enough time on this side of the recruiting process.

While the particular advantages a company can offer will be unique to that company, A's consistently look for these five opportunities:

- Opportunity to grow
- Opportunity to be challenged
- Opportunity to win
- Opportunity to work with the best
- Opportunity for financial rewards

Your ability to demonstrate proof of each of these opportunities will be critical to attracting great performers. The first four opportunities all tie directly to the culture of the business. The best performers know that they can't be successful alone and that they need a great team to reach their maximum potential. This is an area where smaller, faster-growing companies often have an advantage in recruiting over larger, more established entities. It is important to share with potential employees the stories of how employees have grown their skills and overcome challenges and how the company is winning in its market. Exposing potential employees to other A's is also a great way to entice these star performers. And finally, if you want the best, you will have to provide an opportunity for financial reward. However, this does not have to take the form of a giant salary. I find that A players are willing to bet on their ability to make the company successful and will often consider long-term rewards based on that ability. It may require a little creativity on your part, but A's are your source of competitive advantage, so figure out a way to make it work.

Because it is often hard for job seekers to really know a lot about a company from the outside, how the recruiting process is handled is often used as a proxy in the candidate's eyes for the quality of the company and the opportunities it will offer. If you run a really good process with top-notch people in the recruiting position, you will leave a great impression. Your direct involvement will impress almost every candidate, especially if you are a smaller company competing for talent against larger companies.

4. Time is of the essence.

Let's return to our stressed-out manager from the beginning of the chapter. He has now identified a couple of candidates who have the proper check-boxed experiences. The interview process starts with someone from HR reaching out to see if the candidate is still available and interested. The candidate is probably asked to fill out a job application and told that the hiring manager will be in touch. A few days later the manager calls and does a quick phone screen to make sure the candidate has the proper knowledge for the job. If the manager is appropriately impressed, the candidate is brought in for several hours of interviews by the department members and possibly others outside the department. Because the team members often have little hiring experience, the questioning is somewhat random. Because many companies try to interview at least three candidates, it may be weeks before the candidates hear whether they have a job offer or not. Then they may be asked to come back in to meet with the "big boss" as a formality before they get the official offer. It is quite possible that three or four months have passed since the candidates first submitted their resumes.

Now let's think about this process from the potential employee's perspective. Is this how the best people usually find a job? Do the best people usually spend months unemployed? Of course not! This hiring process almost guarantees that the only people hired are mediocre or poor performers who don't have any other options. Most people can't afford to spend months unemployed, waiting for a company to complete their search. The approach also assumes that the open job is highly valuable and that potential employees must compete to get it. While that may be true in rare circumstances, I have always found that top performers are the truly rare commodity and that companies should be competing to get them.

The best people, if they do decide to switch jobs, often have numerous jobs to choose from—former colleagues are likely to be actively recruiting them to their new companies. And I find that top performers are often so busy doing a great job that they don't have time to look for other opportunities. When they do become available, it is often sudden and they want to find a good place to land quickly. Being unemployed is a very stressful situation for the individuals and their families. If they submit a resume, they are looking for quick feedback and someone who can recognize their unique potential.

Potential employees are usually the most excited about working at a company the moment they push the send button and submit a resume. At this instant they have made the decision to make a change and are hopeful that they will quickly be in a new job. Every day that goes by without hearing from the company causes their enthusiasm to wane. The same thing is true once the interview process starts. The longer the time between interview and offer, the less excitement the candidate feels. In my companies I set the goal of two weeks from when we first get the candidate's resume until we have a job offer in that individual's hands. If the candidate is ready to move, we should be able to take care of everything in that time. If a candidate is an A player, hire her; if you don't think she's an A player, move on. However, this only works if you know that the candidates you are considering are high performers and are likely a good fit for your organization. That is why you have to be recruiting always, not passively waiting to see who shows up.

5. One person has to set the bar.

We built NetQoS from start-up to over 250 employees, and I interviewed every potential new hire. As I often joked, I didn't mind interviewing the ones we hired, but I wished I hadn't wasted my time with the ones on which we passed. The problem was that I had to interview everyone to tell the difference. Because I interviewed each candidate, I became pretty good at recognizing the most talented individuals. I knew what to expect for a given position at a given price point in the market.

Any given department of a company might hire people only occasionally. Therefore, it's hard for managers to know what a good value in the market is at any given time. Candidates had to meet a high bar for me to sign off on the hire (I'll describe my criteria in the next chapter), and that helped maintain consistency across the organization. I think it's important to have one person, if possible, interview all potential employees and set that bar for the organization. It doesn't necessarily have to be the CEO, but I can't think of a much better use of a CEO's time. And if your company hires fewer than one hundred people a year, I think you should make the time to meet each serious candidate.

In large organizations, the CEO should absolutely interview every candidate for positions in the top three to five tiers of leadership and should know personally several hundred employees in order to get a sense for the type of talent being acquired and developed. One person in each division or group might interview all candidates for whom he or she is ultimately responsible. The goal should be consistency, so those responsible for holding candidates to certain standards should be trained to interview well and should be coached on how to identify the right talent for the job and the company. If the HR department leads the hiring training program, the CEO should review it carefully. If the CEO offers no input, how can she ensure that her vision for the talent and teams the company should be building is reflected? A good book to consult on this subject is *Who: The A Method for Hiring* by Geoff Smart and Randy Street. Following their methodology will lead to a much stronger hiring process and many more top performers.

SOME CEOS GET IT

In her first eighteen months as CEO of Yahoo, Marissa Mayer saw the company's stock jump by nearly 130 percent. Now, most analysts believe that the jump is only partially a reflection of Mayer's good work (the rest is the company's stake in Alibaba, set to go public fairly soon).

Regardless, Mayer is building the confidence of shareholders, and one way she did that early on, despite a fair amount of criticism, was to begin reviewing every single hire. She reviews every serious candidate's resume. For a company of about 15,000 employees that is hiring all the time, that's a serious endeavor. Sources within the company, though, have made statements that make it clear she couldn't be spending her time better. According to an article in *Business Insider*, "[An employee] says that one of Yahoo's biggest problems over the past couple years has been 'B-players' hiring 'C-players' who were not 'fired up to come to work' and were 'tolerated too long . . . I'd want to review all the talent that comes in the doors, too.'"[14]

Revenue from their core business (ad sales) has been dropping consistently as they lose market share to Google and Facebook. If she's going to turn that around, she needs talented people and experienced leaders who can find a way to make it happen.

Mayer isn't alone in her approach. I was happy to read this headline on *Business Insider:* "America's Hottest CEOs Are Devoting More Time than Ever to Hiring."[15] The article offered some interesting examples: Dave Gilboa, cofounder of Warby Parker, "spends 25 percent of his time recruiting . . . and interviews every potential hire," "Mark Zuckerberg spends up to 50 percent of his time recruiting," and Arianna Huffington interviews "every hire at The *Huffington Post*." This is some proof that it can, and should, be done.

---

6. Look for disruptive events.

The top performers often become available because of what I call disruptive events. I remember that after the events of September 11, 2001, many companies struggled with the resulting recession. I made it a point to stay in touch with the CEOs of companies that might have employees I would want to hire. More than once I had a CEO call and tell me that she was going to be shutting down her business and ask if I would take a look at hiring her top people. When another CEO sends you a resume of one of her best people, that is about as good as it gets in terms of references. Keep your eyes and ears open for these kinds of events. If you hear that a business is struggling, take the time to find out if they have any A's you could pick up, should the worst happen. Acquisitions also may leave A's considering their options. If one of your competitors gets acquired, it's time to go trolling in their waters.

7. Your recruiters must be top people.

The people who represent your company in the role of recruiter—employees or vendors or consultants—must be top-notch talent. First, they must be able to recognize the signs of a top performer when they see it. Second, candidates will spend more time engaged with your recruiters than anyone else in your organization. If your recruiters are not professional and knowledgeable, it will reflect badly on the company. For a fast-growing company, the recruiter role might be the most important individual contributor position in the whole enterprise.

8. Cultivate unique sources.

While every company might like to hire the top graduate from Harvard or Stanford, many companies have no shot at recruiting at those schools. They simply do not offer the money, the prestige, the growth opportunities, or the locations for which those candidates are looking. Of course, sometimes you luck out, but don't make luck your strategy. Instead, look for places that turn out candidates who might have a particular reason to work for your company.

At NetQoS we found two sources that proved valuable but that most of our competitors didn't touch. The first were regional universities in some of the smaller cities around Texas and Louisiana. Because we were located in Austin, many new graduates were excited about the opportunity to move to such a well-regarded city. Also, these smaller schools often were not on the radar of recruiters from the bigger technology companies, because they focused on the major national universities. By building up relationships with the staff at these smaller schools, we often got great candidates without as much competition. My alma mater, Louisiana Tech, was a particularly rich source of talent. The second source of great candidates was people leaving the military. Because I served for four years as an officer, I know how to read military personnel appraisals, or "fitreps." I also know what parts of the military tend to attract the best and brightest. Leveraging this knowledge, we hired several top performers who were finding it difficult to get a job in the civilian world. Of course, we weren't unique in this effort. Walmart has a program for recruiting junior military officers, and GE has a strong track record of acquiring and retaining military talent; and they are not alone. It makes good sense. As a *Harvard Business Review* article so wisely pointed out: "The armed services have been in the business of leadership development much longer than the corporate world has."[16] Think about sources such as these for your business that might be overlooked by your competition.

9. Training is always required.

I have seen many hiring managers make the mistake of hiring the candidate they think will get up to speed in the least amount of time. I believe this is a very shortsighted approach. I always tell managers to assume every employee will take three months of guidance to get up to full productivity. There should be a formalized training program (some call this onboarding) for all employees, covering everything from where is the bathroom to the vision of the CEO. New hires should meet key executives to learn about the company. Every business is unique with its own unique challenges. Spending the time up front to guide new employees is critically important to a successful recruiting process.

10. Track your performance.

I find that while most companies keep metrics on many parts of the business, recruiting is often ignored. I think metrics should be closely tracked and reviewed to continuously improve the recruiting and hiring process. Here are some that I have found useful:

- **Time to fill an open job**: If the company is doing a good job of continuously recruiting, this time can be kept to a minimum. If it is taking multiple months to fill every new position, there is a probably a problem in the recruiting process.

- **Time from engaging candidate to offer**: Moving quickly requires the recruiter and hiring manager to be in sync and prepared if the right candidate is found.

- **Percent of candidates accepting offers**: Hiring is a very time-consuming process, so it is important not to waste everyone's time going through the interviewing process just to have the candidate turn down the offer. Hopefully the recruiter and hiring manager are laying the groundwork for an offer from the get-go and properly selling the company to the candidate. If so, this number should be 80 percent or better.

- **What companies did we lose candidates to**: It's one thing if you lose out on potential employees to other high-flying companies, but if you are losing to Joe's Shoe Emporium, something about your company is not very attractive. I once lost the number-one graduate in computer science from the University of Texas to Google. While I never like losing, the fact that it came down to deciding between NetQoS and Google convinced me we were doing something right.

- **Percentage of new hires rated "A" or "B" two quarters after hire**: Managers should rate their employees each quarter. A-rated performers are those ranked in the top 15 percent in the industry, considering their job and pay. By random chance, therefore, a company would hire an A player about 15 percent of the time. However, because A players rarely look for a job through normal channels, the average company is almost never able to hire an A player. At the very least, you want to ensure that your hires are B's. If you find that you are hiring a good number of C's, you need to reevaluate your process.

One of my proudest achievements as CEO has been the track record at my companies for hiring A's. We were successful about 40 percent of the time, triple what would be expected by random chance and probably ten times the performance of the typical public company. Again, I believe we achieved these numbers (and the resulting business success) because I focused effort and time on the recruiting and hiring process.

—

For a football coach, the right players can make the coach look really smart and make up for a lot of coaching mistakes. How hard is it to have success as an offensive coordinator when Peyton Manning is your quarterback? I would rather make my life as easy as possible and not have to depend on doing a great coaching job. If you get the recruiting process right, you make almost every other part of the CEO job easier. That is the definition of leverage. Of course, if you just take what an average HR department gives you, you had better be a really good coach!

FINDING YOUR BALANCE

1. What role do you currently play in the recruiting process? How are you setting the bar for recruiting and hiring throughout the organization?

2. Is your in-house or outside recruiter an A player? How do you know?

3. What are your primary sources of potential hires? How are you regularly networking with them?

4. What metrics do you have in place for tracking the success of your recruiting efforts?

TALENT VS.
EXPERIENCE/KNOWLEDGE

"Great companies don't hire skilled people and motivate them,
they hire already motivated people and inspire them."

—SIMON SINEK, *START WITH WHY*

I have always been a huge basketball fan and regularly followed the league and the draft. For me, the 1984 NBA draft is one of those events that stick in my mind; 1984 was also an Olympic year and I had followed the Olympic basketball trials closely because my fellow classmate at Louisiana Tech, Karl Malone, was trying to make the team. The coach of the team was the legendary Bob Knight, arguably the greatest basketball coach of his era. The trials were very competitive, and Karl as well as several other future NBA stars, including Charles Barkley and John Stockton, failed to make the team.

During the trials one player stood out above all the others; he was a skinny junior shooting guard from North Carolina by the name of Michael Jordan. Even for the hard-to-impress Knight, Jordan was clearly special. So special that Knight communicated to his old friend Stu Inman, the GM of the Portland Trail Blazers, that Jordan was the best player he had ever seen.

Portland had the second pick in the draft that year and it was well known that the Houston Rockets, with the number-one pick, would draft Hakeem Olajuwon from the University of Houston. Portland thought they needed a center because they already had drafted Clyde Drexler the previous year to play shooting guard. When Knight talked to Inman, he told Inman that they should draft Jordan instead of Sam Bowie, the highest-rated center in the draft. Inman reportedly told Knight, "But Bobby, we don't need a shooting guard; we need a center." To which Knight famously replied, "Okay, then draft Jordan and play him at center!" The rest is history. Jordan went on to become the greatest player in NBA history and Sam Bowie is the answer to a trivia question.

I've made the point a few times now that whenever talent (actually, any highly valuable resource) becomes available, you should grab it. Talent is that important to the success of an organization. However, Knight never would have said, "You have an open assistant coach position, right? Draft Jordan and put him in it." Even as important as talent is, for some positions experience is equally important. You need experienced, successful leaders to build teams, and you need the best talent possible to do the work. The challenge CEOs face is distinguishing one from the other.

THE RESUME SNOB AND THE TEMP ADDICT

The resume-snob CEO is a common occurrence in corporate America. This inclination is often driven by either the background of the CEO or by the belief that an impressive-looking resume actually matters. The CEO is often biased by his own experiences and believes that others with those experiences must be just as wonderful as he is. For example, the CEO spent his formative years at IBM so the CEO heavily favors candidates who also spent their formative time at IBM. If the CEO went to an Ivy League school, all the executives need to have gone to an Ivy League school. By hiring executives with a similar background, the company is handicapped and likely to fall victim to the bias of groupthink. I believe diversity of background and experience, especially among the executive team, is critical to maximize success. If everyone on the team sees the problems the same way, the chance for innovative solutions that provide a competitive advantage is decreased.

Sometimes, these CEOs behave similarly to the black swan CEO. They favor candidates who seem to have the most amazing combination of experiences. "Oh, look, she went to Harvard and she worked for our competitor. We should grab her." Now, either of those experiences might contribute to the candidate's being the right candidate, but on their own, they don't guarantee it. The resume snob tends to be overly impressed with where people went to school, where they've worked, or what titles they've held and less concerned about what they've actually done.

Finally, resume snobs sometimes prioritize experience because they believe that a highly experienced candidate will get up to speed faster and require less training. I have seen this happen often in fast-growth companies in which all managers are so busy that they don't think they have time to train. Simply put, this is almost never true. Every company is different, with different processes, a different culture, and a different approach to the work. You have to invest in every new hire to ensure that he or she is successful.

BUT I DON'T HAVE TIME TO TRAIN

Even though I thought I preached a good hiring process until I was blue in the face, I saw people at NetQoS still fall prey to the influence of classic hiring misconceptions. We were hiring for a quality assurance position to replace an experienced employee who had been let go because of poor performance. Our standard process was to have six to eight employees interview each candidate and then meet to gather input from each interviewer. We went in a round-robin fashion with each interviewer making one comment about the candidate. We used this round-robin method so each interviewer would get their comments recorded without too much influence from what the hiring manager or CEO thought about the candidate.

In the debrief, it was clear that everyone at the table other than the hiring manager thought highly of the candidate. The comments from the interviewers described textbook A-player traits: smart, motivated, creative, passionate. Yet every time it came around to the hiring manager, he would say something negative about the candidate's lack of knowledge in a specific technical area. To me this was a classic case of trying to hire experience when what the position called for was talent. The manager was very busy and thought that if he hired experience he would have to spend less time training the new employee. As I've pointed out, this is a classic hiring mistake. After several rounds of this, I couldn't stand it any longer.

"Hey, I just thought of someone I know who has all this knowledge you're looking for," I said.

The manager clearly thought I was coming around to his point of view, so he took the bait. "Really? That's great. Do you think we could get him?"

I said, "Well, I think he's looking for a job."

You could sense the manager's excitement as he asked, "How can I contact him?"

I pulled the plug: "I think he's down the hall in his office packing his stuff. Apparently his manager fired him because he couldn't get the job done!"

The manager got the point. Experience isn't a guarantee and is often less important than other attributes, especially talent.

FINDING YOUR BALANCE

1. Is it well known in your company that you favor candidates from a particular school or company?

2. Do many members of the executive team share common company backgrounds?

3. Take a look at the last few rounds of candidates you've seen. Honestly, which candidates did you assume would be the best candidates based on their resumes going into the interviewing process?

Some CEOs just don't want to commit. The temp-addict CEO has a standard answer to every hiring challenge: "Let's just get a contractor in here and see what happens." Every time I see this approach to hiring I am shocked. Imagine an NFL team that needs another wide receiver going out to the market and making a random pick from all the people who played wide receiver in college. The temporary outsourcer, like the body-count CEO, often believes that people are interchangeable and one person in a given job is not much better than another person in that job. Any CEO who believes this will not have a very successful career. The individuals who are guilty of this sin wouldn't see it that way. Often they believe that getting the right people is important at the executive level. They then wonder why, when the rubber meets the road, the company is poor at things like customer service, frontline sales, or manufacturing.

If there is need for a person in the organization to do a job, it is worth trying to find the best person possible for that position, and that is almost always a full-time, permanent employee. Now, I understand that in certain locations or industries, labor laws make it so hard to terminate employees that it makes sense to hire people as temporary or contract employees. Fortunately I have spent my business career in Texas, which is an employment-at-will state. Therefore I always hire the best person possible for every position. Every position, from receptionist to CEO, can give you a competitive advantage. Don't be cavalier about hiring for any position, or the culture will develop that regards hiring as a necessary evil versus an opportunity for a competitive advantage.

FINDING YOUR BALANCE

1. Is it significantly easier in your company to hire temporary or contract employees rather than full-time employees?

2. What is your current ratio of temporary employees to permanent employees? What is your ratio of part-time to full-time employees?

3. Is there an attitude in the company that only some positions are worth investing in?

4. What is your turnover rate for the frontline jobs in the organization?

HIRE EXPERIENCE TO BUILD
TEAMS, HIRE TALENT TO DO WORK

For every candidate you hire, it's important to decide ahead of time whether experience or talent is more crucial for success in the position. If you are hiring for a leadership position, you will want somebody with experience. Bringing somebody on board who is new to the company and who has never had experience building a team isn't a great recipe for success. However, if you are hiring for any other type of position, you'll want to hire the most talented person to do the work required in the position. Sometimes that person will have relevant experience and sometimes she won't.

The challenge is that many people equate job experience with talent, which is a mistake. Having relevant experience doesn't necessarily mean that candidate will be effective. A recent *Fast Company* article titled "How to Hire Someone You Won't Regret in a Month" advised against the allure of hiring someone with experience: "On the surface, a candidate who has worked for similar companies or competitors seems like an attractive option . . . The problem with this approach is that relevant experience doesn't always equal success . . . and it can cause you to overlook candidates who possess stronger core traits that will lead to success at the position."[17]

One danger of prioritizing experience is that typically, when you are hiring, you are just adding another person to an existing team. For instance, you need another salesperson, bookkeeper, or software developer. There is already a clear process and workflow in place for how the job is to be done. Hiring managers often think that if they can just find someone with the right experience, that person will be able to hit the ground running. What these managers don't realize is that their approach to the work often differs from the experience of the new employee. The employee comes in and begins doing the job in the way he is accustomed to working, only to find out that the manager wants it done her way. But because the manager hired somebody with experience, she didn't bother to train the new employee carefully. This is very frustrating for both. The manager feels like she is losing time every day, while the employee feels offended that his experience is being discounted. If you hire people with experience, they will expect you to let them use that experience. As the saying goes, "Be careful what you wish for." In my personal experience, it is often far easier to train an inexperienced and talented employee than to retrain a more experienced employee in order to eliminate learned habits that are limiting.

However, in addition to leadership positions, you may need to prioritize experience for jobs that entail doing something the organization either doesn't know how to do or doesn't currently do well. But don't just look for experience; look for experience with being excellent. Many people have experience with being mediocre. The person you want to hire is a person who has delivered exceptional performance while gaining experience. This person will bring not only the skills needed but process and procedure as well. This is another reason why experience becomes very important when hiring executives and senior managers.

Aside from these situations, look for the most productive and talented person you can find without much consideration for experience. The employee with raw talent may create new ways of solving problems and/or develop innovative products or services that the myopia of the more experienced person might overlook. And make sure you have a culture that encourages skills development, creativity, and job advancement. Otherwise, you risk wasting and losing the talent you worked so hard to recruit in the first place.

Regardless of whether you believe you need someone with experience or specific talent, I recommend looking for five traits in every candidate you hire: exceptionalism, job-specific motivation, cultural fit, creative initiative, and value.

FIVE ATTRIBUTES OF EVERY GREAT CANDIDATE

While your company may hire many people in a given year, a particular manager probably hires only a few. Because of this, most managers aren't very good at hiring. If you don't build a culture around recruiting and hiring the best—A's and high B's—your company will quickly fill up with below-average employees—C's—and you will have no competitive advantage. Practice looking for the following identifiers of A's and B's and teach others to do the same to build a top-notch team. These attributes will be more valuable in the long run than straightforward experience.

Exceptionalism

What I always look for in candidates' backgrounds is something that tells me they are or have a history of being exceptional, something that tells me they will contribute a whole lot more to the company than just those skills needed to do the job at an acceptable level. How do you identify exceptionalism? Well, people who are exceptional have a history of being exceptional. Somebody doesn't just wake up one day, play a little golf, and go out and win the U.S. Open. Tiger Woods didn't just show up one day on the golf course and start beating everybody. No. He was on the Johnny Carson show at age five hitting a golf ball. He won three U.S. Junior Amateur Championships and one U.S. Amateur Championship. And only after all that did he turn pro and begin to dominate the professional tour. An exceptional person has a history of being exceptional.

If the candidate is a recent university grad, you may discount his academic experience and say, "Well, what job experience does he have?" Exceptional candidates were usually exceptional when they were young. They were captains of teams, won speech contests, or ran businesses while getting degrees. They programmed robots at age sixteen or won national gaming championships. They were stars in some way. Once people learn how to be really good at one thing, they can often leverage what they've discovered about how they learn to be really good at several things. They have learned how to be great and they have the passion to do it. When you see these kinds of things on a resume, you may not know how this has anything to do with your company, but you know the candidate can be exceptional.

The same traits apply to more experienced candidates. The best people who have worked for me have always had multiple areas of talent. I remember a conversation with my wife when she started training seriously for Ironman triathlons. She found the best swimmers in her age group in town to train with. Austin, Texas, has produced many great swimmers, so the pool was filled with national and even Olympic champions. It was no surprise that they were all amazing swimmers. What did surprise her was that they were almost all high-level executives and CEOs. Exceptional people demonstrate the fact that they are exceptional over and over again. So always look for that on resumes. What stories can they tell you? What have they done to convince you that they are exceptional? Always look for people who strive to excel at whatever they do.

Remember, spending time at exceptional schools or with exceptional companies doesn't necessarily make someone exceptional. I believe we did a tremendous job hiring at NetQoS, but out of 260 employees I would have rated only about 40 percent truly exceptional at their jobs. That's a better ratio than most companies achieve, but it's still less than half. Just because someone was hired by a great company does not make her exceptional. The question to ask is, did she do exceptional things?

Job-Specific Motivation

I want to hire people who will be excited by the opportunity that we can provide. Are they looking for a job to pay the bills, or are they looking for the specific opportunity we are offering? Does our position fit into their career plan? To deliver exceptional performance for the long haul, a candidate will have to feel that he is benefiting from the job as much as the company benefits from having him as an employee. This won't happen if the job is a poor fit right from the start.

Companies often post job descriptions that make it clear they're interested in an exceptional candidate. When you're trying to recruit top performers, understand that they want a new challenge or opportunity. They are highly motivated to learn and grow, so doing the same job they have done before will not likely interest them. If they seem interested, be cautious. They may be trying to get a foot in the door. That's great, until they become disengaged four months in. I have always tried to hire top performers into jobs that *they* considered to be the next step in their career progression.

To discover this job-specific motivation in the interview process, ask questions that reveal how the potential employee sees himself now and in the future. Does he have a five-year plan? What level in the organization does he think is appropriate based on his experience? Three years from now, what would success in the job look like to him? What specific things in past jobs has he enjoyed? What is most appealing to him about the current job? Is it a primary part of the job or a tangential or minimal part of the job?

I have often started interviews thinking a person might be a fit for one job but realized, based on his answers to these types of questions, that he would really be better in another. In every interview, I keep an open mind about how the company might leverage the talents of the exceptional person in front of me.

Cultural Fit

How can you judge if an exceptional, motivated individual will fit in with the culture of your company?

First, ask yourself if you've done the necessary work to develop a culture that is inviting for exceptional people. In the next section of the book, I will explore how to build a great culture that drives engagement and high performance. A high-performance culture gives you the added benefit of being able to hire a wider array of people. Why? Because high-performance cultures tend to value creativity, openness, and talent over conformity. They are more tolerant of differences in personality and perspective. Talented people are often oddballs, and oddballs are more open to working with other oddballs.

That doesn't mean that cultural fit is not important when selecting candidates. It becomes more important to figure out the few issues that are hurdles to cultural fit rather than to look for a candidate who fits a particular model exactly. Two issues I look at are the sizes of the companies the candidate has worked for in the past, and values.

Your company has its own set of cultural norms that every new employee must successfully navigate to be effective. Having spent most of my time in young, smaller companies, I have seen the common cultural clashes that happen when you hire people who have only big-company experience to work in small start-ups. How things get done and what gets rewarded at a Fortune 500 company are far different from those cultural aspects of a young company with thirty people. It's similar to the problem most Americans would face if they went to a foreign country and tried to sell the locals something. Without a strong cultural understanding, it's hard to get people to act. This rule is especially true when hiring leaders.

In the next chapter and in the chapter "Rules-Based vs. Values-Based," I'll address the importance of values in culture building and the importance of having employees (especially leaders) who are aligned with those values. If you get any sense that a candidate may not be able or willing to live your values, you should move forward with caution. Ask questions that can help you discover if the candidate has exhibited your values in her past work or values that you believe are antithetical to the culture you are trying to build.

In the culture discussion, I've referenced the Gallup Q^{12} survey for measuring engagement (and therefore culture) in your organization. The most surprising question for most people on that survey is "Do you have a best friend at work?" A "yes" answer to this question is a leading predictor of company performance. When I am interviewing I think to myself, "Would this candidate be likely to make a best friend in the office?" The question is as good an indicator of cultural fit as most other questions we ask.

Creative Initiative

Philip Delves Broughton, the bestselling author of *Ahead of the Curve*, was visiting with me at NetQoS. I had engaged him to write a history of the company as we prepared for an IPO. He was sitting in my office when somebody knocked on the door and said, "Joel, it's time for your 2 p.m. interview."

Philip started to get up to leave, but I said, "No, stay. I'd like you to hear the interview. Just let me make sure it's okay with the candidate." The candidate agreed and we began.

The position she was applying for was an administrative position supporting the executive team. I began to ask her questions about her most recent job, starting with, "What was the job and what did it entail?"

"I worked as the receptionist in a massage place," she said.

"Did you like the job?" I asked.

"Well, I really got kind of bored," she said, which is what an interviewee says to impress you with his or her diligence and desire for challenge. "Once the person came in for the massage and the massage started there really wasn't much, anything to do. I didn't like not having anything to do so I had to find another job."

We talked for a while longer, covering various topics and then she left. I turned to Phil and said, "Okay, what'd you hear?"

"Well, it sounded like she was eager to work because she was bored at this massage place and she didn't have enough to do."

"Let me tell you what I heard. What I heard is that she doesn't have any creative initiative. I can come up with about ten things off the top of my head she could have been doing at that massage place. She could have been looking at the books to see which customers hadn't come in during the last month and then calling them. She could have been printing out flyers and sticking them on the cars in the parking lot. She could have been creating new displays. She could have been washing sheets. There are a hundred things she could have been doing that would have moved that business forward. She thought of her job as a place where people tell her what to do, not as a place where she is supposed to try to help the business succeed in any way possible."

Creative initiative is the drive and ability to think of ways to do a job better or to contribute more to the success of the organization. The best people are great at consistently coming up with ideas for how to be better at their jobs. Every company needs people with creative initiative. People without a lot of experience but with oodles of creative initiative are more valuable than the reverse (experience, but limited creative initiative) because their ideas for growth or progress are driven by the environment in which they work—your environment. You don't have time to tell everybody in your organizations what to go do every day. You want knowledge workers who can take a set of goals and values and convert them into tasks that move the company forward.

Another way to find out if someone has creative initiative is to ask questions that force them to generate ideas for action, for instance, "Let's say you're hired; what are you going to go do tomorrow, in the first week, or in the first month?" If people are really good at their jobs they can give you a plan. I remember interviewing a public relations person once and saying, "I don't know anything about PR. If you were me, what question would you ask to find out whether somebody was good at PR?"

"Well, I'd ask them what they'd go do."

"Okay, what would you go do?"

The candidate then spent the next five minutes giving me a very detailed, almost hour-by-hour description of the hundred things she was going to go do the first day on the job.

I hired her.

BEHAVIORAL INTERVIEWING IS THE WAY TO GO

Google was once famous for its almost surreal hiring process, during which a candidate might be asked questions like, "How many cows are in Canada?" or posed scenarios that start with "You are shrunk to the height of a nickel and thrown into a blender." But no more. In a public outing of their hiring flaws, Laszlo Bock, senior vice president of people operations, explained in an interview in the New York Times that they had studied the success of their interviews and found that their odd questions or brainteasers were "a complete waste of time. They don't predict anything."[18]

Google has shifted to more straightforward behavioral interviews, structured to allow them to consistently assess candidates. Behavioral interviewing focuses on asking questions about what people do or have done rather than what they *think*. Said Bock, "You get to see how they actually interacted in a real-world situation, and [you gather] the valuable 'meta' information . . . of what they consider to be difficult."

Past behavior is a predictor of future behavior. It's that simple.

Value

The biggest mistake I see inexperienced hiring managers make is failing to understand the business value a candidate provides. It's easy to forget that the fundamental reason to hire people is that they will produce more economic value for the company than they cost. A person who receives $100,000 in total compensation must be twice as productive (in terms of revenue growth, or market share acquired, or productivity improved for the company as a whole, or whatever other measure may be appropriate) as a person who receives $50,000. If you use a team interview approach, the more expensive candidate will often be chosen because of her greater experience, without consideration of her relative value. Sometimes, the more expensive candidate is the right hire because she can help you solve more problems that will lead to greater or faster growth. However, you have to make these judgment calls carefully, and you have to make sure your entire team understands the relative value of each candidate in the hiring process.

—

Every employee in your company provides a competitive advantage—or doesn't. Each time you hire, you have a choice to either hire the best possible candidate or to hire whoever is most affordable or available. Look for talent always, and when hiring leaders, also look for experience.

FINDING YOUR BALANCE

1. In the past year, did you hire somebody who had great experience, yet failed in the position? What was the root of the failure?

2. How many people did you have to let go in the past year because of poor performance (not layoffs)? Do you think you should have been able to predict what happened?

3. Do you have a method for interviewing that is used consistently across the company? Does it reflect the five attributes described in this chapter?

SAVING VS. TRADING UP

*"Associate yourself with men of good quality if you esteem your own
reputation, for 'tis better to be alone than in bad company.'"*

—GEORGE WASHINGTON

I'm sorry to say that during my short tenure in the IT department at AMD,
I learned much more about what not to do than what to do when it came to
managing people. Soon after I arrived, I began accumulating responsibilities and staff. At one point, I had nineteen direct reports (*way* too many for
a single manager), split between Austin, Texas, and Sunnyvale, California.
One of those employees was clearly not carrying her weight in the organization. I began to hear reports that she was getting other employees to do her
job and was accomplishing about half as much as any other person in the
group. I tried to work with her and sent her for additional training, but the
problem didn't improve. I kept my boss informed all along the way and was
ready to terminate the employee. When I mentioned this to my boss, he told
me that she would first have to be put on a performance improvement plan
for a quarter before we could get rid of her. I thought this was likely a waste
of time but complied with my boss's instructions.

One month into the plan, the employee approached me and told me
she had found another job and would be leaving in two weeks. It was all
I could do not to cheer when I got the news. I thanked her for providing
notice and went running across the campus to give my boss the update.

When I told him the news, he didn't seem to be as excited as I was, but I just figured he was busy and I left to celebrate my good fortune. Imagine my shock the next day when I found out that my boss had gone directly to the employee and made a counteroffer. The counter included a significant increase in salary! After a couple of days the employee decided to decline the counteroffer and still leave AMD—but not before she told everyone in the group about how much she had been offered to stay. Needless to say, I had a morale problem of epic proportions. How was I supposed to explain why my boss thought the worst performer in the group should be the highest paid member of the team?

Some leaders, including CEOs, believe that everyone can be saved, possibly because firing someone would require them to admit they made a mistake in the first place. The result is that they fail to save their top performers, who don't want to work with poor performers. On the opposite end of the spectrum, though, are leaders who tolerate no deviation, who expect employees to perform like automatons. The second those employees don't offer consistent performance, the leader boots them out the door. These CEOs care so little about employees, they make layoffs their first course of action at the slightest sign of financial struggle.

Instead, CEOs need to lead the charge to build amazing teams by providing employees with frequent feedback on their performance, working hard to save A's and strong B's and moving poor performers who cannot turn it around on to opportunities elsewhere.

THE SAINT AND CHAINSAW AL

In the summer of 1984 I was lucky enough to go on a trip to Rome with a church youth group. As part of the trip we were scheduled to hear Mother Teresa speak to an assembly of all the youth groups from the United States. At the time I was eighteen, and while I had certainly heard of Mother Teresa, I didn't know that much about her. We crammed into a relatively small, centuries-old church for the event. I arrived early, and as more people came in, I was pushed closer and closer to the front until I was in a pew next to the altar. After a while, a short, wrinkled figure appeared at the back of the church and began to shuffle toward the altar. When she reached the podium and began to speak, the hairs on my arms stood up. Her voice was soft, but there was a presence about her unlike anything I had ever experienced, or have since. The only analogy I can offer is the Force from *Star Wars*. It was like Yoda had walked into the room and you could physically feel the shift in the Force. I listened closely to every word as she presented a simple but powerful message, to love thy neighbor as thyself. It was by far the most moving spiritual experience of my life, and I have always been thankful that I was lucky enough to be in that church on that day.

So, if I love all of my employees as myself, does that mean I can never fire anyone? That is what saint CEOs may think. The saint CEO values harmony over all other things and doesn't want to deal with unpleasant conversations or confrontations. Almost no CEO likes the idea of firing people, but it comes with the job. The CEO who believes in saving everyone doesn't realize the damage he does to employee morale and particularly the morale of the best performers. If you can't force yourself to handle these situations in a timely manner, it will greatly decrease your credibility within the organization.

THE EASIEST WAY TO KILL YOUR COMPANY

I was a member of a CEO peer group years ago. The format of the meetings involved reviewing your current business situation at each meeting and discussing what actions each CEO would take. John, the CEO of a manufacturing company, brought up the same problem over and over again each month—a problem of performance with one of his directors. There was always some reason why he hadn't taken the agreed-upon actions. Finally, the fourth time he raised the issue, the leader of the group looked him right in the eye and said, "John, if I became CEO of your company tomorrow, what would I do to improve performance?"

"Well, you would fire my manufacturing director, who's causing a lot of the problems," John replied matter-of-factly.

"Then why the f*#! haven't you done it already?" the mentor demanded.

The guy knew exactly what he needed to do; he just didn't want to do it. And every day he didn't, he lost a little more credibility with his team and limited the performance of his company. Eventually a downturn hit and he was forced to lay off almost half of his staff. Morale actually improved as the deadweight was eliminated and the company was able to recover when the economy began to grow again.

FINDING YOUR BALANCE

1. Is there someone in your organization who the majority of people in the company think is incompetent? How long has the poor performance been common knowledge?

2. What have you done in the past six months that would build confidence that you will make the right personnel decision in a timely manner, no matter how personally painful it might be?

Chainsaw Al was the nickname given to Al Dunlap, a CEO best known as a turnaround specialist for companies like Scott Paper and Sunbeam. Unlike the saint, Al had no problem firing large percentages of the workforce at the companies he was trying to revive. Unfortunately, Sunbeam ended up in bankruptcy after Dunlap was accused by the SEC of a massive accounting fraud and was banned from ever serving on the board of a public company again. Incidentally, he has been included in a number of books and articles on the parallels between the common traits of CEOs and psychopaths.

I always worry about CEOs who seem to have no feelings about firing large numbers of people. It's one thing to let a poor performer or someone who does not fit with the culture go, but it is quite another to fire thousands of people indiscriminately in one fell swoop. Remember, caring is a necessary part of leadership. Caring is the belief that you will do what is best for the company as a whole, and the company is composed of its employees. Too many companies get in the habit of reflexively cutting headcount just to make a quarterly or yearly number, without any concern for the employees. Employees can sense whether the executive team is making every effort to do what is best for the company or just sacrificing employees in order to make the numbers for their yearly bonus. The CEO is responsible for properly allocating resources in such a way that prepares for all reasonable contingencies. It is one thing when an event like 9/11 happens, but businesses that routinely cut large percentages of their workforce suffer from poor planning at the executive level.

FINDING YOUR BALANCE

1. Do you make firing decisions based on meeting financial goals or on the performance of the people being let go? How many times have you made a decision to lay off people for financial reasons?

2. Does your organization believe you would sacrifice personally before firing members of the team? What have you done to help them trust that you care?

INSTEAD OF LAYOFFS, TRY ENGAGEMENT

Every company faces trying economic circumstances at some point. And when that happens, leaders rightly look at cutting costs to avoid bankruptcy or worse. Often, one of the first options they consider is a set of layoffs. But that is not the direction in which George Mikitarian, president and CEO of Parrish Medical Center (PMC) in Titusville, Florida, led his team.

According to an article in the *Gallup Business Journal*, PMC was facing a double hit in 2008: recession and the planned closing of the shuttle program at the nearby Kennedy Space Center, which would mean the loss of local jobs and fewer patients over time.[19] The executive team knew they needed to cut costs long-term, not just long enough to ride out the recession. Surprisingly, they put layoffs at the bottom of the options to consider. They tried a few approaches, such as a lean Six Sigma process, but weren't able to cut enough costs. So they began to have monthly town hall meetings or "family budget discussions." At these meetings they explained the struggle the company was facing in clear terms to all one thousand employees. And then they asked for help. They needed ideas for cutting costs in a sustainable way, which meant they needed ideas with immediate buy-in from the front lines on up. And that's what they got. Employees submitted more than three hundred ideas via their department heads. They were submitted to the communications and service excellence department, which compiled them and categorized them into certain areas and then sent the list back to the department heads to review and consider for how they would impact patient experience and how likely they were to deliver sustainable cost savings.

The company was careful about the ideas they implemented; yet, in the first round of initiatives, they achieved savings of $3.6 million.

At the same time, the company was focused on improving its workforce by increasing engagement. They wanted to have a stronger full-time staff, use fewer contract workers, reduce their churn, and improve the customer's experience. They used the Gallup Q[12] (which I'll discuss in the upcoming "Build the Culture" section) to guide their actions. While cutting costs, they increased their ratio of engaged to disengaged employees above the world-class ratio of 8:1 to a whopping 10:1. Now they have a waiting list of great local talent ready when they need to fill a position.

And by 2009, those engaged employees had saved the company $7.1 million. Sometimes, saving is the right choice.

SAVE THE BEST, REPLACE THE WORST

The best performers recognize that for them to be truly successful, the team must win, and winning is very difficult when some people aren't carrying their weight. The fastest path to mediocrity as a company is allowing poor performers to remain and pretending that it doesn't matter. The best people will see it for what it is and start heading for the exit.

Tolerating poor performance is not in the best interest of all concerned. Just like every parent knows, while we love our kids, we often act against their immediate wishes. That may mean giving them a swift kick in the rear when they need it. Follow these three steps to ensure that you are addressing performance issues—both high and low—appropriately.

Step 1: Recognize that Annual Reviews Stick You with a Poor Performer for Twelve Months

It has always amazed me to hear a leader talk about doing annual reviews. I always want to ask, "So what were you doing for the other fifty weeks of the year?" Isn't a leader reviewing her employees daily or weekly, or at least monthly? Isn't she always looking for signs of great or poor performance, or at least recognizing the signs when they're shoved under her nose? I recommend building a culture in which employees are constantly evaluated and provided with appropriate feedback, a culture in which employees know that they will not have to carry weak performers for long.

In my companies, we have rated every employee as an A, B, or C each quarter. I'm not recommending a full-blown written performance appraisal every three months, just a judgment call by each leader on each employee, and then some informal conversations to let employees know how they're doing. I review all the ratings each quarter, and if any employee receives a C, I make sure the manager has communicated to the employee that his or her performance is not sufficient and has considered whether the person is in the right position in the company.

Step 2: Focus the Majority of Your
Time and Energy on Your Top Performers

Your best employees are the keys to your success. You must be devoting the necessary time and effort to understand the issues they are facing or the concerns they are raising and do everything possible to address them as quickly as possible. Unfortunately, in most companies managers and leaders are forced to spend about 80 percent of their people management time dealing with issues caused by the bottom 20 percent of their teams—their poorest performers—documenting problems, monitoring actions, fixing mistakes, and so on. I try to flip the 80/20 rule by spending 80 percent of my time with the most valuable employees of the company—to understand how I can help them, what concerns they have, what ideas they can contribute—and 20 percent of my time dealing with the rest. Imagine if a head football coach spent more time coaching his third-string offensive lineman than he spent working with the starting quarterback. That would not be the most productive use of time for the team and it isn't for a company, either.

I would encourage you to meet with your executive team a couple of times a year to discuss all the A performers in the organization. You should spend conscious effort making sure that those top performers have an appropriate career path and are acknowledged by the management team. A nice handwritten note from the CEO to each one also wouldn't be a bad idea.

I have heard managers defend themselves when a star employee on their team leaves by saying that the employee was recruited by another company and got a much better offer. While many managers claim that their employees leave over salary issues, survey after survey has shown that compensation is *not* one of the top few reasons that people change jobs (although since the start of the Great Recession, compensation has definitely been climbing up the list and is now generally in the top five). Lack of leadership and poor management are certainly cited much more often by top performers than salary and benefits. Any time a manager tells me that a top employee left over salary, I am always suspicious.

If indeed salary was a factor, it is likely that the manager allowed the employee's compensation to deviate far enough from fair market value that the employee could receive a much bigger offer from a competitor. Leaving a job is a big decision and most employees won't leave over a 5 percent to 10 percent pay bump if everything else is good. For most people it takes more than 20 percent more pay for them to consider leaving over salary alone. If a company and manager are closely tracking the market, it will be very rare for employees to receive offers that much higher than what they are making. This means companies must base their salary adjustments on market conditions and not merely on a fixed rate of inflation each year, as many large companies do.

Another reason top performers consider leaving is to grow or pursue new challenges. If you want to hold on to them, promote learning and growth at every opportunity. Encouraging employees to continuously improve themselves in their skills and market knowledge not only improves their engagement but also helps the company react to a constantly changing business environment. Supporting employees who want to go back to school, attend training sessions, or expand their knowledge in another way can provide tremendous long-term value to a company. Employees who are growing in their skills and knowledge will be much less likely to consider changing jobs.

Holding on to your best people requires one last effort: Any time you are making a decision, think about how that decision will be received by the A players in your organization, not the average employees or worse, the C players. This tactic will put you on the path to building a high-performance culture that keeps your A's engaged. I'll cover culture in more detail in the next section.

Step 3: After You Give Them
a Chance, Trade C's for B's or A's

If a manager gives somebody a C in two consecutive quarters and hasn't already gotten rid of the employee, you can bet that I'm in his office asking, "Two C's? What's the story here?" This person is clearly hurting the team and there has to be a damned good reason that he hasn't already moved that person off the bus. If you can't get the employees to improve their performance rapidly, either in their current position or in another position that is better suited to their skills or talents, you've got a problem that must be addressed.

Across the organization, lack of performance is the most common reason for making a change in personnel. But employees can damage the health and stability of the company in another way, too—through misalignment with values. Tolerating employees, especially leaders, who behave in ways that aren't aligned with the company's values can be more damaging to the CEO's credibility than tolerating poor performers.

Because you hold the responsibility of owning the mission, vision, and values for the company, the most damaging problem you can face is members of your immediate staff not living the values you are preaching. An employee may be unable to judge the performance of executives in other parts of the company, but everyone hears the stories when an executive doesn't live the values of the company. There are a million little ways in which this can happen, but it is an issue the CEO must address immediately whenever it rears its head. If members of your executive team cannot buy into your vision, I believe they must work somewhere else. This is a lesson that it took time for me to learn in my career. If people were delivering results, I allowed them to hang around even if they couldn't live the values. That was a mistake that cost me credibility with the rest of my team. To be clear, I am not talking about people doing things that are wrong (like stealing). I just mean small things that go against the values. I often see ideas like harmony listed as a core value by a company. I always wonder if the company really means it. Would the CEO fire an executive who delivered superior performance but lost his temper often with employees?

Jack Welch institutionalized the concept of prioritizing living the values alongside performance for any leader at GE. Here's how he explained it in his book, *Winning*:

TYPE 1	TYPE 2
Good values/ Good performance	Bad values/ Bad performance
TYPE 3	**TYPE 4**
Good values/ Bad performance	Bad values/ Good performance

Type 1 bosses [good values/good performance] . . . are the people you want to reward and promote and hold up as examples to the rest of the company. Type 2 bosses [bad values/bad performance] . . . have to go, the sooner the better, and usually do. Type 3 bosses [good values/ bad performance] . . . really believe in the company's values and practice them in earnest, but just can't get the results. Those individuals should be coached and mentored and given another chance or two in other parts of the company. Most bad bosses are . . . Type 4 [bad values/good performance]—and they are the most difficult to deal with. They often get to hang around for a long time, despite their awful behavior, because of their good results.[20]

Be careful that you don't fall into a common trap when you decide to let an employee go for either reason. I often see CEOs who finally make the decision to replace an executive or employee and then allow the person to save face and make it appear that it was her idea to leave. The whole reason you had to make the move was to protect your credibility and then you become complicit in a lie! A lie that every in-touch person in the company can see! I understand not wanting to embarrass anyone, and your lawyers may say "letting somebody leave" is the low-risk approach, but you have to own the decision. The organization must understand that you made a decision to make a change that you believe is in the best interests of the company. Figure out a way to say it to make the lawyers happy, but make sure everyone understands what you did and why you did it.

—

Part of being in command means that you will be held responsible, not only for the decisions you make to hire and fire individuals but also for not making the decision to let people go who are clearly not cutting it. You can't just bury your head in the sand and hope they go away. Every day that a C player remains on the job causes the CEO to lose a little credibility with his team. This will cause the performance bar across the entire organization to gradually sink until mediocre performance is the norm. Living the value that people are our most important asset is not always easy, but it is critical for the high-performing CEO.

FINDING YOUR BALANCE

1. How frequently are employees in your organization reviewed? What is the process like? What are the ramifications of poor performance?

2. How do leaders in your organization support A players? Does the culture support the leadership practice of spending the majority of your time with top performers? Why or why not?

3. Do you have C players on your team right now? How long have they been on your team? What is your plan for moving them off your team?

BUILD

THE

CULTURE

CULTURE IS HOW THINGS GET DONE IN AN ORGANIZATION: HOW PEOPLE communicate, how leaders build and develop teams, and how coworkers collaborate—or don't. It defines the employee's experience, and it heavily influences the customer's experience.

It is important to understand that every organization has a culture and values, whether or not they are explicitly recognized. Your employees will figure out the culture just by observing what gets rewarded. It is better if you make a proactive attempt to define, understand, and communicate key elements of your culture, though. Every leader says he wants a high-performance culture; the test is when performance seems to come into conflict with other positive values.

The challenge with culture is that, while most CEOs recognize that it is critically important, they don't have a model to understand it or a method for measuring it. Culture is a social construct, not a process that can be engineered or a spreadsheet that can be analyzed. It is influenced by the varied behaviors, attitudes, and personalities of the people within it. Which is one reason it's so crucial to hire well. However, neurosocial research has shown that despite our differences, we all ultimately seek out the same things in our interactions with others.

I sold a company not long ago, providing a great return for shareholders. However, because the company had been operating for only two years, many of the employees had not vested in their stock options and so would receive little from the deal. I wanted to be fair—to reward them for their contributions to building a valuable company—as well as provide them with some security (most of the employees would not be continuing with the company after the acquisition). So I visited with all the employees prior to the official announcement to find out what they thought would be a fair severance package. I received answers of three months to six months. After getting that feedback, we decided to give all the terminated employees one year of severance. I felt that this was appropriate because the investors were receiving a great return and the employees would need time to find other employment. When I made the announcement, everyone was very appreciative of the unexpected severance. However, several of the employees were still noticeably uneasy. Even though they had more money in the bank than they reasonably expected, they were disconcerted by the fact that they would soon be unemployed. All of these individuals were talented professionals who would have no trouble finding new jobs. But they were still very uncomfortable with the situation. What explains this reaction?

REWARD VS. THREAT

"Only when we are no longer afraid do we begin to live."

—DOROTHY THOMPSON

I found the answer in a paper written by David Rock called "SCARF: A Brain-based Model for Collaborating with and Influencing Others."[21] Rock also wrote a book that covers the subject, called *Your Brain at Work*. In the paper, Rock provides a model to help us understand the way humans interpret social interactions. The fundamental idea is that the same brain networks that seek to maximize reward and minimize threat for primary survival needs are also used in any situation where people interact. This means that when employees are working, they will constantly evaluate their environment through this filter. If they encounter a reward response they will tend to engage in a particular stimulus; and if they experience a threat they will disengage. Remember the employees in the previous chapter who were losing their jobs? For some of them, their brains were simply more focused on the threat of unemployment than on the reward of a year of security.

The SCARF model lists five common areas of social experience that can elicit the reward/threat response: status, certainty, autonomy, relatedness, and fairness. I was a fan of Daniel Pink's *Drive* before I learned of David Rock's model, and I immediately saw parallels between Pink's model and Rock's. Autonomy is obviously the same; mastery can be linked to status and fairness, and purpose can be linked to relatedness and certainty.

Understanding Rock's more subtle five factors and adjusting decisions, policies, and leadership approaches accordingly will help you build a culture in which people feel respected, secure, trusted, included, and treated fairly—and that will influence employee engagement.

Why is employee engagement so important in driving a high-performance culture? It turns out that the more creative and intellectually challenging the work, the more employee engagement predicts performance. And numerous studies have revealed that the subtle effects of the reward/threat response can dramatically impact cognitive performance. Simply put, if employees feel threatened in any way, they will be less effective in solving complex problems. If your business depends on workers' intellect more than their brawn, you will want to focus on employee engagement to maximize productivity. And that means building a culture in which the perception of threats is minimized and the perception of rewards (those I listed earlier) is maximized. By understanding the real motivation of everyone in your organization, you will be able to build a high-performance culture.

STATUS

Status is the first and potentially most significant of the five areas. Michael Marmot, in his book *The Status Syndrome*, explains that social status has a huge effect on your health and well being. What Marmot shows is that among otherwise very controlled groups, small differences in status have measurable effects on your life span. The concept of social status is woven deeply into our emotional makeup. Seniority, positions, titles, and so on are important to employee engagement. Here's a common example. For start-up CEOs, the number of direct reports one has increases as the company grows. One day, you realize you need to adjust the organizational structure so you have fewer direct reports because you can't effectively manage that many people. This means that people who once reported to you will now report to somebody else, possibly somebody who was already in a leadership position. Even if no title or work flow really changes, people who once reported to you and don't any longer are going to perceive a threat to their status. Conversely, promoting someone directly to your staff even without a change in pay or title can cause a significant reward response. As CEO, you may have wondered why such seemingly insignificant things as the location of someone's office or whether a person was invited to a meeting have such a large impact. Each of these and many more small decisions directly impact a person's perceived status in the organization or on his or her team.

Issues of status can be doubly dangerous when combined with other aspects of the model, such as fairness. Perks can trigger a threat response from employees in both areas. The problem with perks in general is that they divide the workforce into classes: those who get a certain perk and those who don't. For a team to perform at the highest possible level, everyone knows that the team members should have a one-for-all-and-all-for-one attitude. This attitude is really hard to develop when employees are split along class divides. No one expects the CEO to have the same office as the receptionist, but if the CEO feels the need to have an executive wing constructed, it will certainly cause some grumbling. You would think that things like separate executive eating areas and parking spots would have disappeared decades ago, but they still exist in some companies. In many large companies the ultimate perk is use of the corporate jets. I have seen CEOs put a travel ban on all the employees while the executive team is flying around in private jets at $10,000 per hour! Most people do not want to be led by someone who seems to make a habit of separating herself from the people she is trying to lead.

Titles can also be problematic, but there's really no avoiding them. I've heard employees complain that they are at least as good as someone else who has a title they want. Frankly, early in my career I might have told them to quit their whining. Now that I understand the uncontrollable and deeply seated threat response they may be experiencing, I look for more creative ways to handle such issues. Can I do other things to enhance their status? Can I include them in more management meetings or seek out their opinion on important issues? One company I interacted with recently chose not to put titles on employees' business cards because titles don't really matter much in their organization.

Culturally, there are many things you can do to help eliminate or reduce status threats. I personally believe in private offices for everyone. Yep, everyone. I recognize this isn't always possible, but I've been able to make it happen more often than not. Professional development opportunities should be offered to all employees, because reward circuits are activated when people feel that they are learning and growing in their jobs and are offered the same opportunities as others. Being as transparent as possible with all information is also critical. Access to information is a sign of status. Whenever possible—which means almost always—I make sure that everybody has access to the same information (barring any legal limitations).

CERTAINTY

Certainty is another area that can affect employee engagement. The human brain likes to feel that the future is predictable. We get through every day by doing many things from memory. We brush our teeth, we drive to work, and we open a door by recalling patterns that have been ingrained in our neural pathways. When we have to learn a new pattern, for example, driving to a new office, our brain has to work harder and therefore is less able to focus on other tasks. Uncertainty puts our brains on constant alert because we can't be confident in what will come next. This drains energy and makes creative tasks much more difficult. Having been through several acquisitions, both as an acquirer and an acquiree, I can testify that uncertainty in that process can cause almost all productive work to halt. Some companies make reorganizations an almost regular occurrence. A reorg starts as a rumor and then, over time, employees are informed of the changes that are being made. The process drags over months, creating constant uncertainty and stress. And reorgs almost always create status threats as well. It is shocking to me that CEOs don't understand the harm they do as these communications drag out.

Uncertainty can also be caused or diminished by basic operational or leadership approaches. For instance, employees not knowing what criteria will be used to evaluate their performance can cause constant friction in their creative activities. A clearly communicated, consistently applied employee performance model will help people feel secure in their own performance. A strong model also helps minimize status threats because people are more likely to think promotions are warranted. Open-book management is a common approach in many high-performing cultures. By giving employees as much information as possible, the normal uncertainty of business is reduced. Of course there is always uncertainty in business, as in life. A good culture minimizes that uncertainty as much as possible through smart leadership.

AUTONOMY

The third area in the SCARF model is autonomy. People want to feel control over their own work and some control over their environments. The less control they feel they have, the more stress they feel and the less effective they will be on tasks requiring advanced mental processes. Often when people leave lucrative corporate positions to start their own enterprises they are seeking control over their work environment. They want to feel that they have some control over the issues that affect them. Obviously being part of any team reduces the autonomy of the members to some extent. The challenge is providing as much autonomy as possible within a corporate structure. Corporate policy is one area in which autonomy should be carefully considered. I'll explore this issue in more detail in the upcoming chapter.

RELATEDNESS

Relatedness is the fourth item in the SCARF model. It was important for human survival for the brain to be able to quickly recognize others as friend or foe. Almost all people like to be part of a group of people pursuing a common purpose. Once again, the creative, innovative aspects of the brain function best when we are engaged with people we trust, whom we consider friends rather than foes.

It is well known that teams perform better when they have experienced a bonding event. Whether it is a sports team that pulls out an unlikely victory or a sales team that closes a huge sale, the experience of overcoming obstacles together creates a highly positive connection with the other members of the team. This sense of relatedness breaks down the barrier of distrust. It is easy for small companies to create a high sense of relatedness in their culture because everybody is in it together. As a company grows past the size where people can maintain personal relationships with everyone, the CEO must actively look for ways to increase relatedness. One way to do so is to develop and communicate a clear mission, vision, and values. Developing the "we're all in this together" mindset through focused communication, goal setting, and celebrating achievements is key.

In fast-growing companies, new employees arrive every month, sometimes every week. To maintain a sense of relatedness, make new employees part of the team right away. At no time is an employee's stress level higher than the day he starts a new job. He feels uncertain, and he has likely met only a small number of the people he will be working with. Quickly engaging the employee to decrease uncertainty and increase relatedness is important to facilitating a productive work environment. We implemented an onboarding process for new employees, which included making sure they had everything they needed to get started on their first day. I personally taught a ten-hour course each quarter for all new employees that covered the technology and market of the company. Department welcome lunches, shirts with the company logo, and meetings with every executive helped new employees quickly feeling connected to their team and the company as a whole.

The more connected the employees feel in the workplace, the easier it will be to drive high performance.

Stronger cultures are also more open and less political. Workplace politics can divide employees. When politics are minimal, people are motivated by performance. And if performance is what counts, then top performers will always be able to fit in, even if they are outliers. If the culture is weak, the person on the outlying edge (in terms of personality or social behavior) becomes disruptive. In my companies, I have hired some people who were considered to be quite odd. They behaved differently, thought differently, and had curious social behaviors. But they still worked well in the company because we had a strong culture that could accommodate their oddity and help everybody feel a sense of relatedness by focusing on performance, goal achievement, and vision.

FAIRNESS

The last trigger addressed by the SCARF model is the concept of fairness. The desire for fairness shows up early in our development (anyone who has raised children can tell you that) and stays with us no matter how many times we are told the world is not fair. A sense of unfairness can often arise from a lack of consistently applied rules in matters of work assignments, pay, promotions, benefits, rewards, or the use of limited resources. The more objective the rules are perceived to be and the more involvement employees have in decisions (when possible), the less chance there will be that employees will feel they are being treated unfairly.

Pay in particular is one of the most contentious areas for employees. The real problem arises when employees think decisions on pay are made arbitrarily, or that management is showing unjustified favoritism. I have always tried to make pay decisions based on objective data rather than subjective opinions. First, I decoupled pay from the review process so that discussions of performance would be less influenced by thoughts of raises. I tied starting pay and regular raises to data on the value the person had in the market. This was determined as objectively as possible using industry-specific salary surveys. It was amazing how using this objective data took much of the angst out of the regular pay discussions. Fundamentally, people aren't motivated by pay, but they can be demotivated by it if they think that they or others in the organization—including the CEO—are paid unfairly.

The SCARF model provides a set of criteria that explains why a particular culture may be more productive than another and gives a CEO a method to move an existing culture in the right direction. In light of this model, I now understand why many of the approaches and policies I have seen in high-performance companies work so well. Creating a strong culture requires more than just a few policy changes. It requires a consistent and holistic focus on all the factors that affect employee engagement.

Unfortunately, most CEOs struggle with the "soft stuff," according to former Campbell Soup CEO Douglas Conant. "Your EQ [emotional quotient] has to keep up with your IQ," he told *Bloomberg BusinessWeek*.[22] He's right. Understanding what motivates you as well as your team is critical to success in the CEO role. In fact, according to an article in the *Wall Street Journal*, business schools are starting to test for emotional intelligence to "identify future stars."[23] Emotional intelligence is defined as the ability to identify, assess, and control the emotions of oneself, of others, and of groups. According to Daniel Goleman, who has done seminal work in this area, emotional intelligence requires self-awareness, self-management, social awareness, and relationship management. And understanding how we and others are driven to seek rewards and avoid threats in the five areas of social experience can put us on the right track.

Now that we have a model for developing a high-performance culture, the next question many CEOs ask is "Can I measure my culture?" Well, like many things, you may not be able to measure culture specifically, but you can measure the outcome—employee engagement. In 2001, I read *First, Break All the Rules: What the World's Greatest Managers Do Differently*, by Marcus Buckingham and Curt Coffman. This was the first business book that satisfied my desire for significant analytics that support employee performance. The research for the book was conducted by the Gallup organization and resulted in the now famous Gallup Q^{12}. You can closely correlate the responses to twelve simple statements with superior workgroup performance. Workgroups that have better scores on the Q^{12} deliver higher employee retention, higher customer satisfaction, higher productivity, and higher profits. After using this model for more than a decade, I am convinced that it is highly accurate and that it reflects the strength of the culture.

The biggest proof of this methodology occurred after a much larger firm acquired one of the companies I had founded. We had been conducting the Q^{12} survey every six months for years and had been closely monitoring the results and working to improve any weak areas. The scores had been consistently positive and had been stable, with little variation for the last two or three years. When the ownership transaction closed, the acquirer initially made very few changes in personnel. The vast majority of people were still working for the same boss doing the same thing six months after the transaction closed (although I was no longer running the operation). The biggest difference is that they were now part of a much bigger entity with less defined vision, mission, and values. I expected the survey results to move slightly after the acquisition, of course, but I was shocked when the results came back. Employee engagement had dropped 30 percent to 40 percent across the board. In six months, the organization's workforce had gone from highly engaged to a very mixed level of engagement.

Although people make a company, good people are not enough to make a good company. Without clear vision, mission, and values, good employees have no sense of purpose or relatedness, they will not engage, and productivity will suffer dramatically. The biggest difference I see between highly successful companies and less successful companies is not necessarily the quality of the people. It is surprising to me how many great people stay with poorly run companies, at least initially. The biggest difference between great companies and mediocre companies is the quality of the leadership within the organization. Without the proper leadership, even the best people will gradually disengage and lose direction.

By leveraging the extensive work done by the Gallup group, every organization can measure the engagement of their employees and quantify the impact of culture in terms of the performance of the organization. For too long CEOs have talked about culture as a theoretical construct without finding ways to manage it as they would any other critical asset. With these tools, culture should become a critical part of your toolbox as a CEO.

In the rest of this section, I'll explore the key challenges we face as we work to build a high-performance culture: leveraging procedures and values effectively and focusing on relationships while achieving results.

RULES-BASED
VS. VALUES-BASED

"Where 100 people think, there are 100 powers;
if 1,000 people think, there are 1,000 powers."

—SOICHIRO HONDA

You may have heard this story before, but I love it. One day a researcher put five monkeys in a cage. In the middle of the cage he placed a ladder that provided access to a string of bananas that were tied to the top of the cage. Monkeys are pretty smart, so they quickly saw the bananas and recognized that the ladder was the only way to reach them. However, as soon as one monkey would begin to climb up the ladder to try to get to the bananas, the researcher would spray all the monkeys with ice-cold water. It took only a few tries for the monkeys to realize that going up the ladder was not worth getting sprayed by the water, so they began to avoid the ladder.

The researcher then replaced one of the five monkeys with a new monkey that had never experienced being sprayed by the water. As soon as he was placed in the cage, the new monkey began to eye the bananas and then started to head for the ladder. This time, instead of spraying the cage with water, the researcher watched as the other four monkeys rushed the newcomer and dragged him off the ladder. They understood the linkage between climbing the ladder and getting sprayed with water. The researcher continued to replace monkeys in the cage with monkeys that had never been sprayed before. Each time, the same scenario developed. The new monkey would eye the bananas and begin to climb the ladder only to have the other monkeys beat him down. Eventually all the monkeys in the cage were monkeys that had never experienced the ice-cold water. But they still avoided the ladder and would keep any newcomer off of it.

After a while, one of the monkeys turned to another monkey and said, "Why do we always beat up a monkey if he tries to go up the ladder?" The other monkey replied, "That's just how we do things around here."

While obviously fictionalized, this story is loosely based on research done by psychologists and social learning experts throughout the latter half of the twentieth century. It has been used many times to describe how rules develop in organizations and carry on, even when no one knows why the rule was created in the first place.

As companies mature, they often transition from a pure values-based approach to a more rules-based approach to getting things done. The whole process of growing from start-up to successful company with a long-term future is one of learning what works and trying to institutionalize those successes. Early in the life of a company, no one, including the CEO, knows exactly how things are going to work. Every time a new challenge occurs, the founding team jumps in and figures out how to handle the situation based on their unique approach to the market and their collective experience. This is often a competitive advantage for start-ups as they invent new and better ways to engage their customers. Of course, this process doesn't scale.

As the business grows, more and more transactions have to happen automatically for the business to prosper. At this point a balance must be struck between trying to create a rule-based process for everything and trying to make every decision based on the values of the organization, while still balancing the needs of all the stakeholders. On one hand, going too far over to the rules-based side will lead to an organization that is inflexible, with employees like the monkeys in the story often doing things that no longer make sense. On the other hand, a purely values-based organization would spend so much time figuring out how to act in each situation that they would struggle to get much done. The question for the CEO is, How do you achieve the efficiencies of a rules-based culture while leveraging the flexibility and openness of a values-based culture?

Using what we've learned about employee engagement and the SCARF model, the best path is to do what is necessary to ensure that employees feel respected, secure, trusted, aligned, and treated fairly. In this chapter, I'll offer some methods for striking the balance.

THE BUREAUCRAT AND THE ANARCHIST

For some, the process is everything. Like the micromanaging CEO who wants to be involved in everything, the bureaucrat CEO obsesses over the manner in which everything gets done. Process is king and following process is more important than anything else. This CEO wants workers who act like robots and can carry out the same tasks over and over again. While there are certainly some businesses that might lend themselves to this approach, most workers will find this kind of job to be most dissatisfying. Tasha Eurich, author of *Bankable Leadership*, described a ten-page dress code she once experienced that specified everything from the length of pants to the openness of female employees' shoes—and how she spent a considerable amount of time finding ways to subtly break the rules to see if anybody would notice. Keeping employees engaged with this overly oppressive rules approach would be almost impossible. As changes occur in the market, it will be hard for the company to adjust; top-down processes are slow to change. Without input from and flexibility for the frontline employees, the business will suffer.

The bureaucrat CEO never evolved her leadership skills beyond the traditional approach to management, which emerged with the start of the industrial age and the advent of assembly line manufacturing. The paradigm dictated that management was responsible for the thinking and frontline employees were responsible for the doing. Management was responsible for the creation of processes that workers were then required to implement. Management's job was to monitor how accurately the workers executed the processes and make corrections as necessary. This approach was very efficient when the job of the employee was simply to repeat the same process over and over. Unfortunately, this top-down management approach is still practiced today in many companies, even when it is totally inappropriate to the type of work being done.

FINDING YOUR BALANCE

1. Do you have processes that were drafted by management for how to do almost everything in your business?

2. How long are the policy or procedure documents for individual departments in your company?

3. How often do you review or adjust the procedures in your company? Who is involved in the process?

New companies are often founded by entrepreneur CEOs who wanted to escape the bureaucracy of corporate America. While this can be strong motivation, it can also lead to a management approach that says all process is bad. You primarily see these anarchist CEOs in small companies, because when all process is eliminated or avoided, it becomes very difficult for the business to scale and grow. Every task takes longer than it should, employees never feel certain about their work or their performance, and it is impossible to establish meaningful metrics because everyone does things differently. While employees will initially feel empowered because they are given wide latitude to perform their jobs, they eventually become discouraged as the chaos of the workplace overwhelms their ability to get things done. They may try to invent their own processes, but that is difficult to pull off without management support.

FINDING YOUR BALANCE

1. Do you eschew process in order to prevent bureaucracy?

2. Do you have documented policies and procedures? How long are the documents?

3. What metrics do you consistently track, other than basic financials? What do they tell you about how consistently work is being performed within or across teams?

CLARITY AND EMPOWERMENT

Researchers say that 28 percent to 45 percent of employees in the United States are knowledge workers. However, I define a knowledge worker as anyone who must make decisions based on a unique set of conditions that change from situation to situation. I think that applies to a much higher percentage of workers than the researchers allow. With the daily customer demands for better products and services, companies need most of their employees to make smart judgments to achieve the best outcome. This is how companies foster innovation and succeed in the market.

If you want to build a high-performance culture that leverages the efficiencies of process and the flexibility of values-based decisions, try the following approaches.

Create Values Specific Enough
to Guide Decisions and Apply Them Consistently

Values are crucial to a high-performance culture—because they can promote autonomy while also building a sense of relatedness. However, they have to be aligned with the business beliefs of the CEO, they have to be behavioral and universally applicable, and they have to guide every decision, not just some decisions.

If values have to be applied consistently to be effective and to create a foundation for the culture, then values must communicate the *unique* views of the CEO. If the CEO does not buy into the values, how can she expect any other employee to do so? It is critical for employees to understand how the CEO views the world of the company, what the CEO believes should be prioritized in day-to-day operations, particularly when those views may be different from what employees might expect. In this way, employees are guided toward decisions that are consistent with those the CEO might make.

Do you have specific values? Are they abstract concepts or are they specific enough to provide real guidance when an employee is struggling to make a decision in a new or challenging situation? If you do a quick search for company values, you will find that many of the Fortune 500 proudly display them on their websites. The problem with many of these statements is that they don't really provide any guidance in decision making. Here is a list from one company: leadership, collaboration, honesty, accountability, passion, diversity, and quality. Employees don't need to be told to be honest. Not that I am saying everyone will be honest—I'm not naïve. I do know telling employees that honesty is a core value doesn't necessarily help them make most practical, day-to-day decisions.

In the previous section, I wrote about Jack Welch's grid of values and performance. Ken Blanchard, author of *The One Minute Manager* and many other management and leadership books, has adapted the idea to build a model for a high-performance, values-aligned culture. He charges that values must be defined in behavioral terms: "Without clearly defined behavioral guidelines describing exactly how a 'great corporate citizen' behaves, each leader and staff member can define those values as it suits their personality, role, and activities . . . Values defined in behavioral terms describe how team members should behave as they pursue their team goals."[24]

I have seen many companies whose values tilt more in the direction of one stakeholder or another. Young start-ups are often employee or customer centered, while many large, established companies tend to become very shareholder focused. For a company to reach its full potential, I believe it is critical that the company properly consider how the values will be applied in achieving the interests of all stakeholders.

At NetQoS we had documented values that were specific enough to help guide decisions. For instance: "We attract, cultivate, and retain exceptional talent"; "We act as company owners and hold ourselves accountable"; and "We are easy to do business with." I would go over the values with every new employee and emphasize them in many of my company presentations.

However, I'm not sure employees understood the power of the values until they were tested. In late 2002 we had to let go seven employees to get our expenses in line with revenue as sales remained slow due to the recession. Earlier in the year, before we realized how badly things were going, we had made an offer to a college student to start in January 2003. We thought she was an exceptional candidate and were excited when she accepted our offer. When it later became obvious that we were going to have to fire some employees, many people assumed we would rescind our offer to this college student and save an existing employee. It was clear to me that this was not consistent with our first value. The existing employee who would be saved had been with us for a couple of years and, while a competent worker, had not proved to be an exceptional talent. Though it was harder to fire the existing employee because of the stronger emotional connection we had to him than the college student we barely knew, the right answer was to keep the college student and let the existing employee go. The student turned out to be an exceptional talent and was instrumental in the success of the company.

It is often easier to be consistent with your culture and values when things are going well. At many companies, their true values come out when things get tough. You can achieve the benefits of having strong, clear values only if you use them to guide every decision, not just *some* decisions.

Any time a decision is made by a member of management, employees will assume that the CEO sanctions it. This is one reason the values-performance grid is so essential for hiring or retaining the right managers. It's also critical to have an anonymous feedback mechanism so that you can hear from all parts of the organization. Employees need to be able to alert the CEO about issues with management (and any other concerns) without worrying about repercussions. If your team is healthy, they should be able to come to you directly without worry, but some employees come to a company with baggage and have learned to keep their mouths shut. While employees may not always be right in their assessment of a situation, getting their feedback will let you know where potential issues could develop. If you put such a feedback mechanism in place, all comments should go directly to you and not be pushed off on lower-level staff.

Let Those Who Have to
Follow the Rules Make the Rules

In a recent *Harvard Business Review* article titled "Creating the Best Workplace on Earth," researchers Rob Goffee and Gareth Jones described their three-year quest to identify the traits of the very best workplace: "an organization that operates at its fullest potential by allowing people to do their best work."[25] They identified six imperatives based on hundreds of interviews with executives. Number six was "no stupid rules."

If you want to avoid a rules-based culture that breeds disengagement, yet still operate efficiently, change who owns the rules. If the rules are owned and dictated by management, frontline employees will mindlessly execute those rules, whether they make sense or not. How many times have you experienced this as a customer? A company has a particular rule that makes sense in most cases but doesn't fit a particular situation. The employee is powerless to make a change and doesn't even seem to care about the issue. Instead, the paradigm should be flipped. Management should facilitate the development of the rules and processes but the employees in the group performing the function must take ownership. Ownership implies the ability not only to set the rules but also to change them based on circumstances. The role of management changes from dictating procedures to verifying that the procedures created are consistent with the goals and values of the company.

The manager is a conduit that ties the frontline employees to the rest of the organization, aligning their efforts to achieve bigger-picture goals.

For employees to effectively own the rules of their group or team, they must understand the why of what they do from a bigger-picture perspective, which demonstrates the need for a strong vision and mission. But having ownership of their procedures also helps build an understanding of why they do what they do on a more granular scale. Understanding this *why* is critical if you want creative, innovative, productive, and valuable employees. Instead of being merely programmable robots, these employees can leverage their natural problem-solving abilities to improve things across the business. Who knows better how to do a particular task than the person who does it over and over again? Driving this "why" thinking throughout the organization will pay tremendous dividends in the productivity of the business.

Of course, some corporate policies will always be necessary, and employees may not always have a say when those policies are developed. A company is not a democracy. However, I have found that the CEO can do many things to help people feel a sense of control, even with broad policies, by making them flexible. For instance, at NetQoS, I created a policy that every new employee would receive $250 when he or she started to decorate his or her office. This small gesture allowed employees to create their own unique work environments. We also had a flexible work hours policy and an "unlimited" vacation policy. If you want engaged employees, give them control when possible.

Align Corporate-Level Policies with Values

Corporate policies and procedures often just pile up over the years, one on top of the other. As CEO, you will be held responsible by the employees for all the policies of the company and even the procedures of their teams, whether you created them or they were in place for years before you arrived. Examine the policies and procedures at your company and how they're developed, and look for situations in which policy isn't aligned with stated values.

Build a Transparent Work Environment

Do your employees have the information they need to understand the true state of the business and how best to contribute to its success—and their own? Some CEOs foster a culture of secrecy by holding on to information and encouraging other leaders to do the same. However, if you want to build a high-performance culture, employees should have access to every bit of information that might help them do their jobs better, make better decisions, or innovate better solutions. Whether they are being guided by values or procedures in any given situation, they need knowledge, too.

Transparency is a hallmark of most high-performance cultures. Yet in many private companies, financial information is guarded like the queen's jewels. It's like asking someone to play in a football game but not allowing them to know the score. You may have heard of the concept of flow, developed by Mihaly Csikszentmihalyi, called the father of positive psychology by some. Essentially, flow is a mental state of uber-engagement in or focus on an enjoyable activity, during which you feel motivated and energized. Wouldn't it be great to have all your employees exist in this state most of the time? Well, one of the requirements is immediate feedback that helps a person know if and how he should change his behavior to continue to succeed. I'm extrapolating the idea a bit, but if you want engaged employees, you need to share information that helps them understand how successfully they are performing. If they don't have that feedback—in a variety of forms—they'll disengage. If you want employees to emotionally engage in and be committed to the business, share all the details about how the business is doing. It builds a sense of autonomy as well as certainty, because they aren't left to guess about the future prospects of the business.

I also made it standard policy in my companies that anyone could attend any meeting they wanted, unless specifically excluded. Obviously some discussions of employee pay and other personnel issues must be kept private, but the vast majority of meetings don't deal with these sensitive issues. I would invite my entire staff to board meetings as well. Many of them had never been in a board meeting, and by seeing my interactions with the board and knowing what interested the members, they felt more tied to the shareholders.

The sense of openness I tried to create reduced status threats and helped people feel more certain about future events. When a culture is secretive, employees can waste energy and creative resources worrying and gossiping about unknowns. Or they perform poorly because they don't have the necessary information to make the best choices.

—

Efficiency and creativity. Predictability and flexibility. Any good leader sees the value in all of these potential attributes of a company. Growth and profitability require that you know when and how to build each into the culture and operations of your company. As your company grows and changes, though, your focus will have to shift. But be careful that you don't inadvertently cause your high performers to disengage along the way.

FINDING YOUR BALANCE

1. What are your organization's values? Consider a recent decision and determine if the values, as they're currently written, provided clear and appropriate guidance.

2. Are all of your decisions aligned with the company's values?

3. Who makes the rules in your organization? How would you change the current pattern of operations and management?

4. What information is shared with employees in your organization and how? Do you believe that all employees have the information they need to make decisions that lead to company success?

REQUIRING VS. RELATING

*"You can make more friends in two months by becoming
interested in other people than you can in two years
by trying to get other people interested in you."*

—DALE CARNEGIE

I started my first business, the custom PC business, with capital that my wife, Cathy, had saved prior to our marriage. Borrowing money from your wife is one way to provide extra incentive to make sure your business is successful! I managed to make a little money, but I felt that I was never able to do things right because I lacked enough capital to invest in the best people. The foundation of my most successful company, NetQoS, was a network management product and methodology that Cathy had developed. We were able to secure $11 million in funding in 2000, just before the tech bubble burst.

NetQoS was my chance to run a business "right." I could hire the best people. At the time, I was only thirty-five years old and I hired many people who were older and more experienced than I was. I'm sure some of them looked at me and thought they could do a better job as CEO than I could. It didn't help that our offering had been developed by my wife; while she clearly needed a business partner, they probably thought I was just riding on her coattails. I knew I had a lot to learn, but I had been running businesses and studying for this job my whole adult life. I had strong ideas about how the business should be run and the culture I wanted to build. Inevitably issues would arise with some of the older management team that would test my authority and management capabilities.

We made it our top priority to hire the best talent into every available position. When you hire really talented people, they expect the other people around them to be just as talented, and that includes their managers. Unfortunately, hiring experienced and successful executives does not necessarily mean that they will be great managers. While I had some hiring experience, I had never before hired management-level people. Through discussions with employees and our employee surveys it became obvious to me that some of our executives could improve their management skills. They weren't incompetent or ineffective, but I knew we could do better. The problem I faced, however, was that these people were much older and more experienced than I was and felt there was no need to change their style. Because they had always been successful, they had convinced themselves that their methods were the right methods.

Two particular executives provided a study in contrasts. One was the consummate people person and focused exclusively on the needs of his employees from both a professional and emotional perspective. He knew the names of their kids, their career goals, and everything going on in their lives that might affect their work. The problem was that when it came to the actual work of the employees and delivering results for the business, he was totally disconnected. He believed that if everyone was happy, the work would take care of itself. In many cases this is true, and employees liked working for him. But over time performance issues arose in his area. If an employee was a weak performer and needed coaching, this executive couldn't help. He didn't track the details of projects and therefore didn't know when issues were developing. I tried to guide him, but it was difficult for me to teach a different mindset. The other executive was a master strategist. He had no relationship with his people and little impact on his team. He was so out of touch, it was almost like having no one in the position at all. He was a valuable member of the executive team from a strategic perspective, but he provided no coaching, no mentoring, and no value to the employees.

Most leaders tend to lean in one direction or another in terms of where they focus their attention: results, or relationships. I have learned that any of us can be more balanced in our approach if we understand where our natural tendencies lie and put in the effort to improve our management and leadership skills.

THE BEST FRIEND AND ATTILA THE HUN

For some CEOs, building relationships comes naturally. They have no problem engaging personally with employees at all levels of the organization. Employees like the attention they receive from these personable CEOs and return the affection—their desire for relatedness is fulfilled, and they get a status bump every time the CEO delivers kind words of praise. There's nothing wrong with this, but there is a problem when the relationship impacts running the business. Although the media often portray CEOs as hard-charging, win-at-all-costs creatures, I have observed many CEOs who failed because they were everybody's best friend. Their primary motivation is the desire to be liked, and that will hamper their performance of core responsibilities. They become so close to employees that they struggle to make changes in personnel or provide any critical feedback. If the CEO cannot hold people accountable for a high level of performance, the organization suffers and gradually sinks to mediocrity. Employees see the company beginning to fail, lose their sense of security, and begin to jump ship.

FINDING YOUR BALANCE

1. Have you ever struggled to make a personnel move because of your feelings for the people involved? How often has that happened?

2. When was the last time you gave critical feedback to an employee?

3. Do you tend to move people around the organization to avoid firing them? Do you let your managers handle all the dirty work?

Attila the Hun as CEO is the character often portrayed in movies and the press as the prototypical CEO. While I won't argue that this type of CEO doesn't exist, I will say he is probably less common than the public perception. One reason is that after his behavior becomes known, it becomes hard for him to attract competent employees. For Attila nothing is ever good enough. He requires exceptional performance at all times while treating employees like minions. This focus on outcomes without building up any personal relationships convinces employees that he really doesn't care. They perceive threats at every turn—to status, certainty, relatedness, and fairness. Attila never earns the trust required to have real influence in the organization. While he may think that he's driving the ship, he is not building buy-in from employees and is often getting far less than their best effort. The top performers will usually flee, knowing they will be better treated in another environment.

FINDING YOUR BALANCE

1. How do you let your employees know that you care about their success as much as your own?

2. Do employees discuss personal problems with you?

3. How many employees would follow you if you were to leave to become CEO of a different company?

BUILDING RELATIONSHIPS, ACHIEVING RESULTS

When I was struggling to figure out how to coach my two very different executives, I discovered a great book by Peter E. Friedes titled *The 2R Manager: When to Relate, When to Require, and How to Do Both Effectively.* The fundamental theory of the book is that the best managers relate well to their employees but also set strong requirements for performance. There is no balance to be struck between the two: you have to do both well. But in either area—relating or requiring—a manager can be too weak or too strong. For example, while it's important to relate to your employees, you can't become their best friend or managing them will be difficult. And while many managers are scared to require enough because they want to be liked, no one wants to work for Attila the Hun.

These two ideas tie directly to statements on the Gallup Q[12]. For example, relating well can be linked with statements such as these:

- "My supervisor, or someone at work, seems to care about me as a person."

- "In the last seven days, I have received recognition or praise for doing good work."

Requiring well can be linked with statements such as these:

- "I know what is expected of me at work."

- "In the last six months, someone at work has talked to me about my progress."

- "At work, I have the opportunity to do what I do best every day."

- "My associates or fellow employees are committed to doing quality work."

Friedes provides a simple assessment in the book that can be given to a manager's reports so that she can understand where she is on the spectrum in these critical areas.

THE 2R SURVEY

The following survey was adapted from *The 2R Manager* by Peter Friedes.*
Questions 1, 3, 4, 6, 8, and 10 are statements about relating, while questions 2, 5, 7, 9, 11, and 12 concern requiring. You should look at both an average score across all respondents for each question and a total score for each group of questions to see how you score in each area.

Score your manager in each of the following statements on a scale of 1 to 5.

1	2	3	4	5
Never	Seldom	Sometimes	Usually	Always

1. Relates to employees easily.   _____

2. Sets clear priorities.   _____

3. Includes employees in decisions.   _____

4. Listens to employees.   _____

5. Insists on high performance standards.   _____

6. Empathizes with and understands employees.   _____

7. Is comfortable with disagreements and conflict.   _____

8. Encourages and compliments employees.   _____

9. Creates a sense of urgency.   _____

10. Shows a need to be liked by employees.   _____

11. Is comfortable making demands of employees.   _____

12.. Addresses performance problems quickly.   _____

This survey was adapted with permission from Jossey-Bass (a registered trademark of John Wiley & Sons, Inc.).

It's critical, if you want honest feedback, to find a way to guarantee that the responses are confidential. You might consider using an online survey tool that can be set up to make all responses anonymous. You could also give the responsibility of administering the survey to another person in the organization, such as someone in human resources.

Another great resource that takes a similar approach to Friedes's (because both are based on essential management research that began in the 1960s) is from *Bankable Leadership* by Tasha Eurich. Her model addresses the fact that we tend to pit good relationships against great results, but the solution is to understand that you can have both through simple, modern management practices, which she covers in the book, offering many helpful tools and approaches. She also has an assessment on her website (bankableleadership.com) that allows you to ask others to assess your skills.

Often managers are surprised to discover that their employees perceive them to be strong in one area (requiring or relating, relationships or results), but weak in the other. Very few managers will be well balanced naturally—our personalities and experiences usually push us in one direction or another. The 2R Survey or the Bankable Leadership assessment can help you discover your natural tendencies so that you know where to focus your efforts to improve as a leader. These tools also do an excellent job of identifying the best managers, so it may be something that leaders who are responsible for coaching other leaders may want to review. Any time I was considering moving someone from an individual contributor position into a management position, I thought about how she would perform across the two dimensions of requiring and relating. If I didn't think she would do well in one area or the other, I coached her on the issue before moving her. This is one reason to identify the A's in your organization and ensure that they are being coached so that they can grow their skills and move into appropriate positions over time.

—

Let's face it; we all like to be liked. There is a term for people who have no interest in what others think of them: sociopaths. However, we also think we have to forgo being liked in the workplace in order to earn respect and to achieve goals. What we have learned from management theory and practice over the last five decades is that it isn't necessary to forgo one for another. We need to relate well to the people on our teams and also do a good job of requiring that they fulfill responsibilities and meet goals. Understanding our personal, natural tendencies toward one end of the spectrum or the other helps us understand how to build on our strengths and address our weaknesses.

FINDING YOUR BALANCE

1. Do you believe you are better at requiring or relating? Why do you believe this?

2. How do you think your leadership style affects the culture of your team?

3. Have you ever asked members of your team to fill out an anonymous questionnaire about your leadership style and effectiveness?

MAKE

DECISIONS

DECISIONS ARE THE FUEL ON WHICH EVERY ORGANIZATION RUNS. THE quality and speed with which decisions are made determine the productivity of the organization. Decisions are made at every level of the organization, even if the decision made is only to pass the issue along to someone else.

There is a clear trend away from the command and control models of the past to new models that empower employees to make decisions at the lowest level possible. I am a big supporter of this trend. The people closest to the situation will generally have the greatest knowledge of the particular issue. However, merely changing the level at which a decision is made does not necessarily lead to a better decision. Moving the decision making to the lowest-level, least experienced employees would most likely lead to poorer decisions. And for many companies, efforts to move decision making down the organization has failed miserably, which is why they revert to command and control. This failure often results when employees do not have the proper context to make good decisions and so they just default to a model of whatever is best for them.

The challenge for the CEO is to find a way to balance the greater knowledge of the particular situation that a lower-level employee may have with the bigger-picture strategy that the CEO is trying to implement. Is it easier to transfer the strategy down to the lower-level employee or to transfer all the domain-specific information of each employee to the CEO? Once a company reaches any significant size, it is almost always easier to transfer knowledge of strategy than knowledge of detailed operational issues. Therefore the goal for the CEO is to create an organization in which each employee makes the best decision possible by combining knowledge of the company's mission, vision, values, and strategy with knowledge of the particular situation. This is why it's so important for the CEO to own the vision. But managers must constantly work to make sure the overall strategy is driven down to every corner of the organization while sharing critical information back up so that the outcomes of decisions and plans are known at all levels. A process of open communication and continuous learning for everybody in the organization will result in better and better decisions over time.

If you drive the strategy throughout your organization, does this mean that you won't have any decisions to make? Hardly. There are many decisions that should only be made by the CEO and many others that will land on your desk anyway. Training your people to make the decisions they should while quickly escalating the rest to you is the challenge that CEOs face on a daily basis. The CEO should make the decision when the outcome affects multiple functional areas. The vice president of sales shouldn't be able to make a decision that commits the VP of manufacturing to doing something to which he hasn't agreed. I always encourage my direct reports to quickly escalate any issues they have with other departments, because the CEO is the only one who can allocate resources across the company. Additionally, the CEO should be involved in key personnel decisions (which is why I devoted five chapters to human resources). Obviously any decision that commits the company to action, such as mergers and acquisitions or strategic partnerships, must be taken to the CEO. As I explained in the "Build the Culture" section, it's also critical for the CEO to take responsibility for all decisions regarding corporate policy. I have seen too many CEOs leave this responsibility to their HR and legal teams. Having enough decisions to make is not a problem many CEOs have to deal with, particularly because it isn't always easy to make a quick judgment call. I'll address this issue in much more detail in the next chapter, offering a balanced system for decision making that can be used by you and any leader in your organization to foster a high-performance culture.

An even bigger challenge CEOs face is the fact that many of us (humans, not just CEOs) are very poor at making decisions, as Chip and Dan Heath point out in their excellent book *Decisive: How to Make Better Choices in Life and Work*. They describe what they call the "four villains of decision making" that strike across a wide range of decision-making processes. I think they map particularly well to the way most CEOs approach decisions. The villains, according to the Heath brothers, are "narrow framing," "confirmation bias," "short-term emotion," and "overconfidence" about the future.[26]

Let's say a CEO is asked to make a decision about an acquisition. We encounter the first villain in how the question is posed: "Should we buy company X?" The decision has been framed very narrowly, often because it is reactive. A company becomes available, and so the question is a response to a situation. It isn't spurred by a proactive discussion of whether the company should consider acquisitions given the current strategy or market conditions. Instead of asking, "What is the best way to invest a certain amount of money to get a strong return for the business?" the question narrows the decision to a simple yes or no. The CEO's first responsibility in every decision-making process is to widen the scope of the decision and make sure it is framed as broadly as possible so that the discussions get to the root of the issue rather than focus on a tangent. Allowing your team to narrowly frame a decision will lead to a poor outcome based on an answer to the wrong question.

Even if the question is properly framed, it is easy for people to search out only the information that confirms their preferred course of action. Confirmation bias happens every day in companies, from hiring decisions to large-scale strategy decisions. In mergers and acquisitions, I've seen companies assign huge teams of people to collect thousands of pages of information during their due diligence. The problem is that 99 percent of that information is not relevant to the decision-making process. All it does is make people feel more certain of their positions. The right approach might be to decide before you begin what assumptions need to be tested to gather specific proof in support of doing the deal *and* what factors, if discovered, would cause you *not* to do the deal. One team should test the assumptions while another team that has no bias toward the deal should be charged with uncovering reasons not to proceed. This search for information on the opposing side of an issue is critical for good decision making.

Any time a lot of work is put into an effort people will become emotionally invested in the decision. No one wants to do months of work only to decide not to move forward. The vast majority of CEOs are predisposed to action, so when it comes down to a decision, their default position will be to do something. The driving force of short-term emotion can cause bad decisions that have long-term implications.

Finally, after a decision we convince ourselves that we made the right decision regardless of any future data. In a study from KPMG regarding mergers and acquisitions, 82 percent of CEOs reported that a major acquisition each one had led was a success. When KPMG analyzed the objective data, they found that "83 percent of the mergers were unsuccessful in producing any business benefit as regards shareholder value." Talk about a disconnect between beliefs and reality. Not only do we make poor decisions, we also tend to deny it when we do. It is very hard to predict the future, so it is critical that CEOs continue to look for objective data after a decision has been made to adjust to changing conditions as quickly as possible.

Being aware of the common biases and issues in decision making can make you more effective in your own process and in demanding rigor from the leaders in your organization. You can also regularly seek out information from other CEOs about their past decisions and how they could have been better. Studying game theory can also help broaden your perspective. Game theory is the area of mathematics that explores conflict and cooperation between intelligent, rational decision makers, especially efforts to make the best possible decision without complete information.

I have seen CEOs who try to put off decisions, hoping they will get more information to make the decision easier. Unfortunately, while they are looking for more information, the employees are sitting on their hands waiting for direction. Colin Powell, the former secretary of state, is famous for his 40/70 rule. He said that a leader should make a decision when he has between 40 percent and 70 percent of the information available. If you make the decision with less than 40 percent of the information, you are shooting from the hip; but waiting for more than 70 percent of the information delays the decision unnecessarily. While a CEO can make both mistakes, I have seen more CEOs who wait to accumulate far more than 70 percent and hurt their organizations' productivity. Your job as CEO is to make the tough calls; don't wait too long to pull the trigger. Failing to take action on an obvious issue is just as bad as, if not worse than, making a bad decision.

The unique challenge for CEOs is that amid all the difficulties of decision making—battling the four villains and knowing when it's a decision the CEO should make—they also have to balance the interests of multiple stakeholders and develop buy-in among all of those stakeholders. Throughout this section, I'll describe a process that takes the four villains into account and I'll explore how to balance the unique interests of and pressures from various stakeholders in your efforts to make the best decisions possible.

DECIDING VS.
BUILDING CONSENSUS

"The price of inaction is far greater than the cost of a mistake."

—MEG WHITMAN

I came across an excellent blog post by Bryan Goldberg, the founder of Bleacher Report, not long ago on the most important managerial skill. He calls it "battle-picking," or the skill of knowing when to let employees make decisions, even decisions that the manager believes to be incorrect, and when to jump in and dictate a solution.[27] On one hand, jumping in all the time would obviously be detrimental to morale and would not allow employees to engage and grow in their own decision-making abilities. On the other hand, just going with the flow and accepting everything your subordinates want to do would diminish alignment of teams and make you irrelevant to the enterprise. Goldberg writes, "My goal is for employees to say, 'Bryan is really easy-going, and he lets us manage our own affairs . . . except when something really big happens.'"

Along the same lines, good CEOs recognize that not every decision is a bet-the-company decision. In fact, few decisions are. Sometimes the right answer is to give an executive or other leader a chance—to make a winning decision or a mistake.

In the early days of NetQoS, my sales executive came to me to propose that we use a then-small company I had never heard of called Salesforce.

com to track customer information. I had extensive experience in the information technology area, and I "knew" that using a remote data center to store critical corporate information was dangerous. At the time, the idea of software as a service for mission-critical applications was not a proven concept. I was pretty confident that the right answer was to host our own data. While an internal system would be slower and more expensive than a native Web application, I would know the data was secure and available. However, my sales executive had experience using Salesforce.com and believed it would help the business. So I went against what I thought I knew and I let the executive make the decision.

The decision to use Salesforce.com turned out to be a very smart one. Over time we built more and more of our infrastructure around the Web application, which provided tremendous value to the company and helped put us way ahead of our competitors. All because I gave my executive a chance to make a decision that I wouldn't have made.

While overruling people constantly is not good, it doesn't mean that you will always have consensus. Consensus can be valuable, but it is not always possible. The problem with consensus is that true consensus is not easy to obtain and it often slows down the decision-making process. My dad used to say, "The most efficient form of government is a benevolent dictatorship, where I am the dictator!" While dictating is more efficient, if the CEO is constantly dictating decisions without getting input from all involved, he can alienate his team and run off his best performers. People don't like to work in places where their opinions are routinely dismissed and their actions are dictated without their input, as I explained in the previous section. Balancing these two extremes is critical for success. There will be times when the CEO must make a dictatorial decision and move on. When the decision is not as time sensitive or important, the CEO should look for ways to build consensus. Regardless of how a decision is achieved, the CEO must always consider how to grow the decision-making abilities of his team and build buy-in for final decisions.

Finding the balance requires a process. I needed a process to help me decide to let my executive decide, and I needed to know that he was following a process to come to his decision. It helped me have enough faith in his decision to move forward. Without a process, our approaches are erratic or stifling and our outcomes are poor. With a process, we enable high performers to make smart decisions, we limit overreliance on the CEO decision-making power, and we achieve better results.

CARPET BOMBERS AND BLACK HOLES

The flyby carpet bomber: that's what I call a CEO who is too busy most of the time to pay attention to the business or involve herself in important decisions. But then suddenly when she thinks things are not going as she planned, she comes in barking orders like a Marine drill sergeant. This behavior puts tremendous stress on the organization. This type of CEO often hasn't been paying enough attention to even make reasonable decisions. Employees are caught between doing what is best for the business and saving their hides by doing what the CEO is ordering—obviously not a good way to engage employees. Different CEOs have different styles in terms of how much time they spend on the day-to-day operations of a business. I think a fairly wide range of styles can be successful, depending on the nature of the company. But whatever your level of involvement, it is important to be consistent. The team needs to know how and when the CEO will engage and on what issues.

FINDING YOUR BALANCE

1. How hard is it for your direct reports to schedule one-on-one time with you?

2. Do you engage with your team only when there is a problem to solve?

3. Do you think you learn about issues early or late, once they have escalated into major problems?

Some CEOs allow appropriate issues to land on their desk but then stifle the progress of the organization by not making decisions. They serve as black holes in their organizations. A black hole is an area of space in which gravity is so strong that nothing, including light, can escape. Issues or ideas sent up to the black hole CEO disappear and are never seen again. Often, the indecision results from either a desire for consensus where none is possible or a fear of making the wrong decision—what some people call analysis paralysis. After some period of time without an answer, the organization just muddles through or a functional executive takes charge and makes a decision. If the CEO doesn't act, this lower-level executive will effectively take over as CEO, yet may lack the big-picture view necessary to make good decisions. The company will flounder as all key decisions begin to reflect only the interests of one area of the company. It's hard to be successful in the CEO role unless you are willing to make decisions. Making decisions is fundamental to the job, and the failure to make decisions in a timely manner causes huge problems throughout an organization.

FINDING YOUR BALANCE

1. How long is your current decision to-do list? How many people on your team are currently waiting for responses or decisions from you?

2. Do you make it a practice to communicate decisions at the end of or shortly after any meetings?

3. Do the same issues seem to linger without clear resolution for months at a time?

DECISION TRIAGE

I have found it helpful to institute a two-stage decision-making process. The first stage is triage, which helps me decide how to approach the issue and how to work with my team to reach a final decision. The second stage is communication and analysis, which helps build buy-in, even when consensus isn't possible, and helps the organization learn from the decision. Let's look at the triage breakdown first.

The triage procedure prompts you to sort decisions into one of three categories based on their impact on the business:

- **Less significant**: The decision, on its own, won't impact the business overall in a considerable way.

- **Easy but significant**: The pros and cons of various options are clear, but it's important to get the decision right because it will affect the entire business.

- **Difficult and significant**: The options are complicated or it isn't clear if you are even considering all the options, and the decision will make a difference to business operations and results.

Less Significant Decisions

Less significant decisions present coaching opportunities. I force people who bring me these issues to make decisions and explain to me how they arrived at their conclusions. I never change these decisions, even if they are very different from the solutions I would have proposed. Different isn't necessarily better, and I want to build employees' confidence in their decision-making abilities.

In *The Decision Maker*, Dennis Bakke, the highly successful CEO of AES, wrote: "Nothing tells you more about an organization than the way it makes decisions. Do leaders trust team members? Do the people closest to the action get to make the call? Do team members have real responsibility and real control? All of these questions can be answered by one other one: who gets to make the decisions? . . . Few business leaders tap into the value created by putting important decisions in the hands of their people."[28]

I agree. However, building a decision-making culture is often easier said than done. Many employees want to bring decisions to your desk instead of making decisions themselves. Don't let them get away with this. It is perfectly fine for someone to run a decision by you or talk it through with you. You should encourage that behavior. But don't allow people to drop problems on your desk that are totally within their area of responsibility. It is highly likely that they know more about the issues than you do. You pay people to be experts, so you should not allow them to bring issues to you without proposing a well-thought-out position. Your job is to then push and prod on that position. Check to make sure they have considered all factors. If the issue can be quantified, have they run the numbers and made reasonable assumptions? What is the worst case? Does the decision take into account the interests of all stakeholders—customers, employees, and shareholders? Are any of the four villains of decision making obviously present? By being thorough in your questioning you will teach your team to put in the work so that you can trust that their decisions are appropriate.

If the decision is successful, you should give credit to the people who proposed the solution. If it isn't, you should still support them. You agreed with their proposal, so you should have their back if things don't go well. Only if they lied or intentionally withheld information can you blame them if things turn out badly. If you didn't think their decision was correct but you didn't have a better answer and so went along with what they proposed, you must still show your support and you must take responsibility for any failure.

ASK MORE THAN TELL

Instead of dictating decisions, Meg Whitman, Hewlett-Packard's CEO, asks questions of her leaders, forcing them to explain issues and verbally analyze them until the best decision becomes clear. What types of questions does she ask?

- What does this do for the customer?
- Do we understand the problem?
- What's the opportunity here?
- How can I help you get that accomplished? [29]

Studies have shown that talking is important for clarifying ideas and learning. Talking forces us to process information with a different part of our brain—the part that governs verbal communication—that requires us to consolidate our own learning, giving structure and meaning to what we know and formulating ideas into a message. If you want to help your leaders achieve greater clarity, get them to talk through their thinking by asking questions.

Easy but Significant Decisions

Easy but significant decisions require the input of the executive team. Because the decision could have a significant impact on the business, you must make sure the final decision is correct, and you need to build buy-in. If the decision affects multiple groups, and most do, I engage all the appropriate executives to find out what decision they would make. The executives may have additional information on the problem that sheds new light on the issue or other ideas not yet considered. This process either leads to a consensus decision or a new option for me to consider that is strengthened by additional information and an opportunity to create buy-in.

Training your executive team to make good decisions is a key requirement to building an organization that can support rapid growth. If you find yourself constantly making decisions that are different from those solutions proposed by your executive team, there is a problem. Decisions are made by understanding and applying the vision, values, and goals of the organization in combination with market conditions. If an executive is not able to consistently make good decisions either on his own or as part of the executive team, first ensure that he clearly understands the vision, values, and goals. Then ask yourself if you think he is falling victim to any of the "four villains" and coach him to identify and avoid them. Finally, ask yourself if he has the appropriate knowledge and experience to be the expert you need him to be.

As Bryan Goldberg points out in his blog, if you have hired well, the people on your team are smarter than you in their area of expertise. What you typically have over them is experience—usually—or big-picture vision. What you should try to do is meld your experience with their smarts to make the best decision possible. As CEO there are certain decisions that you will need to make for the company. Strategy, resource allocation, hiring, firing, and many other issues often reach your desk for a final decision. However, in most of these cases there is already a consensus within the organization as to the right course of action, if you are encouraging open discussions among and between teams. If you arbitrarily change these decisions you will find yourself at war with your own team. However, there will be times when you have to make a tough call that goes against the general consensus. When you make these decisions it is important to respect people's opinions by explaining why you are making the decision to overrule the general consensus. Hearing them out and then explaining the *why* will help build buy-in among your team for an idea not their own.

I didn't overrule others often at NetQoS, but I remember a few cases. At one point, we were hiring a new recruiting coordinator. As I discussed in the chapter "Recruiting vs. Hiring," the recruiting coordinator is a key position in any company because that person is often the first person a potential hire engages with and therefore influences early opinions of the company. We had interviewed three candidates for the position. The first candidate had significant HR and recruiting experience but was in my opinion a very mediocre talent (per my five attributes). The second candidate had some HR experience and was somewhat more talented than the first candidate. The third candidate had *no* recruiting or HR experience but was clearly an exceptional talent. As we progressed through the debrief, it was clear there were differing opinions on who should be hired. All of the HR team wanted to hire candidate one because she had the most experience. All of the non-HR people who participated in the interview process wanted to hire the second candidate because she at least had some experience and was clearly more talented than the first. I was the only one who wanted to hire the third candidate because I didn't care that she didn't have experience, I just cared that she was an exceptional talent. The coordinator wasn't responsible for building the HR team, and so experience wasn't very important to me. Needless to say my decision to overrule the entire room and hire the one candidate no one else wanted to hire was not popular. Hopefully I did a good job explaining why it was critical that the person in this position (or any other for that matter) be exceptionally talented. In case you are wondering, the new hire did an exceptional job. Not only that, but she met and married a fellow NetQoS employee. I often remind them of my role in creating their family.

Difficult and Significant Decisions

Difficult and significant decisions, more than any others, require the CEO's active involvement in the decision-making process. I would still follow the process described in the previous section, gathering input from the executive team to ensure we have considered all options and to hear opinions, but I know that ultimately I will have to make the final decision. I recommend beginning by determining the level of risk inherent in the decision, and so I split this category into two sub-categories based on how easy the decision is to correct if the wrong decision is made.

Some decisions, while difficult to make and significant, are low risk: they are relatively easy to reverse. For these issues, the CEO should focus on making a quick decision that allows the organization to move quickly. I almost always encourage quick decision making, but CEOs often get hung up on difficult and significant decisions, dragging their feet and causing the organization to lose valuable momentum. No one wants to make a bad decision because she decided too quickly, but in most cases a quick decision is critical to keeping the organization functioning at top efficiency. I often took comfort in the fact that if the other smart people in the organization didn't agree on the course of action, it was probably close to a 50-50 call. So I could just pick one and move on.

The thing to remember about low-risk decisions is that bad decisions should be changed just as quickly as they were made. You can afford to make decisions quickly only if you are also willing to quickly admit when you make a mistake. This is true of all decisions, of course, but we seem to shy away from admitting we are wrong the more significant the decision is. Overconfidence kicks in—we believe that eventually things will work out. But as new information comes in you must reevaluate your decision. You cannot be emotionally tied to the old decision. Admitting you were wrong and moving on will allow you to maintain credibility with your team. The longer you let an obviously bad decision stand, the more credibility you will lose. Remember, as CEO you are responsible for every decision. Don't allow bad decisions to fester and diminish your credibility.

Other decisions—for instance, moving forward with a major acquisition—are almost impossible to reverse and therefore carry tremendous risk. Difficult, significant, and risky decisions should be made carefully, with careful analysis and thorough discussion. They can determine the ultimate success of a CEO. Obviously, there is no magic pill for making them. When you talk to CEOs about these kinds of decisions, they will often refer to relying on their gut instinct or a special feeling that something was the right course. When I faced these decisions, I relied on two resources to test my thinking and my instincts.

First, I assigned a devil's advocate for every big decision. Originally, the devil's advocate was a Catholic church lawyer appointed to argue against granting sainthood to any candidate. The purpose was to thoroughly test the evidence for every candidate. Appointing a senior person to fill the role of devil's advocate for key decisions can be a very valuable tool in decision making. By looking for all the things that can go wrong and probing the assumptions, they will make the proposed decision better thought-out or reveal that the decision was ill-conceived.

I have also found it critical to get the perspective of people who are not emotionally attached to the decision. Often, their wider perspectives will provide a better path forward than would views from individuals who are in the heat of the battle. Reaching out to mentors and peers who have faced similar issues can provide key insights that might otherwise be neglected. For example, one of the biggest decisions of my business career involved negotiating the sale of NetQoS. After a little back-and-forth with the acquirer, we had received a "final" cash offer of $180 million. This was in

May 2009 and the economy was still sputtering. M&A activity was near an all-time low as companies hoarded cash in the face of the recession.

We had set a goal of selling the company for $200 million, so the question was whether to take the offer as is or walk away from the $180 million and hope the acquirer would raise the offer. There were no other acquirers in sight, so if they didn't raise their offer, we would have missed out on a big deal and who knew when another acquirer would show up—or how we would continue to weather the recession in the meantime.

I owned a significant portion of the company, so from a personal perspective it would have been easy to take the offer and declare victory. However, something bothered me about settling for an offer that, while reasonable, was short of the goal. I reached out to the members of my CEO peer group for guidance.

Without revealing the acquirer, I was able to walk them through the issues involved. While more of them would have taken the $180 million than pass, the process of talking through the issues with a group that was not emotionally connected to the transaction provided the clarity I needed. I recommended to the board that we pass on the offer. Six weeks later the acquirer returned to the table with an offer of $200 million. While things could have turned out differently, I was confident that I had made the best decision possible and could have lived comfortably with either outcome.

COMMUNICATE AND ANALYZE

I have seen many CEOs have a discussion with one or two people, make an important decision, and then fail to communicate it clearly to everyone in the organization who is or might be affected. Decisions drive action in an organization. Without clear communication, valuable time is lost while the decision slowly leaks out to the rest of the organization. Just like a children's game of telephone, the decision is often changed in the transmission process. When you make a decision, immediately communicate that decision to everyone affected by the decision. Don't force other people to communicate your decision. You made it, so you should explain to everyone what you decided and why.

Always communicate the basic reasoning you used to reach each decision. For example, if you are operating under the idea that growth is more important than profits at this time in your business and you make a decision because of this fact, it's critical to remind people of this operating principle. If you don't, not only will they possibly not understand the decision or how they can act to support it, but also they won't buy into it. Smart, talented people operate on more than blind faith. They need the "why" in order to process change and shift their opinions.

By clearly stating your reason for any decision, you will also help your team make better future decisions. By constantly reminding your team of your core operating principles, you will allow them to consistently act in ways that promote those principles. Over time fewer decisions will reach your desk because the organization will understand your intent.

As I've already explained, it is critical to admit when you've made a bad decision, in order to correct it. Sometimes it's obvious when you need to change course. But the best way to know for sure is to conduct an official postmortem for every significant decision. Decisions that are strategic in nature should be reexamined as a matter of process simply through the regular review of key metrics and overall performance. For decisions that are less strategy-centric yet still significant, if a formal postmortem process is not put in place, it is easy for the issues to never be reexamined. The organization would never learn anything from the decision. With a formal postmortem the organization will be able to grow in its ability to make decisions. It should answer questions like: What factors should we have considered in making the decision that we missed? What assumptions did we make that turned out not to be true? How could we have implemented the decision more effectively? What did we do that worked particularly well? These postmortems also help build buy-in for future decisions because people trust that if you make a decision that doesn't work out, there is a process in place to analyze it and change it if necessary or at least improve on it. There is always something to learn from every change an organization endures, no matter how successful.

—

None of us will have a perfect decision-making record. The four villains of decision making that the Heath brothers identified are fairly universal, which means we all fall victim to them. Our best option is to work with our teams through a process that helps us avoid these pitfalls as much as possible, trusting in the talent and experience of our people to balance our own biases.

FINDING YOUR BALANCE

1. What process do you follow for decision making in your organization? How does it leverage the talent of your teams?

2. How often are you involved in decisions that you think should have been made by executives or other leaders?

3. When was the last time you reversed a decision you made?

4. How do you analyze the outcome of decisions? What questions do you ask? What data do you gather?

EMPLOYEES VS. CUSTOMERS
VS. SHAREHOLDERS

"Your employees come first. And if you treat your employees right, guess what? Your customers come back, and that makes your shareholders happy. Start with employees and the rest follows from that."

—HERB KELLEHER

When I was working at AMD in the late '90s, most of the people I worked with had never run their own businesses and they were curious about how it compared to working in a large company. It struck me one day that the most essential difference was the way they had learned to make decisions versus the way I had learned to make decisions. They almost always framed decisions in terms of their own interests or of the interests of their departments or bosses. They would say things like "I have too much on my plate to do that" or "We don't have budget for that." Every decision seemed to reflect the interests of the individual, the boss, and the department. I rarely heard a discussion about whether a particular course of action was good for the company as a whole.

Unfortunately, this is our default decision mode. Of course our starting point in any situation is to view it from our own perspective. That's human nature, and the SCARF model I described in the previous section explains why it is so. If we are given no other perspectives to consider, we will base our decisions on what is best for us. The job of the CEO is to provide those other perspectives so that employees can make decisions based on the interests of customers and shareholders as well as their own. Of course, CEOs have to walk the same path if they want to encourage others to follow it, and that's not always easy.

START-UP, GROWTH, AND ROI

Where the company is in its life span often has a dramatic impact on whose interests dominate the decision-making process. When a company is first formed there are often no customers to worry about. Because all the employees are well known by the CEO and can fit in a small room, employee concerns tend to take precedence in the CEO's mind. He's trying to build a team, he has no operational redundancy, and so it seems critical to keep every employee happy and productive. The only thought given to shareholders is whether they have provided enough money to make payroll. If the CEO is smart, he has created a product based on an analysis of what potential customers want, so the initial offering is designed to fill unmet needs. Belief in the product is the extent of consideration for the customer.

Over time, if the company is successful, it will reach a growth phase during which it adds customers rapidly. With this new attention *from* customers, many companies will begin to focus strongly *on* customers. Variations of the slogans "the customer is always right" or "the answer is always yes" will become common, and stories about employees going out of their way to meet the needs of customers are celebrated. If the balance goes too far in this direction, you end up with issues of employee burnout and low profitability (poor shareholder return) as no expense is spared to treat customers well.

Finally, as the company achieves more economic success, the shareholders will begin to press for plans and actions that deliver a return on their investment. Even in companies that are bootstrapped, the founders will eventually need to recognize returns from their efforts. For companies that make it to the public markets, the pressure for shareholder return often becomes all-consuming and very short-term focused. If you spend time within most public companies, you'll get the sense that decisions are made based almost solely on their impact on earnings in the current quarter and year. Customers and employees are sacrificed at the altar of making the quarterly number. Although this shareholder-focused approach will initially show financial results as the emphasis moves away from customers and employees, the business will begin to erode. A few quarters of good performance turns into a death spiral of dissatisfied customers and unmotivated employees.

It's critical for the CEO to understand the natural pressures that exist in organizations as they mature and to balance these pressures in the company's decision-making process.

SHAREHOLDERS MAY REVOLT

Some CEOs tend to think that if they have the board's approval, that's all they really need to worry about. But that's not always the case. Shareholders occasionally rise up and wield their power to block a move or change a practice they don't like. In October 2013, the shareholders of Alco Stores voted down a merger proposal, going against the unanimous recommendation of the CEO and the board, as well as industry groups. They didn't like the share price being offered, which seemed to devalue the company, or the move by management just two weeks before announcing the merger to grant itself additional stock. So they voted the move down.

Another hot button for shareholders? Executive pay. Shareholders have attacked companies like Oracle, WPP, BSkyB, Aviva, Anglo American, and others when they didn't believe that executive pay was well aligned with performance. If shareholders think their interests aren't being cared for, they'll find a way to let you know it.

FINDING YOUR BALANCE

1. Have you made a decision in the past six months designed to keep either employees or customers happy, even though you doubted the long-term wisdom of it?

2. What stories or proof of success do you share at meetings? Is there a particular focus on either customer service stories or on financials?

3. Do you neglect training for employees because you can't calculate the return on the expense? Do you try to keep your salary expense as low as possible?

THE DECISION NEXUS

The best CEOs grow the "big picture" thinking of their employees, and I believe that the three-way balancing act of good decision making is one of the most important pieces of that skill. I use the graphic shown here to encourage people to frame a decision based on the interests of employees, customers, and shareholders. Any time an employee is faced with a difficult decision or is in conflict about what to do, he or she should think about what would be the best course of action for each of the constituencies. What would the shareholders as a group want me to do in this situation? What would the employees as a group want me to do? What would the customers as a group want me to do? The right answer is most often found by seeking the solution that best reflects the interests of all three groups.

If you explain important decisions that you make using this method, employees will begin to understand how to act in the best interests of the company as a whole. When this methodology is not taught, you will see employees act in a way that is locally optimized. This is how silos develop in an organization. In heavily siloed companies, only the CEO and board are looking out for the company as a whole. Let's explore how the interests of the primary stakeholders compete and overlap.

THE DECISION NEXUS

Employees

We have already discussed what employees are looking for and how to meet their needs in the "Provide the Proper Resources" and "Build the Culture" sections. The challenge for the CEO is to maintain a high-performance culture as the company grows and matures. This is why it's so important to constantly gather feedback on employee engagement and to wear the priest hat as often as you can. When employee morale dips, the customer experience will take a hit and so will shareholder return. Great CEOs understand the importance of creating great jobs for their employees. If you are starting from scratch, I would start with that set of constituents; without highly engaged employees it will be very difficult to ever have happy customers or maximize value for shareholders.

Customers

Customers are the people who pay the bills for successful companies. No matter how much money is raised at start-up or during an IPO, if a company is to be successful in the long term, customers should be providing the vast majority of the capital for the business. Just like the importance of surveying for employee engagement, it is important to survey customers to get reliable feedback on their satisfaction with the company. This isn't news. Most companies already do this. With the ease of creating and sending Web-based surveys, companies are constantly asking for feedback. The problem is that the surveys are typically poorly conceived and ask too many questions of the customer without giving anything in return. Most of us regularly pass on these surveys and the companies lose an opportunity to actually gather valuable feedback.

In the December 2003 *Harvard Business Review* article "The One Number You Need to Grow," Fred Reichheld describes the results of his research on the best metric for measuring customer satisfaction. His work on tracking net promoters—"the percentage of customers who are promoters of a brand or company minus the percentage who are detractors"—provides a simple yet powerful way to measure customer satisfaction across a wide range of industries. To find out whether a customer was a promoter or a detractor required only a single question. "How likely is it that you would recommend [brand or company X] to a friend or colleague?"[30] Customers respond based on a scale from *not at all likely* to *extremely likely*. Customers who answer with a high score are considered promoters while customers who answer with a low score are considered detractors. To calculate the Net Promoter Score (NPS) you subtract the percentage of detractors from the percentage of promoters. The more positive the number, the better.

In addition to being quite simple to implement, the NPS can reveal your competitive advantage with customers because it's often possible to find out the NPS of other companies. You can easily survey your target customers and calculate the NPS of your closest competitors. By keeping the survey to a single question you will ensure broader participation.

Once you have your NPS, the next order of business is to convert those who are not promoters into the promoter category. You can follow up the NPS survey with more targeted questioning of select customers as a way to explore issues and improve your decision making.

One way to ensure that you're building good relationships with customers that will lead you to more promoters is to have customers represented by an executive who reports directly to the CEO. This executive should not be responsible for any sales effort; she should be focused on customer satisfaction and the customer relationship. The head of sales cannot represent the customer effectively and still worry about closing revenue. Many companies make the mistake of expecting salespeople to maintain the relationship with the customer. The problem with this approach is that customers never fully trust salespeople because of the nature of the sales job. And salespeople are often not available to assist customers when they need it. Every customer should know whom to call when they need assistance, and those employees must be empowered at the highest level to resolve almost any issue. Having an executive focused on customer satisfaction, free of any revenue goals, is a valuable differentiator in the marketplace.

Again, though, the theme here is balance. Customer service is a critical component of any great company, but it must not be the only goal. Because, frankly, the customer is not always right, and trying to please every customer in every situation will bankrupt a company. To help your employees achieve the right level of focus on customer interests, begin with a clear definition of your core customer. You might find in your detractors people who are not your core customer. It's unlikely that you will ever be able to sufficiently meet their needs to make them a promoter because you haven't designed your products or services to do so. If you aren't focused in your approach to the market, you won't be able to identify your most valuable customers for long-term growth and make decisions based on their unique interests.

When a relationship with a customer becomes strained, don't be afraid to consider the shareholders' interests and ask, "Is this customer improving our profitability now or in the long term?" Sometimes, you can't afford to do business with a customer. I learned this lesson in my first business building custom PCs. After delivering a computer, it was not unusual to get a call about some issue the customer was having or occasionally even have the customer show back up at the office with the computer in tow to demonstrate a problem. Most customers realized that I merely assembled the units and didn't have control of the operating systems or other software they might install. For one customer, however, this concept was too difficult to grasp. For the first several days after he bought a computer, he showed up in my office asking me to solve issues with his Windows software or other applications. Though I sold consulting services, he of course had no interest in paying for them. He believed that a free computer expert came with the purchase. After helping him for a time each day, I would explain that I needed to help other customers and that he should purchase consulting services if he needed more help. The message was not being received. On the fifth consecutive day he came in to get help, I reached under the counter and pulled out my checkbook, wrote him a check for the entire purchase price, and told him that I had decided I couldn't afford to do business with him. He was shocked that anyone would not want his business, but I stuck to my guns.

Not every customer is the right customer. Your job as CEO is to help identify and focus your resources on the right customers and encourage your employees to do the same.

Shareholders

In the introduction, I mentioned my favorite movie about business, *Barbarians at the Gate*. Early in the movie, the CEO of RJR Nabisco, Ross Johnson, is playing golf with a representative of one of his largest shareholders. The rep begins complaining, in a friendly way, about the fact that RJR stock has been flat and asking what Johnson is going to do about it, saying, "All we want you to do is make us rich. That's all we're asking." To which Johnson slyly observes, "Or you'll find somebody else who will."

My experience with shareholders is that most are relatively simple in their motives and interests. They want you to make them a lot of money. Except in rare circumstances, how you do it is much less interesting to them. While obviously this is a broad generalization, it does frame the nature of the relationship.

I have played the role of investor many times, and I've observed how different CEOs handle the relationship. The CEO is often the only employee who interacts with shareholders (although I don't think this is necessarily wise). Consequently, making sure that shareholders maintain their investment and don't feel compelled to wreak havoc is a prime responsibility for the CEO. You accomplish this by reassuring them that their interests are consistently top of mind in the company.

Like most Americans, I distinctly remember where I was on September 11, 2001. My wife, Cathy, and I were attending an industry trade show for NetQoS where we were launching our second product. I was watching CNBC because they were going to have an interview with Jack Welch, when news of the first plane crash came across the screen. When the second plane hit, everyone knew that the world had changed. Later that week, as we drove home, we discussed what the horrible events might mean for both the country and our business. As CEO I knew that just surviving the next twelve months would be an accomplishment. At the time, the company was just beginning to ramp revenue and was burning cash on a monthly basis. Unfortunately my worst fears were realized. As we went into 2002, it became almost impossible to sell our products. One customer told me that our product was the best product he had ever seen from a new company, but that if it cost a dollar he couldn't buy it. As 2002 continued to challenge us, I knew it was time to consider the interests of our shareholders.

We had been funded by a single firm, Liberty Partners. They had invested a total of $11 million in the business, and it seemed likely that they would lose the entire investment if we continued. I entered the board meeting in the fall of 2002 with my mind made up. The right answer was to make a recommendation that we return the remaining funds to Liberty and shut down the company. While I believed that the company had two great products and a strong team, the economic environment was preventing us from having any success. There is nothing tougher for a CEO than contemplating the death of his company, but I thought it was clearly the right thing to do. "If it was my money, I would take it and go home," I said. I will never forget the words of Tom Greig, a managing partner at Liberty, "If you need more money, we have a checkbook." Sometimes in business the only thing that matters is having the right partner on the board.

Just as with any other group, maintaining a strong relationship with shareholders requires influence. Credibility, competence, and caring form the basis of the relationship between the CEO and shareholders. Credibility means that the shareholders can trust that everything you communicate to them you believe to be absolutely true. Of course this implies that you are regularly communicating to them. For private companies this is one of the biggest mistakes I see CEOs make. Once they have received money from investors they often disappear until they need additional funding. This approach fails to build credibility with shareholders and often leads to a deteriorating relationship. Regular communication presents an opportunity to show your competence in the business. The more competence you can demonstrate, the more comfortable shareholders will be in staying with your company through thick and thin. Almost all businesses experience difficult times, and it's important that shareholders be supportive. CEOs can encourage this behavior by showing that they care about the shareholders as well. CEOs who at the first sign of trouble start talking about their bonus or reputation instead of about the shareholders' investment won't hold on to that investment for long.

The biggest challenge for a CEO is determining the appropriate time frame for measuring returns. Some investors have a long-term outlook and are just looking for steady progress, but others want to see great results every quarter. The CEO must deliver short-term results without harming the long-term growth potential. That's why you get paid the big bucks. Objective measurements for customer and employee satisfaction can help ensure that any improvements in financial performance are not merely because the pendulum has swung from a balanced approach to favoring shareholders at all costs.

In an article titled "Shareholders First? Not So Fast . . ." Jeffrey Pfeffer wrote, "Consider that there are literally scores of recent studies showing the gains in profitability and productivity that companies have made—not by putting investors' interests first but by implementing high-commitment work practices."[31] Pfeffer explained that the pendulum of corporate focus was directed toward all stakeholders in the '50s and '60s, swung heavily toward investors in the '70s, and is now rightly swinging back toward a more balanced approach. He went on to quote Dennis Bakke, the cofounder of AES and author of *The Decision Maker*: "'Why should past labor [capital] receive so much preference over current labor [employees]?'" I don't believe it should, which is why I have always done my best to follow the same balanced approach that I ask of my employees.

Of course, to help ensure that the shareholders' interests are being represented, a company employs a board of directors. The relationship between the CEO and the board of directors is unique in the business world. The idea of reporting to a committee of people instead of to a single individual makes managing this relationship much more challenging, particularly for new CEOs with little experience working with boards. The composition of the board will have a big impact on the relationship as well. The trend over the last twenty years has been to diversify the composition of boards and to include more functional expertise. I have always thought that the job of the board should be to select and monitor the CEO in their efforts to represent shareholders' interests, not to become involved in running various areas of the company. It is impossible for a group that meets once a quarter to have the same understanding of the business as the people who are working in it every day. For this reason I like to see boards that are primarily composed of people with CEO experience. If you have a board with mostly subject-matter experts, for example, CFOs or CIOs or CSOs, the board can quickly morph into a super executive team. People will naturally gravitate to their area of expertise and the board can become an operating entity. This is dangerous and undermines the credibility of the CEO. The problem can be exacerbated if any executives in the key positions are weak.

If you are running a private company, spending time to get the right board members in place is a valuable use of your time. Even in public companies, the CEO will likely have some influence. Aim high. Most people are flattered that you would consider them for a board position, and while they may not always accept the position, they will often have recommendations for others who would be a good fit. I think it is a good idea to have board terms expire every year or two and require unanimous approval to renew then. Sometimes, board members remain long past their useful time just because there is no easy mechanism for replacing them.

In the end, the best way to maintain a strong, positive relationship with the board is to show them that you are balancing the interests of shareholders with the interests of other stakeholders.

—

You will be much more successful and your job as CEO will be easier over time if you and your employees are consistently balancing the interests of your employees, customers, and shareholders. When this approach is the model, decisions are made faster, are undone less often, and lead to better results overall.

FINDING YOUR BALANCE

1. How do you encourage balanced decision making in your teams? How often do you talk to people about the interests of the stakeholders in the company?

2. What tools do you currently use to assess employee and customer satisfaction?

3. Who represents the interests of customers on the executive team in your company?

4. Do you regularly assess your customers to determine which are the most profitable and make decisions accordingly? Do you ever "fire" customers because of a poor return, because of how they treat employees, or for other reasons that make them a poor fit?

5. Do you view the role of CEO as being flag bearer for shareholders?

6. How often and in what form do you communicate with shareholders?

DEPARTMENT VS. DEPARTMENT

"In organizations, real power and energy is generated through relationships. The patterns of relationships and the capacities to form them are more important than tasks, functions, roles, and positions."

—MARGARET WHEATLEY

Being a CEO has certain similarities to being a parent. As parents, we love all of our children. In our efforts to be good parents, we avoid playing favorites, we try to make all of our children feel special, and we devote relatively equal time to each. Good CEOs face the same challenges with the departments or divisions in the company, represented by direct reports on the executive team. Unfortunately, many CEOs fail at this basic task. Think of how many times you have seen a CEO paired at the hip with her CFO, COO, or VP of sales. Favoritism doesn't work in a family or in a company.

We spend our entire school career being judged almost exclusively on our individual work abilities, and then spend much of our work career being judged almost exclusively on our team-building capabilities: how well we assemble and lead a team to perform. The composition and quality of the executive team may be the most important decision a CEO makes. But a team full of talented individuals doesn't necessarily deliver great results.

In *The Five Dysfunctions of a Team*, Patrick Lencioni provides a model for building an effective and productive team. What kills teams? According to Lencioni, it's absence of trust, fear of conflict, lack of commitment, avoidance of accountability, and inattention to results. Only the CEO can lead a team to top performance by creating a healthy environment. I address the last three issues in other chapters. The first two factors, though, are dramatically affected by the CEO's leadership style, approach, and capabilities, which are evident in the decisions he makes about where he spends his time, who reports to him, and how he balances resources across the company.

MY FAVORITE CHILD

In my early days of being a CEO, I would attend many events around town to hear speakers and network with other CEOs. I wanted to learn everything I could from their experiences. I would often see one particular CEO at these events, and every time I saw him, his CFO was by his side. The first few times, I didn't think much of it; but after a while I began to wonder, Does this CEO go anywhere without his CFO? There he was, event after event. I never saw any other member of the management team out with the CEO. I suspected the CEO likely had a problem with his executive team. Favored execs often take advantage of their close relationship with the chief executive and act like mini-CEOs, wielding influence far outside of their areas of responsibility. Other members of the executive team then become resentful of their second-class status. If this CEO spent much of his time with his CFO, he was likely neglecting the other members of the team. I suspect the CFO was positioned as "first among equals," acting as proxy for the CEO when he wasn't present and exerting influence way beyond his financial responsibilities.

FINDING YOUR BALANCE

1. Do you receive complaints that some departments always seem to get what they want while others are neglected?

2. In the past two months, with which members of your team have you spent the most time? Why?

3. Are you friends outside of the office with a member of your team? Are you related to any member of your team?

BATTLE ROYALE

Sears Holdings is slowly circling the drain, and everybody seems to agree that it's Eddie Lampert's fault. Lampert, the slightly eccentric investor-turned-Chairman and CEO, has been named worst CEO of the year by columnists for *MarketWatch* and *Forbes* in the past. As I'm writing this, investors with ESL Investments, Lampert's hedge fund, have decided to take their money and go home, forcing Lampert to surrender majority control. Sears stock has been plummeting for years as the company sinks deeper and deeper into the red every quarter. Some believe the 120-year-old brand might have had a shot until Lampert's confounding organizational move five years ago.

An exposé in *Bloomberg Businessweek* by Mina Kimes reveals the brutal realities of Lampert's decision to take one company and turn it into *more than thirty autonomous business units.*[32] A free-market hardliner, Lampert believes that decentralization will reveal which units can survive in the market, but he can't seem to see that all efficiencies have been lost and the intense competition between the units for limited resources is causing them to sabotage each other. Amazingly, each unit has its own leadership team and board of directors, and some executives are on a number of boards, so they spend much of their time in meetings. The salaries for all of these executives certainly isn't helping Sears's bottom line. Performance is judged separately for each unit, so whatever a unit needs to do to improve financials, it will do. Writes Kimes, "Appliance maker Kenmore is a widely recognized brand sold exclusively at Sears . . . The appliances unit had to pay fees to the Kenmore unit. Because the appliances unit could make more money selling devices manufactured by outside brands, such as LG Electronics, it began giving Kenmore's rivals more prominent placement in stores." Business units didn't even have easy access to essential administrative functions, such as IT or human resources. If they needed those services, they had to enter into formal agreements or outsource.

Lampert doesn't appear to be playing favorites among the business units. In fact, he doesn't seem to like any of them at all.

THREE WAYS TO MAKE BETTER DECISIONS ACROSS DEPARTMENTS

1. Have the Right Direct Reports

According to a Harvard Business School working paper entitled "Who Lives in the C-Suite?" the number of direct reports for the average CEO doubled from five in the 1980s to ten by the mid-2000s.[33] My thought is that ten is on the high end and approaches the maximum number of direct reports a CEO should ever have. The purpose of the paper is to study, in part, the centralization of decision making at the executive level in some firms and the drivers of that centralization, including improved IT, that make information more available at higher levels of the organization. The study also examined less diversification in products, services, and operations, which increases synergy among functional managers and makes it more possible for them to serve directly on the executive team.

Although I don't necessarily agree with overly centralized decision making, I do believe that the executive team is the most important unit in the company and that the right functions should be represented. However, if the executives aren't capable of removing their functional hats and putting on their company hats, they probably don't belong in the C-suite.

Often-neglected functions that I think should always report to the CEO include customer experience (which I explained in the last chapter) and human resources. People are so important to the success of an organization—so much so that the head of HR should have a close relationship with the CEO. Too many organizations bury the HR function under a CFO or other executive, often treating it as a cost function instead of an area for strategic competitive advantage. In an interview with CNN Money, Alan Mulally, the CEO of Ford credited with turning the company around and guiding it successfully through a tough recession, said, "'When I arrived, there were six or seven people reporting to Bill Ford, and the IT person wasn't there, the human resources person wasn't there . . . So I moved up and included every functional discipline on my team because everybody in this place had to be involved and had to know everything.'"[34]

Another role that I see underutilized in the C-suite is that of chief technologist or strategist, depending on the nature of the business. Intel and some other companies have "futurists." The purpose of this role is to have someone focused on future developments in the industry. The executive team members are often so involved in the day-to-day operation of the business that they are unable to see changes coming in the market until it is too late. Having a deep thinker on the team who is anticipating future advances is critical to your efforts to adapt to the next major trend. In some companies, this executive is also responsible for ensuring execution of the strategy, although I believe that if you have the right leaders in place and have done a good job of aligning strategy with group goals, good execution should not consume the chief strategist's time.

2. Spend Your Time Impartially

Simply put, don't play favorites. Find a way to spend quality time with each member of your executive team. It will help head off departmental rivalries before they develop. Your executives will trust you and each other more, and they will be more likely to raise concerns that you need to hear or to address conflicts that you need to help resolve.

Be careful that in your efforts to spend time with executives individually you don't end up spending time with them *only* individually. The entire team should be meeting on a regular basis to encourage discussion between executives and address issues as a team. Alan Mulally meets with leaders from Ford's four profit centers and twelve functional areas every Thursday. Open discussion with everybody in the room, where people feel comfortable raising concerns and recognizing problems, will help you be seen as impartial and will help you make better decisions across departments.

3. Manage Conflict and Trade-offs

It is the CEO's job to manage, not eliminate, conflict in the organization. A certain level of tension will naturally exist between departments because they are always competing for limited resources. The question for the CEO is how she handles this tension when it develops. I have found that one of the hardest things to teach new executives is that they should immediately escalate any cross-departmental conflicts to me. Top performers often think it is their responsibility to solve these issues without involving the CEO. The problem is that only the CEO is in the position to make trade-offs between the conflicting demands of two different parts of the organization. (I've addressed how to consider these trade-offs in the first two chapters of the "Provide the Proper Resources" section.) If a conflict can be resolved quickly and easily through collaboration and cooperation between departments, great! But often, executives end up with an uneasy détente in which neither side is happy and the fundamental issue is unresolved.

It is your job to make difficult decisions and trade-offs, and to do it in a way that creates buy-in so that your team trusts you and follows your lead. Too many CEOs bury their heads in the sand when it comes to making judgments between departments. But making these decisions allows the organization to move forward quickly. And when your executives feel comfortable bringing issues to you for a fair hearing and a logical decision, emotional mayhem will be diminished. The faster you resolve these conflicts, the better for everyone and the company.

—

Eventually, you will face decisions that only the CEO can make, and that is especially true when it comes to resolving conflicts between departments or allocating resources appropriately across the organization. How you build your executive team and how fairly you direct your time, energy, and focus will have a big impact on the health of your team, the quality of the decisions you make, and the results you achieve together.

FINDING YOUR BALANCE

1. How many direct reports do you have? Which functional areas do you think may be underrepresented on your team?

2. If you tracked the time you spent with your executive team, would it be balanced across all members?

3. How often do you meet with your entire team? How productive are these meetings?

4. Do you find that you are constantly mediating squabbles between departments? Are you actively creating a team environment that mitigates or encourages tension?

DELIVER

PERFORMANCE

AT THE END OF THE DAY, CEOS ARE JUDGED ON THEIR ABILITY TO DE-liver performance. Some CEOs focus on nothing else. The challenge is that good performance is a goal, not a behavior that can be taught. In sports the goal is to win, but a good coach doesn't say, "Go win!" and leave it at that. Great coaches break down the fundamentals that are necessary to winning and train their players to execute those fundamentals at the highest possible level. Great CEOs must do the same thing. They must break down the business to the fundamental behaviors necessary to be successful in the market. Bad CEOs tell their employees to "win" but don't help them develop an understanding of the fundamentals necessary for success. The result is inconsistent performance because some employees can't translate the desire to win into execution that moves the business forward.

How does the CEO break down the business to the fundamental behaviors? I'm not saying that the CEO has to personally teach every employee how to do his or her job. Only in the smallest of companies would this be possible, and even then it's unlikely the CEO would know the best methods for accomplishing all tasks. Instead, the CEO has to lead the charge to help employees align their behaviors with the overall goals of the organization. The CEO is responsible for maintaining the company's focus on its big-picture strategy, while employees are responsible for leveraging their expertise to complete the necessary individual tasks. The key for the CEO is to make sure that he is growing and empowering that expertise at the individual level and harnessing it for the bigger purpose of the organization. The entire management team must embrace its role in coaching employees on these fundamental behaviors. If the team fails to do this, then the company will become highly inefficient; each individual or department will begin to act as they see fit, totally detached from the direction the CEO is trying to establish. How many times have you seen employees do things that you know are bad for the company, yet they seem oblivious to the harm they are doing?

To ensure alignment in the companies I have run, I focused on clarifying and communicating intent, which I described in the chapter "Growth vs. Profitability" under the topic "Clarify and Communicate Your Goal." In order to facilitate the process of breaking down the corporate goals into actual behaviors that individual employees can undertake, I created a software-based management system called Khorus. The purpose of Khorus is to clearly show each employee how he or she is contributing to the goals of the organization, while allowing the CEO to verify that each group is working on the right fundamentals. Each quarter, the CEO enters a set of corporate goals for the company. (Most of the businesses I have operated work best on a quarterly time frame, but some early-stage businesses might be better suited to a monthly tempo.) These goals were specific; for example, "Generate $20 million in revenue," "Launch new product, Cosmo," "Complete headquarters move," or "Improve operational efficiency by 2 percent." Typically there were about five to eight corporate goals each quarter.

The corporate goals take on two forms. The first type of corporate goal is called a priority goal. These goals are new initiatives that the CEO is asking the company to undertake. These goals set the priorities for the specific quarter. It is important that any department have two priority goals at most in a given quarter. The second type of corporate goal is a sustaining goal. Sustaining goals capture the normal operations of the company on an ongoing basis. For example, I would often use a goal of "Continuous improvement in operational excellence" to align employees who didn't have a direct tie to the priority goals.

Once the corporate goals were entered into the system, each executive worked with his or her teams to develop departmental goals that were tied to those corporate goals. Each lower level in the organization then worked with their manager to develop goals that supported their manager's goals. The system allows for each employee to contribute to the development of his or her own goals and to see everyone else's goals. By being able to see everyone's goals, employees understand not only how their efforts contribute directly to the success of the company, but also what other groups are doing to contribute to the same corporate goals. The final piece of the puzzle, and what is incredibly valuable to the CEO, is that each employee receives an email at the end of each week asking them to update the status of their goals. Instead of having to create some complex "TPS reports," the employee has only to answer two questions on each of their goals. The first question is: "On a scale of 1 to 5, how likely is it that you will complete this goal in the quarter?" The second is: "On a scale of 1 to 5, how do you feel about the quality of the work you have completed toward this goal so far?" The employees can, in a couple of minutes, update their status; when that information is combined with everyone else's updates, the CEO has valuable insight into what goals are in danger of not being completed. Instead of most of the typical corporate systems that provide only historical data, this system gives the CEO valuable foresight, which can allow him to take action to solve issues before deliverables slip and goals are missed. (For more information on how Khorus can be used in your business, check out the system at www.khorus.com.)

Many people struggle to set the right goals. The best goals align with the priorities of the organization and optimize the fundamentals that drive success in a given business. For example, a corporate goal might be to reach $100 million in revenue in the current quarter. As that goal is cascaded down the line first to a regional sales manager and eventually an individual salesperson, the individual goal should not be just to deliver a proportionate part of the $100 million in revenue. A better set of goals for the individual salesperson would be to identify how many qualified prospects she needs to meet with in the quarter, how many demos she should install, or how much pipeline is needed to reach the number. By working with individuals to understand these fundamentals that drive the business, the goal process ensures that individuals are working on the highest-priority items.

Priority is a key word here. Goals can be extremely valuable in keeping an organization on track, but if they aren't developed thoughtfully, they can actually limit performance. In their book *The 4 Disciplines of Execution*, Chris McChesney and Sean Covey write, "Practicing Discipline 1 means narrowing your focus to a few highly important goals so you can manageably achieve them in the midst of the whirlwind of the day job. Simply put,

Discipline 1 is about applying more energy against fewer goals because, when it comes to setting goals, the law of diminishing returns is as real as the law of gravity."[35] Generally, you can accomplish two goals very well if they fall outside of your day job. If you have more than two goals that aren't directly related to performing your core responsibilities, the chances of achieving them with excellence diminish, and you'll likely accomplish only one. If you are going to establish, say, three to five goals, only a couple should be outside of the realm of daily activities. The rest should be focused on executing daily activities at a level that ensures the success of the company goals.

For a system like Khorus to be most effective, it is critical that management engage employees in a mutual goal-setting process. At the end of the conversation, the employee must take ownership of the goal and agree that it is achievable and worth pursuing. In my opinion this conversation is one of the most critical roles that managers in a company fulfill.

As an example, I recently had a conversation with a product management executive at an early-stage software company. We had not worked together before so I had asked him to think about the key responsibilities of his job. He told me that his number-one priority was to deliver an exceptional product. I agreed that this was the most important responsibility of his position. But then I asked, "How would we know if it was an exceptional product?" He said he thought an exceptional product would be easy and quick to implement. I suggested that an exceptional product would also have a high conversion rate from demo to purchase. We also agreed that the better the product, the fewer support calls the company would receive, and the higher the renewal rate would be. We then set metrics for each of these areas. For this start-up we went from a high-level corporate or departmental goal to specific, measurable, individual goals that highlighted the fundamentals for this area of the business. One of the biggest mistakes I see companies make is not taking the time to go through this process of identifying the business fundamentals with new employees. They bring on new employees and have no training process in place to make sure the employees know their role and how it fits into the bigger picture. Without this preparation, employees will make mistakes and struggle to succeed.

Part of the preparation for all employees should be calibrating "performance." The issue reminds me of an old joke about two hikers who come across a vicious grizzly bear. One hiker turns to the other and says, "What are we going to do?" The second hiker says, "Run." The first says, "We can't outrun a grizzly bear." To which the second slyly responds, "I don't have to outrun the grizzly bear. I just have to outrun you!" Many times people talk about performance like there is an absolute standard that must be met. You can sense this in slogans like "Quality is Job 1" or "The Relentless Pursuit of Perfection." In reality, making a product that is of higher quality than the competition's has value, but making a product of *much* higher quality than any competitor can be a quick path to bankruptcy. Almost every business exists in a highly competitive market with both direct and indirect competitors for the customer's dollars. Performance in a competitive business environment is relative. As I mentioned earlier, if your company is growing at 10 percent while the market is growing at 25 percent, you are clearly underperforming. But the same 10 percent growth in a declining market might be exceptional. Executing the plan requires delivering results compared to objective measures in the appropriate industry. As you build a performance culture and establish appropriate goals, always look for ways to compare your company's performance to that of competitors and other related companies.

Without a formal system of goals and clear communication about vision and values, the CEO risks playing a giant game of telephone, in which company direction is passed down verbally; by the time it makes it to the frontline employee, the meaning has been so contorted as to be unrecognizable. Then the CEO is surprised when he finds out employees aren't accomplishing his key initiatives. Additionally, the CEO is not getting direct information from the people who know the most about what is happening on the front lines of the business.

Some might argue that a goal system this detailed diminishes an employee's autonomy and potentially reduces engagement, thus harming the high-performance culture. In the earlier "Build the Culture" section, I described the natural human desire for autonomy. All people want to have control over how they perform their jobs, no matter what the job may be. Most CEOs and managers understand that employees would prefer not to be told what to do every moment of their day. Initially a new CEO may allow his employees plenty of autonomy. He then begins to observe that people are not making the decisions he would like them to make. He thinks to himself, "I can't believe all the bad decisions my employees are making. I have to rein them in." Much as he would prefer not to, he begins introducing rules that define what employees can and cannot do. The new policies and procedures multiply as more and more problem areas are discovered. The decreased autonomy causes employees to disengage and make even poorer decisions.

The bigger the company, the greater the disconnect between the executive team and the rest of the organization. The people who interact with the CEO regularly are most closely aligned with the CEO. Their decisions reflect a greater understanding of the vision and culture. The further you move away from the CEO, the more local optimization rather than global optimization guides decision making. This is the scenario when you lack the alignment created by a system of interdependent goals.

Many researchers have studied employee engagement from the perspective of customer experience. One in particular, Bruce Temkin, has proposed that truly engaged employees are empowered (autonomous) and aligned. Autonomy without alignment results in entitlement, and alignment without autonomy results in marginalization. Either way, performance suffers.

In *The Art of Action* by Stephen Bungay, which I first mentioned in the chapter "Planning vs. Action vs. Results," Bungay explains how this problem is common in almost every large organization, and that the solution has been understood in the military since the nineteenth century when Field Marshal Helmuth von Moltke applied the insights of Clausewitz to develop a highly effective operating manual for the Prussian army. Von Moltke recognized that autonomy and alignment are actually inversely related. Problems with autonomy are inevitably due to lack of alignment. The more alignment you have, the more autonomy you can grant. Additionally, because no battle plan survives first contact with the enemy, autonomy is critical to reaching high performance.

Once you have clear alignment throughout the organization, you have to ensure that the company executes the goals within a continuous cycle of improvement. Innovation and improvement can come from all levels of the organization, but there are certain responsibilities the CEO has in this area. The CEO sets the bar, and by ignoring poor or mediocre performance in a particular area the CEO lowers the bar across all areas. When the performance of a given area is not good enough, it's often necessary for the CEO to highlight that area for improvement and possibly to look outside the organization for additional expertise and personnel.

It is crucial to identify, monitor, and constantly refine the fundamentals that lead to business success when additional data is gathered about the business and market. This is what delivering performance is all about. In the first chapter of this section, "Trust vs. Verify," I'll address the struggle to trust employees to do their work and still verify that the work is being done well, by pairing goals with strong metrics.

As CEO, you are responsible not only for continuously improving the performance of the company, but also for continuously improving your own performance as CEO—which will affect the performance of the company. As I mentioned in the introduction, you have no immediate boss to provide regular feedback on your performance. If you want to deliver great performance personally, you will have to establish a relationship with your board that encourages them to provide appropriate and helpful feedback. The board is also there to help you guide the organization to high performance.

The right board can be a powerful multiplier of your efforts as CEO, with knowledge, connections and experience that will make you better. Of course, if you want the board to be helpful in improving the performance of the company, you have to give them the right information. The vast majority of what the board members know about the company is what you tell them in the board meetings. It's very important to think about what you present and how you present it. I have been in far too many board meetings that sound like infomercials—the CEO presents each department in the best possible light and never mentions any problems. This is pointless if you actually want help from your board.

What the board needs to know is how you, the CEO, run the business, not what each department does day to day. You and the department heads should identify a few metrics (which I'll discuss more in the next chapter) that reflect how they are doing. For the board, understanding how these metrics are tracking and what issues need to be addressed is much more interesting and important than hearing about all the deals that might close next quarter. If your board members do not know the issues that are keeping you up at night, they can't provide their full value. Abstract the information to a general business level at which the board members can reasonably contribute, and stay away from the intricate details. For example, discuss your overall sales process and how the key metrics at each stage are tracking. Board members should have experience with sales processes across many industries and can add value. Talking about a specific deal, unless you are asking for a board member to help with closing it for some reason, is a waste of time and will often lead down a rabbit hole.

Expecting the board to help you improve as CEO is tricky. Unfortunately, studies have shown that boards are not very good at assessing the work of CEOs. They tend to focus primarily on financials—the outcome—rather than the behaviors that lead to strong financials. According to a study conducted by the Center for Leadership Development and Research and the Rock Center for Corporate Governance, both at Stanford University, as well as The Miles Group, boards include issues of customer service, innovation, and workplace satisfaction in their evaluations of CEOs less than 5 percent of the time. And about 10 percent of boards don't evaluate the CEO at all![36]

Even though the board is technically the CEO's boss, the CEO provides leadership in relation to the board. A group of people making a decision tends to be much more risk averse than an individual making the same decision. Therefore boards are often very reluctant to replace CEOs, even when performance is not up to expectations. The CEO job is very difficult and good boards recognize that. As long as the CEO can still provide leadership to the board, they will often stick with the CEO through difficult times. However, once one or more of the 3C's—credibility, competence, or caring—are violated, all bets are off. As a board member, I have been in favor of replacing a CEO only when the CEO failed on one of the 3C's. For instance, too many CEOs make presentations to their boards that are far too optimistic in their assumptions. Over time as each forecast is missed or revised downward, the board loses confidence in the CEO. Either the CEO is lying to the board or the CEO is incompetent, and both are bad.

If you want your board to help you perform well, I would encourage you to adopt two methods for gathering feedback. First, after each board meeting, try to give your board members a homework assignment to identify three things you are doing well and three things you or the company can improve. After gathering their feedback, you should spend some time addressing those issues at the next board meeting and repeat the process. Closing the loop on this feedback and taking action on the items will dramatically strengthen your relationship with the board and will help you improve your performance as well as the company's.

The second way you can gather feedback from your board is to ask each of them on an annual basis to fill out a scorecard, grading you as I've recommended that other employees be graded. The form I like to use follows the outline of this book; it is shown on the CEO Scorecard that follows. I would ask each board member to provide a simple grade—A through F—for your performance in each area of responsibility. You should also rate yourself in each area. Comparing how the board rates you to your own ratings should raise issues for reflection. Once the scorecards are completed, you should have a session with the board or a subset of the board and discuss the grades.

CEO Scorecard

Responsibility	Personal Grade	Board Member Grade
Own the vision		
Provide the proper resources		
Build the culture		

Make decisions		
Deliver performance		

In the last chapters of this section, I'll address the biggest challenges CEOs face to their own high performance, including fulfilling internal roles and external roles appropriately and balancing the needs of the company with their personal needs.

TRUST VS. VERIFY

"The best executive is the one who has sense enough to pick good men to do what he wants done, and self-restraint to keep from meddling with them while they do it."

—THEODORE ROOSEVELT

Ronald Reagan famously said, "Trust, but verify" when referring to an arms agreement with the Soviet Union. As CEO you should have the same attitude. The struggle to find balance, though, comes when we trust too much and don't track progress toward critical goals or hold people to high standards for achieving goals. We're afraid to hold people accountable because it implies conflict. The alternative is that we trust too little and we demand more and more information and data to verify that work is being performed on time and to high standards. People become overwhelmed by the process of tracking data and their attention and time are diverted from what you want them to be doing—the work you hired them to perform.

While you should trust all of your people to deliver results (if you've hired well), you should also create a culture in which progress is consistently measured and constant improvement is the norm. The best way to do this is by making sure that all goals are clearly measurable using metrics that help predict business success. Choosing the right measurement is critical to making the goal process as valuable as possible.

THE GRANDPARENT AND THE AUDITOR

Grandparents have the best job in the world. They get to enjoy the kids when they want but don't have to deal with issues when they arise. Spoiling the grandkids a little and letting them get away with something is part of the fun. This works great for grandparents, but not so well for CEOs. One of the key roles of the CEO is to set the bar for the quality of the work in the organization and then hold people accountable. If the CEO lets people get away with not meeting their deliverables, for instance, her credibility will suffer. Setting up good metrics, although challenging, is the easy part compared to consistently holding everyone to the high standards required to be a successful company.

FINDING YOUR BALANCE

1. How do you respond when people on your team miss key deliverables?

2. How do you apply standards for performance? Would people in your organization say that you hold some groups to higher standards than other groups?

Auditing can be a valuable function in any business, but it can also be a waste of resources. Good auditors understand the larger purpose of the business and look for ways to improve the efficiency of the operation. Bad auditors are overly focused on form over function and waste time gathering excess data that validates bad processes. Some CEOs fall into the bad-auditor trap—they focus on form, not function. I have seen companies make the collection of data a full-time effort for a whole department of people and burden the rest of the organization with fulfilling requests for more and more information. While it is important to have good data in a business, data collection must be built into the systems and processes without interfering with the actual work that people do.

The other threat of too much data is that it can actually reduce your ability to make good decisions rather than enhance it. I'm going to quote from a paper written by chemist Michael Schultz: "Decision making is impeded when evaluating information that is wrong or excessive, and thus [data] should be limited to the absolute minimum and most relevant available. As [biologist Yuri] Lazebnik described, sometimes the more facts we learn, the less we understand."[37] Even scientists agree that too much data is a bad thing!

Don't allow your desire for hard numbers to decrease the productivity of your workforce or the decision-making abilities of your team.

FINDING YOUR BALANCE

1. Do you have employees who spend all their time gathering data for you?

2. What type of documentation requirements do employees face when they complete tasks?

THE BEST METRICS TO ENCOURAGE PERFORMANCE

The backbone of any smart verification system is a set of metrics that effectively reflect the essentials of business performance. We have all heard the saying, "You get what you measure." Executing on your plan well demands that you determine what measurements are important and relevant for your particular business. Constantly driving and refining the operational metrics are a key part of any CEO's job.

Picking the right metrics is critically important. Ideal metrics possess five characteristics:

- **Easily measurable**: If you have to build a new system or implement a complicated process just to measure one aspect of performance, it's probably not worth it in terms of what you'll learn.

- **Directly correlated with business performance**: Remember the fundamentals of business success I discussed in the opening of the section? Remember the goals that emphasize the fundamentals? Well, the metrics should be tied to the goals you establish for the department, group, or company. They will tell you if you are successfully executing the fundamentals.

- **Predictive of future business performance**: Most metrics reflect past performance. This is particularly true of financials. For instance, revenue tells you how many deals your sales team closed or how well your frontline staff pitched a new service—last quarter. It doesn't tell you anything about what might happen in the coming quarter. The best metrics don't tell you just how well you've done (your financials tell you that), they tell you how well you're going to do—in the next month, quarter, or year.

- **Isolated to factors controlled by the group that it is measuring**: This one is tricky and difficult to achieve. Everything a team does is interrelated with the actions of other teams in a business. However, identifying fundamentals that pertain primarily to a particular group will tell you much more about the strength and performance of that group.

- **Comparable to competitor's metrics**: It's helpful to track your progress against your competitor's so that you can judge how well you're building or maintaining an advantage in terms of operations, holding on to top talent, and holding on to top customers.

Now before you get all excited about finding "ideal" metrics, let me tell you that I have never found one that fully meets all five criteria. Instead, you look for as many matches as possible. The first conversation I have with every new manager that works for me revolves around the questions, "What goals should we set for your department that focus on the fundamentals?" and "What metrics can we come up with that tell me whether you are doing a good job achieving those goals?" This should be a collaborative discussion between the CEO and the manager, not a dictated decision. Often it will take some trial and error to find metrics that are as ideal as possible.

Let's look at sales as an example. I distinctly remember the first time my head of sales at NetQoS and I discussed metrics for his sales group. When I asked him what was the most important metric for sales he quickly fired off the obvious answer: revenue. While it's true that the job of the sales team is to deliver revenue, that doesn't make it the best metric. First of all, as I mentioned earlier, revenue is not predictive. Second, sales often depend on far more than the effort of the sales group. How good is the product? What are the economic conditions? What is the price? Is the market growing or shrinking? All of these things and more affect whether a sales team generates revenue. Therefore it's not a good metric for the sales team because low revenue doesn't necessarily correlate to a bad team or poor effort. I remember after the events of 9/11 that it was damn near impossible to sell anything. Many companies saw revenue drop dramatically. Did this mean their sales groups suddenly became incompetent? Of course not.

If revenue is not the best metric for sales, what is? As any good salesperson knows, making a sale is a process. The better you understand the process, the better you will be at maximizing the revenue possible with the given market conditions. So what metric would measure how good a sales team is at understanding the sales process? I would argue that really good sales teams excel at predicting revenue, which is why the number-one metric for the sales team at NetQoS was accuracy of revenue forecasts (I describe this in more detail in the "Budgeting vs. Opportunistic Investment" chapter). At NetQoS, final numbers were expected to be within 5 percent of the forecast given at the beginning of the quarter, and they were, more than 90 percent of the time.

You might think that this approach would promote sandbagging or holding orders or sales at the end of the quarter in order to hit the projection. Because each individual salesperson was paid a commission on total revenue, he or she had a strong incentive to close every deal possible. While obviously an upside surprise was easier to swallow than a downside miss, both were damaging to the business. It's hard to properly allocate resources when you don't know what resources you will have. Building excellent forecasting into the sales culture of the company gave me a strong competitive advantage.

Another of my favorite metrics for sales is a combined sales and marketing metric. We calculated the metric by taking the total software license revenue (new revenue as opposed to maintenance revenue) sold in a quarter and dividing it by the total sales and marketing expense in that quarter. This metric captures the resources it takes to sell your product. In my industry, established software companies should have a number greater than one. You wouldn't want to spend more than one dollar to get a dollar's worth of new revenue. If a software company reaches a ratio of 2, things are going very well. I like this measurement because it is easy to compare your results to any public company and get a sense of how you are doing. Young companies should see steady progress in this metric quarter over quarter; if not, it may indicate a serious problem in the business model. It's true that this metric isn't predictive, exactly, and it isn't dependent on only the groups involved. But having a metric that involves both groups may help sales and marketing work together instead of complaining about each other!

More Metrics to Consider

I turn to a handful of metrics again and again to help me verify certain organization-wide fundamentals.

One metric that I include for every department is employee satisfaction. We use the Gallup Q^{12}, as I described in the section "Build the Culture." By giving this survey anonymously every six months, you can closely monitor employee morale. Every manager in a company is responsible for helping the CEO create great jobs and build a high-performance culture with engaged employees. It's easily measured, it's predictive, and it's somewhat reflective of factors unique to individual departments.

Some metrics can work for almost any executive. The most important to me is the number of A-rated employees who leave the company. Any time an A-rated employee leaves, a thorough postmortem should be done to understand why she left and what can be done in the future to prevent further losses. When top performers leave for other jobs it is often an early sign that things are going wrong in a department. As CEO you should make an effort to build relationships with the top performers at the individual contributor level to try to head off problems before they occur. These outstanding employees are the source of your competitive advantage. A related metric is how long it takes leaders to fill open positions and how many positions are filled with internal promotions. Hiring and development are key parts of any leader's duties, and leaving positions sitting open is often a sign of neglect in this critical area.

Using Metrics

Metrics should be visible to everyone who can impact those metrics. I have all departments post their metrics for everyone to see. It's good for the employees in the department to understand how they as a group are being measured and to understand the key drivers of success for other departments.

Posting metrics, however, puts even more pressure on leaders to respond when performance falls off and the metrics start to slip. Holding people accountable begins with the CEO. It is critical for an organization to know that the CEO will constantly hold everyone to a high standard. The rest of the organization will never set the bar higher than the CEO does. Too many CEOs think that following up on these performance details can be left to someone lower in the organization. The result is that the level of performance in the organization slips to mediocrity.

Holding people accountable doesn't require you to be a jerk. In fact, having the right goals and metrics in place and tracking them consistently allows leaders to hold employees and each other accountable in a non-emotional way. You learn of performance issues before they become catastrophes that put people into panic mode. People cannot be unemotional when they're panicking. Accountability is also much less scary in healthy team environments with high levels of trust and open communication. If you've built a high-performance culture, accountability won't be a four-letter word—never uttered except behind closed doors.

METRICS CAN IMPROVE
PERFORMANCE—EVEN IN GOVERNMENT!

Many people have heard of Mitch Daniels, former two-term governor of Indiana. Republicans were pushing him to run for president for a while, primarily because of the "miracle" he wrought in his state. He turned a $600 million budget deficit into a multibillion-dollar budget surplus, cut property taxes, and improved services across the state. You may not agree with all of his tactics, and Indiana is still a struggling state in many ways, but the improvement in performance cannot be denied. Under his leadership, agencies—including the Department of Corrections, the Department of Child Services, and the Department of Motor Vehicles—were transformed from the worst performers in the country (compared with other states) to national award winners.

In interviews and a book, *Keeping the Republic*, Governor Daniels describes how he and his team instituted a management-by-measurement approach, creating performance metrics for every agency aligned with the most important goals, like reducing the number of child deaths or vehicular deaths, or increasing the number of jobs in the state. Budgets were linked to improvement on metrics (if agencies dramatically improved their metrics, they were asked to reduce their costs by a smaller percentage); pay and promotions were linked to job performance metrics; and so on. In fact, Governor Daniels had on his desk a dashboard of twenty-five key metrics updated weekly, and that dashboard was posted on the government's website for all citizens to see.

Governor Daniels's chief of staff, Earl Goode, former president of GTE Information Services (which merged into the new company Verizon in 2000), told a story about the difference the metrics and dashboard made in terms of real-time oversight in the book *Leadocracy*:

> One of our cabinet members was recruited to a much larger state than ours . . . He was back for a visit a couple of months later, and I asked him how it was going. "One thing is really different," he said. "When I did something in my agency you guys knew about it within twenty-four hours. Now, it might be three years before they know what I've done."[38]

—

You absolutely want to trust your executive team members. You should give them wide latitude on how to accomplish agreed-upon goals. At the same time, you want to build a culture in the business that is constantly seeking to understand and improve performance by measuring it intelligently. If people understand that they will be held to a high standard, the productivity of the company will be maximized. People want desperately to be part of a winning team, and building a culture that verifies performance is one of the most important ways to build a winning team.

FINDING YOUR BALANCE

1. How many metrics do you currently track for each department or group and for the company as a whole, other than financials?

2. How well do your metrics follow the five characteristics outlined in this chapter?

3. What do you do with the data you gather? How do you analyze it? How does it guide decisions?

4. Is everybody in your organization privy to all the metrics you track?

INTERNAL VS. EXTERNAL

There are many unique facets of the CEO role, but the most surprising for many new CEOs is the role the CEO plays as the interface between the external environment and stakeholders, and the internal operations and people. This role becomes only more complex as the company grows. I remember talking with one CEO about the process of going public. When I asked him about it, he responded that it was like he had personally gone public.

It's important to realize that the brand of the company and the personal brand of the CEO are often hard to separate, particularly if the CEO is the founder. It will be many years before people will think of Apple and not think of Steve Jobs. Jack Welch is still tied to GE in people's minds, more than a dozen years after he left the company. People are more likely to know the name Warren Buffett than Berkshire Hathaway. The CEO is the one person in the organization whose every action reflects on the company. A VP who does something stupid that reflects poorly on the company can be replaced and the company can move forward without taking much of a hit. If a CEO commits some grievous act, it often impacts the entire company.

Of course, CEOs can also use their positive personal brands to provide value to the company, and many do. However, if the CEO becomes overly focused on playing a role in the external environment, she risks neglecting internal operations, losing touch with the day-to-day of the company, and limiting her ability to make good decisions.

Finding the right balance between internal and external issues can be a challenge for any CEO. The key is to use the needs of the company to judge the best use of your time and attention.

THE CELEBRITY AND HOWARD HUGHES

One of the interesting things that happens when someone becomes CEO is that he becomes much more popular. It can start small, with more invitations to speak at conferences, to attend customer appreciation weekends held by vendors, etc. But it often balloons quickly. Suddenly he starts receiving invitations to events with all the "cool" people. For many CEOs, the chance to hang with other high-profile businesspeople, politicians, and even celebrities is too much to resist. It's easy for them to justify one more trip, one more charity golf event, or one more local board that needs their guidance. They're representing the company to all the movers and shakers, and that could help the business. Right? Of course the more opportunities that are accepted, the more opportunities that are presented. Often the CEO's spouse may enjoy the newfound status and encourage the behavior. The celebrity CEO spends far more time—and sometimes money—than appropriate on things that don't move the business forward. Modern CEOs don't have resources or time to waste on unproductive endeavors.

Being a celebrity also comes with a steep price. You put your every action in the spotlight, even more than would naturally be the case. You subject yourself to media attention—and the attention of employees and shareholders. Too much attention, and you could find yourself without a job.

To maintain trust in your credibility, competence, and caring, you have to be a role model all the time. Your employees pay very close attention to *everything* you do, and your actions or inactions can dramatically affect the culture and employee engagement. An offhand comment can cause people to spring into action or make them wonder about the future of the company. People will want to do things to please the boss, and as CEO you must treat that respect like gold. How you treat your family, what you do in your spare time, and how you spend your money can all affect your ability to lead an organization. In short, don't do anything you wouldn't want on the front page of the newspaper.

FINDING YOUR BALANCE

1. How many events or engagements do you have this week that will take you out of the office? How many this month?

2. Have you recently been covered in the media in a way that you wish you had not been?

THE FOUNDER WITHOUT A FILTER

Some people in the media wonder how it is that John Mackey, cofounder and CEO of Whole Foods, still has a job. He's known for his erratic behavior and his off-the-cuff remarks that send everybody into a tailspin. After reading a book that promoted veganism and elimination of all processed foods, he told the *Wall Street Journal*, "We sell a bunch of junk."[39] He got caught in a sock puppet scandal, entering Yahoo message boards under an alias to promote Whole Foods stock. He wrote an op-ed for the *Wall Street Journal* rejecting the national health care proposal, enraging the more liberal Whole Foods customers and prompting boycotts. In an article in *The New Yorker*, he made statements like, "'[I can't] embarrass the company,'" "'I have to grow up,'" "'I can't have affairs with women,'" and "'I no longer drink alcohol around journalists.'"[40] Well, duh. It's hard to say whether the Whole Foods brand has been helped or hindered by Mackey's exploits, but over the past few years, Mackey has faded out of the limelight a bit. He brought in a co-CEO who has taken over the day-to-day operations of the business, leaving him the opportunity to think about future changes in the industry. He seems to be learning an important lesson.

Howard Hughes spent the last ten years of his life moving from hotel penthouse to hotel penthouse with his entourage and rarely engaging anyone outside his personal aides. It's not unusual to see CEOs of major companies get trapped in the same existence. While most CEOs may not be as extreme as Howard Hughes, they may surround themselves with a small group of handlers, limiting their contact with external resources and even employees. A CEO's time is very valuable, but if it is entirely scripted and controlled it will be impossible to build the relationships throughout the organization that are necessary to really manage the business. It's hard to provide leadership if you spend all your time isolated in your office or with a very small entourage. Get out and engage with the world and the people that affect your business.

A PUBLICITY RECLUSE EMERGES

In a move similar to Willy Wonka's emergence after decades in seclusion, Ren Zhengfei, founder and CEO of Huawei, gave his first press interview in May 2013, twenty-five years after founding the company. If Huawei was a small company, this might not seem particularly odd. But Huawei, based in Shenzhen, China, is the largest telecommunications equipment producer in the world, with revenue in 2012 of $218 billion.

Clearly Zhengfei's recluse-like behavior hasn't hurt the company's value in the market. So why did Zhengfei break his media silence? It's hard to say, except that Huawei had been trying to break into the U.S. network market and was receiving opposition from Congress. Zhengfei had "embarked on a campaign that emphasizes openness and transparency."[41] It's hard to refuse to give interviews and remain that reclusive in today's world. Eventually, every CEO needs the reach that media provides.

FINDING YOUR BALANCE

1. When was the last time you met with key vendors that serve your company?

2. Would employees in your own company know who you were if they saw you in public or even in the hallways of the company?

3. Can you immediately recognize your company's top 100 employees by name?

GIVE YOUR COMPANY THE ATTENTION IT NEEDS

How CEOs should split their time between internal and external roles depends on several factors. In general, the earlier the company is in the traditional business life cycle, the more time the CEO should spend focused on internal issues, building the right teams for growth, verifying the business model, etc. The more the company matures, the more time the CEO can afford to devote to external issues and the more that effort can bear fruit.

As CEO you can help the company through external relationships in numerous ways, but the following four groups should receive regular attention:

- Customers and potential customers
- Shareholders and potential shareholders
- Strategic partners
- Experts

Customers and potential customers are obviously important to any business and deserve some of the CEO's time. It is important for the CEO to maintain a constant sense of the market—how it's changing, whether it's growing, influences on customers that could impact their interaction with the company—and talking directly with customers is a key way to do that. When visiting with customers, the CEO needs to stay "in character" as the CEO. I have seen many CEOs quickly become VP of sales and try to close a deal on the spot. This behavior undermines the authority of the sales team and makes the company seem small and immature. Unless the deal is one that falls into the strategic partnership category, leave it for the sales team and maintain your position as CEO.

Shareholders and potential shareholders will also require time from the CEO, as I covered in the chapter "Employees vs. Shareholders vs. Customers." In the early stages of the company's development, when raising money is a regular activity, CEOs can get trapped into spending almost all of their time in this endeavor. Unlike visiting with potential customers, where you may learn something even when they don't buy, spending time trying to raise money only to be told no is not particularly valuable. Before you spend much time with a potential investor, make sure there is a reasonable chance he or she will fund the deal. Having money is not enough. As I mentioned previously, once you have shareholders, it's important to establish a regular communication pattern that they can count on for updates. If you are "fortunate" enough to reach public company status, you will have a whole department dedicated to investor relations. Unfortunately. you will still be required to visit with certain investors and analysts because only the CEO can speak authoritatively for the company.

Strategic partners represent an often-neglected resource that CEOs can tap to make a tremendous difference in the performance of their companies. Working jointly with other companies is always challenging. Getting your own people to act like a team is tough enough, but getting someone else's team to think that way is even more challenging. The CEO is the one person in an organization who can drive these kinds of relationships. By working directly with his peer at the partnering company, the CEO can gain the commitment necessary for joint projects to work. Also, these strong relationships with CEOs in closely related companies can often pay off in strategic opportunities.

Small companies can rarely afford to hire all the experience and expertise the CEO would like to have available. The CEO should seek out advisors who can provide value. Many experienced executives are flattered to be asked to help out in an advisory role in their area of expertise. If you ask for the occasional lunch or coffee, they will often provide advice free of charge. If you want to engage them in a more formal and regular process, you'll have to offer some form of compensation in either cash or stock. I always found that the more people I engaged to discuss my business, the better my strategic thinking became. Spend time discussing your business problems with people outside the bubble—and listening to their feedback. They usually won't have the exact answer, but the process will move you forward in your thinking.

In my experience, one highly underutilized resource that every CEO has access to—usually for free—is the myriad of potential vendors that want to sell you something. Now if you took every meeting requested by a potential vendor, you would have no time for anything else. However, building up a relationship with key vendors can provide a tremendous education in a short period of time. I believe CEOs should develop a broad range of knowledge across all the key functions of their business. This can often be facilitated by vendors who can be used as a resource to understand the latest thinking and trends in their areas of expertise. When we were building NetQoS, I met annually with our benefits provider to stay current on the latest trends in health care and other employee benefits. After salary, the benefits package was the area that employees cared about the most. Making sure that our package was competitive was important to our success in hiring the best talent. While I allowed my HR team to make the detailed decisions, I felt it was important that I understood the inevitable trade-offs that we made in selecting a particular plan. Each quarter I would identify an area of the business to learn more about, and I often fulfilled this goal by leveraging a vendor's or potential vendor's superior knowledge of their industry.

BIG PERSONALITY, BIG VALUE

In an article in *Wired*, Chris Anderson wrote, "[Entrepreneurs] have an extraordinary ability to believe in their own visions, so much so that they think what they're embarking on isn't really that risky . . . I have never met an entrepreneur who fits this model more than Elon Musk."[42] Musk is a serial entrepreneur (PayPal, Tesla, SpaceX, and others) who seems to sweep naysayers to the side and energize his believers with his straightforward, high-energy attack on "problems that really matter." Musk's personal brand has brought incredible value to Tesla. His success with PayPal and SpaceX (he built and launched a rocket that then docked with the International Space Station and orbited Earth) builds trust in his competence. He's involved in the minute design details of every car. He lets no criticism slip by, going on the well-reasoned attack whenever it's warranted. But he's also brutally honest—he's not afraid to tell the media that the Tesla stock is overpriced. The Tesla business model doesn't make sense to a lot of people, yet people still seem to want to give the company money. Sometimes a company's success has everything to do with the CEO's brand and how they leverage it in the external environment.

Much of this book is about the type of work the CEO should be doing when focusing on internal issues and opportunities. Keep in mind that, when working within the organization, the CEO is constantly in the spotlight. Your employees will watch everything you do. Behavior that would be dismissed as just an odd quirk in someone lower in the organization takes on major importance when exhibited by the CEO. A VP might be able to get away with not having a relationship with some people in the company, but as CEO you are the leader of everyone in the organization. This constant attention from employees can be draining on CEOs who would prefer less scrutiny. But being comfortable in the spotlight is critical for being a great CEO.

Like a general on the battlefield, the CEO needs to be seen and heard. Get out with the troops and practice management by walking around. If you do this consistently, people will begin to feel comfortable with you and share key things about the business that you might otherwise never know. To develop credibility, respect, and trust, people must see you not just on the stage, but also in day-to-day situations where they can engage with you personally. People want to like their leaders, but they can only do that if they have some personal connection. Spending time with your employees in informal settings will do much to drive this connection.

—

Your purpose in the company is to deliver great performance. When making decisions about whether you should be more focused on playing an internal role or an external role, ask yourself two questions: "What issues and opportunities do we currently face? What do we need to solve them or take advantage of them?" Your job is to remove obstacles and provide resources for growth. From month to month, where your attention is needed may change.

FINDING YOUR BALANCE

1. How often do you meet with customers or potential customers? What do you attempt to learn in these meetings?

2. How much of your time is required for raising capital? Do you expect that to change in the near future?

3. What relationships have you developed with CEOs of related companies or leaders in vendor companies? What opportunities exist in those relationships?

4. How often do your employees see you out and about in the offices or on the front lines? Do they approach you, or do you have few interactions other than those you initiate?

PERSONAL NEEDS
VS. COMPANY NEEDS

"Nearly all men can stand adversity, but if
you want to test a man's character, give him power."

—ABRAHAM LINCOLN

I was on my way to Las Vegas to attend a major trade show; the company I worked for had a large presence there. I had become friendly with the head of the company's public relations department and we found ourselves on the same flight out to Vegas. Because of her role, she often dealt directly with the CEO, and during the flight and on our taxi ride to the hotel, I learned that these interactions were not always pleasant.

Because of budget issues the company required people to share rooms at a rather modest hotel. I didn't think too much about having to double up. If budgets were tight, that seemed like a reasonable way to save money. Once our group checked in, a few of us went out to try our luck and then walked back to the hotel and said our goodnights at around ten o'clock, knowing we had to be up early the next morning.

The next morning, I climbed on the bus to the exhibit hall. Soon after I sat down I saw the PR head walking down the aisle toward me. She had the unmistakable look of someone who had gotten very little sleep. I teased her, asking if she had headed back to the craps table. "No," she said, clearly fuming. The CEO had called her at 2 a.m. and screamed at her for fifteen minutes because his suite, which happened to be in the nicest hotel in town, only had one bedroom and there was no place for the nanny to sleep.

It was bad enough that he was traveling in luxury with his entire family while the rest of us were doubling up at a modest hotel. But to call and berate an employee when there was nothing she could do really took the cake. Needless to say, any respect I had for this CEO went out the window that day. If the CEO doesn't care for his people, who will?

THE PLAYBOY KING AND THE MARTYR

I spent some time recently in England and experienced the true concept of monarchy. Touring the Hampton Court Palace, built during King Henry VIII's rule, brought home the opulence of the sixteenth-century monarchy. Clearly there was no distinction between the possessions of the monarchy and those of the country. Some CEOs seem to share this view. They make no distinction between the personal resources of the CEO and the resources of the company. This attitude often develops in the early days of a company when the founder/CEO is personally providing the resources. It's understandable if all the capital for the business is coming out of the CEO's pocket. Unfortunately many CEOs continue to blur this line after taking on investors and even public shareholders.

Some people enjoy the position of CEO too much. These CEOs spend most of their time enjoying the pay and perks of the position. While the rest of the company may be under tight expense limits, the CEO knows no limits. First-class travel or worse, the corporate jet; suites instead of regular hotel rooms; and only the best restaurants with the finest wines—nothing is too much for the playboy king. It's understandable for the CEO to have a nicer office or a dedicated assistant, but many CEOs lose all touch with what the average employee's work life is like. This behavior is probably the fastest way to lose the respect of employees.

FINDING YOUR BALANCE

1. Do you cover family travel with company funds when your family accompanies you on business trips?

2. Does the company cover membership fees for groups or organizations that don't directly benefit the company?

THE CORPORATE JET—
TAKEN ONE STEP FURTHER

I once saw a presentation by Warren Buffett to a group of Harvard MBA students. When it came to the Q&A section, many students wanted to ask questions about what it was like to have so much money. Buffett is well known for having a very modest life style, particularly for a billionaire, but he admitted one indulgence. He said, "The only difference between you and me is that I don't fly commercial." Ah, the private jet. The hallmark of having made it. I've been fortunate enough in my life to be able to afford private aviation on some occasions, and I can say it is one of the world's great luxuries. The problem for CEOs is that there is rarely a justifiable *business* reason for using a private jet.

Clearly Michael Jeffries, CEO of Abercrombie & Fitch, doesn't see it that way. Not only does he regularly use the company's private jet, but he and his partner also developed a lengthy manual for the onboard flight crew, outlining their seemingly obsessive-compulsive personal preferences and standards. The manual sets clear rules for the placement of specific magazines, what phrases should be used when responding to a request, what song should be played during landing, and the seating arrangements for Jeffries's three dogs.

It specifies what cologne the male crew members should use and what under-wear they should wear—boxer briefs.

Not surprisingly, the document was leaked as part of a lawsuit brought by a pilot charging age discrimination.

I would hate to leave the impression that I see only self-serving behavior from CEOs. You will often encounter a CEO who is so focused on the success of the business that it consumes her whole life. This is most common in first-time or serial entrepreneur CEOs. CEOs must be able to drive the success of the business without allowing any setbacks—and there are always setbacks—to become physically or emotionally crippling. While I have had two very successful business exits, in growing both businesses there were times when I thought they would totally fail. For some people, dealing with these inevitable difficulties causes unhealthy amounts of stress. It's also often hard for a CEO to separate personal life from business life. If a CEO is having personal issues, he will often be closely followed in the business and the media, causing additional stress. It's sometimes hard to know how you will be affected by the challenges of the CEO position until you have experienced them. Some people can find appropriate ways to manage the stress while others lose their health, their friends, and their families as they push harder and harder to make the company a success.

In her book *For Better or for Work: A Survival Guide for Entrepreneurs and Their Families*, Meg Cadoux Hirshberg, wife of Stonyfield Farm founder Gary Hirshberg, describes in brutally honest detail the struggles families can face when one person is an entrepreneur. Often those struggles lead to resentment, estrangement from spouse and children, or possibly even abuse. One female entrepreneur told a sad story: as her husband felt more and more sidelined by her focus on her business, he began to abuse her emotionally and physically. The most extreme entrepreneur CEOs described in Hirshberg's book throw themselves on the pyre of business and have little left to offer outside of it. Make sure you're not in that category.

FINDING YOUR BALANCE

1. Does the performance of your business affect your physical and emotional well-being?

2. How much time do you spend each week on pursuits or relationships outside of the business?

3. Are you more worried about failing than you are about running the business?

MATERIAL NEEDS

Modern CEOs have to avoid circumventing the normal processes in the company or receiving greater benefits or perks than all other employees. Often CEO perquisites start small and grow over time. These perks can have a negative impact on your ability to lead. It's hard for employees to believe you care as much about their well-being as you do your own when you regularly receive fringe benefits that they do not. Few employees will ever directly comment or criticize, so it's important to be self-aware enough to recognize these issues before they become problems. Any benefits you receive that are above and beyond those of the normal employee should be closely scrutinized. Reserved parking spots, assistance with personal errands, and special travel privileges are all things to be avoided.

These days, CEO pay is an area of special concern, especially for CEOs of public companies. I believe CEOs should negotiate for an appropriate market-based compensation package, but it looks bad when the company pays for additional items outside the normal salary or pays bonuses that aren't closely tied to the true performance of the company. When CEOs receive additional compensation for home security, personal travel, or help with tax compliance, employees question the motives of everyone involved. Negotiate an appropriate compensation package, but keep all the extras out of the deal. If you make so much money that you need security or special tax help, you should be able to pay for it yourself.

One last point of caution: some CEOs enjoy the attention they receive from making charitable contributions and use these contributions to support their personal entertainment and lifestyle interests. Some CEOs could qualify as professional golfers for all the time they spend at charity golf tournaments—at the company's expense. I am a big believer that corporate contributions should be tested against the same decision nexus as other business decisions. How does the action balance the interests of employees, customers, and shareholders? Some charitable contributions may. But if the contributions of your company are overly tied to you, as CEO, you may be slipping into a danger zone of receiving too many personal benefits from company resources.

EMOTIONAL NEEDS

Sometimes people asked me how it feels to be CEO. While every CEO brings a unique personality and approach, I think there are common emotional issues that we all must learn to deal with. Paul DeJoe, the CEO and founder of Ecquire, answered the question on the website quora.com. He wrote that it's like being a duck, smooth and calm on top of the water while paddling like crazy beneath the surface. He also addressed the personal responsibility of the CEO job that is not usually felt by any other member of the team. "You feel guilty when you're doing something you like doing outside of the company. Only through years of wrestling with this internal fight do you recognize how the word 'balance' is an art that is just as important as any other skill set you could ever hope to have."[43]

Some CEOs, especially entrepreneurs, have talked about the fun of it all. I have often felt anxious. I often wished I could fast-forward six months to see how the things we were doing to improve the business would turn out. I have felt deeply satisfied after achieving a major goal, or elation at getting an unexpectedly large order. But fun is not the first word that comes to mind. I do think it is important to stop and celebrate with the team; "work hard and play hard" is a great motto. But as CEO, the weight of command always tempered my enthusiasm. I knew that any success was fragile and it was my job to make sure we remained focused and didn't run into the proverbial iceberg.

Everyone has heard the phrase: it's lonely at the top. As CEO, you have no peer in the organization with whom to share your thoughts and doubts. I think it's important for CEOs to build a network of contacts outside the business that she can use as a sounding board. If you live in a major metropolitan area, there are likely many CEO peer groups. These can be valuable organizations if you select the right group for you. I have been involved in several, and the two factors that determined the value for me were the quality of the group leader and the quality of the other members. The group leader faces a challenge trying to corral a group of CEOs. Look for leaders with significant real-world experience. They should have numerous references you can talk to who can validate their leadership abilities. When it comes to the members, look for a group that consists of CEOs running somewhat similar businesses to your own. I have found that the biggest similarity should be in size of the business. A company with twenty employees is far different from a company with two hundred employees, and the CEO perspective for each is unique. Also, businesses that are growing rapidly present a different set of challenges from businesses that are in a relatively steady state. If you can find the proper group it can be an extremely valuable resource for achieving success as a CEO.

—

As CEO, your personal success and the success of the company are so closely entwined that it can be difficult to differentiate between your personal needs and the needs of the company. You must strike the right balance for the company's sake and for your own.

FINDING YOUR BALANCE

1. What benefits or perks do you have as CEO that no other employee has or that only a handful have?

2. What limits do you place on others in the organization that you do not place on yourself?

3. How do you feel about your leadership position? What word would you use to describe it?

4. What type of support system do you have in place?

HOW TO IMPROVE AS CEO

If you have made it this far in the book, I hope you have a better under-standing of the role of the CEO and have come away with ideas for improv-ing your own productivity as well as the productivity of your company. The business world is constantly changing and brings new challenges every day. The best CEOs recognize that continuous learning is a must if they want to stay on top of their game. With so many things on your plate, how do you find the time to get better? The best CEOs look at continuous improvement as an investment in themselves and their company that will pay off in real dollars down the line. Building a cycle of continuous improvement into your companies, as well as personally, is critical to your long-term success.

So what specifically can you do as a CEO to improve? I am going to borrow a list from my friend Mike Hawkins, president of Alpine Link Cor-poration, a coaching and consulting company. Mike is also the author of *Activating Your Ambition: A Guide to Coaching the Best Out of Yourself and Others*. I have customized his list to make it apply directly to CEOs.

1. **Learn from experience**: In the "Make Decisions" section I discussed the importance of performing a postmortem on all the important decisions you make by actively looking for evidence that would prove you were wrong. This willingness to examine past actions for ways to improve distinguishes great CEOs from good CEOs and will allow you to provide leadership in your company for the long haul.

2. **Attend training programs**: Over the past several years I have given an annual seminar on the CEO job. The biggest excuse I hear from CEOs for not attending is that they don't have time. From my experience, the CEOs that do attend are typically the ones who are already better than most and because of that know how to make time to improve their skills. If you think you don't have time to get better at your job, you are not doing your job properly.

3. **Read**: The fact that you are reading a book on the challenges of the CEO role puts you a step ahead of many CEOs. As the author I can tell you that this book, like others, captures decades of experience and research. While the advice I uncover in the hordes of business books I read may not be perfect for every situation, I can honestly say that I almost always come away with a couple of ideas that make a difference in my business.

   Reading is also a great way to learn the history of your industry and others, which is important for a great CEO. I read a lot of business-related histories and biographies, and I use them to draw parallels to my businesses and the market today. Understanding the history of your industry will prepare you to deal with the inevitable changes you'll face.

4. **Write**: The most challenging thing I have ever done was write this book. Writing forces you to clarify your thoughts in a way that is highly beneficial for future action. Taking the time to write a regular email to your company explaining your thoughts and actions can do a lot to improve your thinking as well as align the team with your vision. Many CEOs blog regularly, commenting on issues they find interesting or relevant to their work and companies. Formalizing your writing schedule will pay big dividends.

5. **Meet with wise people**: Find people from outside your company who can bring knowledge and experience to bear on your problems. Make an effort to get to know people in your community who have

relevant experience. Seek out the other leaders in your industry to establish relationships. Many times the relationships I formed within my industry provided tremendous value to the company. As CEO it is easy to get trapped into thinking that you should have all the answers. It is much more efficient to find someone who already has them. Of course, you have to be willing to listen.

6. **Teach**: I spent my first four years out of college teaching for a living at Naval Nuclear Power School. That experience taught me that you never really learn material until you are forced to explain it in front of a group. Teaching requires you to communicate about a subject in a way that you can understand, but also in a way that everyone can understand. There are many opportunities in business to teach what you know to others, both inside and outside the company. It's a great way to deepen your knowledge and improve your communication skills.

7. **Study yourself**: There are a lot of different self-assessments available, and I have taken many of them. Learning about yourself, how you think and react, is critical to developing as a CEO and overcoming your internal biases. Many firms specialize in this area and may offer a free interpretation of your results in order to pitch for more business. If you find one you like, expand it out to your team so you have a common language to address personality and communication issues.

8. **Gather feedback**: If you are not getting regular feedback from your teams and board, you have a problem. It's not enough to ask for feedback and hope it comes. You should actively solicit feedback from your employees as well as your board. Getting feedback from employees will often require an anonymous feedback mechanism or third-party gatherer. Feedback from your board should be both informal and formal.

9. **Seek out mentors**: You are not the first person to go down the CEO path. The problem is that most CEOs are first-time CEOs. Reach out to those who have gone before you to learn from their experience.

The CEO job is unique, so make sure you have in your circle people who have been in the chair and understand the challenges of the job.

10. **Apply your knowledge**: As soon as you uncover a nugget of wisdom from one of these sources, try to put it in action. Teach your executive team the concept so they can use it as well. Train your team to expect new ideas on a regular basis, but don't throw them out and then abandon them. Without follow-through, the efforts are meaningless.

Continuous improvement is vital to your success as CEO. If you are not improving in your knowledge and experience, you are stagnating, which means your company may be, too. Instead, choose one responsibility to examine this month. Assess yourself. Ask others for their thoughts. Take it step-by-step, just as every good CEO has done, and you'll find the job becoming more rewarding day by day.

PREPARE YOURSELF FOR
TOUGH, REWARDING WORK

When a much larger company acquired one of my software businesses, I saw the impact of poor leadership on a massive scale. The company was going through a CEO transition, and no one was really in charge. It seemed like everywhere I turned I was confronted by some group that had its own set of goals, which ultimately worked against the fundamental goal of trying to build and sell more and better software. The most amazing example occurred in the facilities group.

We had a remote office that held about a dozen software developers. Most of these developers had ten-plus years of experience and their average pay was well into six figures. For the acquiring company, there was no more valuable group of employees than these talented engineers. In fact, we had established this remote office specifically to hire this particular team.

The acquirer also had a small office in the area. Since both leases were near renewal, it was decided that we should combine the groups in a new location. This was a perfectly reasonable thing for the company to do, and while the new location might cause some hardship—longer commutes and the like—I knew everyone would understand why the move was necessary.

So I was a little surprised when I received an urgent call from our lead developer, complaining about the plans for the new office. He had just received a presentation from the facilities group on the new layout. I assumed he was upset that the new location wasn't convenient for the team.

Instead the problem was far more significant. The facility group had decided that the cubicles for the developers would be 6 feet by 6 feet. Now, cubicle size seems like a small issue in the grand scheme of mergers and acquisitions, right? But those cubicles were the smallest I have ever seen—so small that the standard computer system that most of our developers used, a powerful workstation with two large monitors, would not fit in the cubicle.

Thinking that surely someone would recognize the foolishness of the decision, I scheduled a call with the appropriate facility planners to try to improve the situation. I was shocked to find out that, not only were they not interested in hearing a different view, they had managed to convince themselves that they were giving the developers what they wanted! They claimed they had surveyed the development community and developers wanted more open workspaces. Of course, it took a giant illogical leap to go from more open workspaces to 6 x 6 cubicles, but that didn't stop this facility group. Soon after the merger, key developers from this team began to leave. They found companies where they felt more valued.

What does this have to do with the CEO? you might be asking. Everything. The cubicle debacle was one issue in a wide range of problems that beset the company. As CEO, you are responsible for the policies you approve as well as those that others invoke in your name. There was no active management of the culture, and that falls on the CEO. Maybe he hadn't communicated a strong vision for how the acquisition would benefit the company and employees. Maybe if he had provided appropriate resources, the facilities team wouldn't have tried to cram bodies into a tiny space. Maybe if he had built a culture in which high performance and great talent were valued above all, the managers would have listened to the concerns of the affected employees. Worst of all, though, I don't think he understood that creating a system of communication and alignment was necessary to ensure performance and strong decisions. I doubt anyone ever knew why the most critical team members of a company they had just bought for hundreds of millions of dollars were jumping ship. And that was just one more corporate acquisition than didn't achieve its full potential.

It's easy to lose sight of what matters to a company's success. It's easy to head down a rabbit hole and emerge months later to a company you no longer recognize. Being a good CEO means doing the hard work of aligning teams, moving the company forward, and balancing, balancing, balancing every day. It requires constant vigilance.

The challenges of the work are balanced by the rewards, though—and I'm not talking about money or power or other perks. For me, special moments stand out: thank-yous I've received from employees, days when I felt I had done a better job than the day before, high returns I've delivered to investors, but especially moments when I knew I had provided great jobs in a great environment for great people. As much as some people may fantasize about spending their lives on a deserted beach, most of us need a purpose in our lives, work by which we make a difference. Providing a way for people to wake up every morning excited to make that difference is as noble a calling as I can imagine.

I hope that being a CEO is just as rewarding for you. I hope you find your balance and achieve the mastery your company needs from you.

Good luck, and stay in touch.

THANKS

This book is a result of interactions with many special people over my career. It is always dangerous to mention people by name because there may be some I have inadvertently overlooked. Most recently partnering with my editor, Lari Bishop, has been a wonderful growth experience. I often felt that she could have written twice as good a book in half the time; however, like your favorite high school teacher, she guided me to produce something that is clearly my own, warts and all.

I want to thank all the employees that have worked for and with me over my career. Each one of them has helped me gain a little better understanding of how to balance the CEO job. Even now when I interview potential employees and they accept an offer, I am a little amazed that they would put their livelihood in my hands.

I was first inspired to pursue a career in business by Ronnie Hathorn and Don Boyett. The fact that they took an interest in a young high school kid was critical to showing me a path that I would otherwise not have found.

I was also inspired by Captain Gary Jensen, my commanding officer for most of my time at Nuclear Power School. He demonstrated that great leadership is a noble cause and makes people glad to come to work in the morning.

Although my mom and dad have passed on, they were critical in giving me the confidence that a kid from a small town in Louisiana could dream big.

My most important partner, not only in business but also personally over the last twenty-five years, has been my wife, Cathy Fulton. Her standards of perfection and brilliance made me work harder to just try and keep up. Without her none of this would have been possible.

And finally, I must mention our three kids, Caitlin, Ryan, and Stephen. While they are too young to have an interest in this book or what Daddy does for work, I hope someday they will be able to read it and have a little better understanding of dear old Dad.

If you have made it this far, I should thank you for spending your time with me, and I hope the ideas here will help you become a better CEO.

NOTES

Stepping Onto the Rope

1. Daniel Gross, "Fast Times in the Corner Office," *Newsweek* (online), May 6, 2013.

2. Ginka Toegel and Jean-Louis Barsoux, "How to Become a Better Leader," *MIT Sloan Management Review*, March 20, 2012.

3. Ellen McGirt, "Most Innovative Companies 2012: 05_Square," *Fast Company*, February 7, 2012.

Own the Vision

4. Kim S. Nash, "CIOs Share How They Made the Leap to CEO," *CIO Magazine* (online), September 25, 2013.

5. Ram Charan and Geoffrey Colvin, "Why CEOs Fail," *Fortune* (online), June 21, 1999.

6. Carl von Clausewitz, translated by Michael Eliot Howard and Peter Paret, *On War* (Princeton, NJ: Princeton University Press, 1989, reprint), 119.

7. Bob Knight and Bob Hamel, *The Power of Negative Thinking: An Unconventional Approach to Achieving Positive Results* (New York: Houghton Mifflin Harcourt, 2013), viii–ix.

8. *NBA Encyclopedia Playoff Edition*, "Riley Guarantees a Repeat," NBA's Greatest Moments, NBA.com, accessed on December 6, 2013.

9. Wojtek Dabrowski, "RIM Co-CEO Doesn't See Threat from Apple's iPhone," *Reuters* (online), February 12, 2007.

Provide the Proper Resources

10. Geoffrey Tate with Ulrike Malmendier, "Who Makes Acquisitions? CEO Overconfidence and the Market's Reaction," *Journal of Financial Economics*, 89 (1; July 2008), 20–43.

11. Neil Amato, "Forward roll: How companies can move beyond traditional budgeting," *Journal of Accountancy* (online), October 2013.

12. Marguerite Imbert, "Groupon Manager Attacks 'Slavedriver' CEO Daniel Glasner with Two Leaked Emails," VentureVillage, February 17, 2012.

13. Andrew Ross Sorkin, "The Missed Red Flags on Groupon," DealBook (blog) *New York Times*, October 17, 2011.

14. Nicholas Carlson, "Marissa Mayer Reviews Every New Hire at Yahoo," *Business Insider* (online), September 4, 2012.

15. Vivian Giang and Gus Lubin, "America's Hottest CEOs Are Devoting More Time than Ever to Hiring," *Business Insider* (online), May 23, 2013.

16. Michael Useem, "Four Lessons in Adaptive Leadership," *Harvard Business Review*, November 2010.

17. Corey Weiner, "How to Hire Someone You Won't Regret in a Month," *Fast Company*, December 13, 2012.

18. Adam Bryant, "In Head-Hunting, Big Data May Not Be Such a Big Deal," *New York Times*, June 20, 2013, F6.

19. Jeannie Ruhlman and Cheryl Siegman, "Boosting Engagement While Cutting Costs," *Gallup Business Journal*, podcast, June 18, 2009.

20. Jack Welch, *Winning* (New York: HarperCollins, 2005), 305–306.

Build the Culture

21. David Rock, "SCARF: A Brain-based Model for Collaborating with and Influencing Others," *NeuroLeadership Journal* (neuroleadership.org), issue 1, 2008.

22. Elizabeth Rowe, "Conant: What Derails Most CEOs Is the 'Soft Stuff,'" *Bloomberg Businessweek* (online), July 25, 2013.

23. Melissa Korn, "B-Schools Know How You Think, but How Do You Feel?" *Wall Street Journal* (online), May 1, 2013.

24. Ken Blanchard Companies, "Perspectives: Creating a High Performance, Values-ligned Culture" (whitepaper), 2010, www.kenblanchard.com.

25. Rob Goffee and Gareth Jones, "Creating the Best Workplace on Earth," *Harvard Business Review* (online), May 2013.

Make Decisions

26. Chip Heath and Dan Heath, *Decisive: How to Make Better Choices in Life and Work* (New York: Crown Business, 2013).

27. Bryan Goldberg, "The Most Important Managerial Skill," PandoDaily.com, July 29, 2013.

28. Dennis Bakke, *The Decision Maker: Unlocking the Potential of Everyone in Your Organization, One Decision at a Time* (Seattle, WA: Pear Press, 2013), 9–10.

29. George Anders, "Meg Whitman Has a Few Questions for You," *Forbes*, June 10, 2013 (also online on May 22, 2013).

30. Fred Reichheld, "The One Number You Need to Grow," *Harvard Business Review*, December 2003.

31. Jeffrey Pfeffer, "Shareholders First? Not So Fast. . . ," *Harvard Business Review*, July 2009.

32. Mina Kimes, "At Sears, Eddie Lampert's Warring Divisions Model Adds to the Troubles," Bloomberg Businessweek (online), July 11, 2013.

33. Maria Guadalupe, Hongyi Li, and Julie Wulf, "Who Lives in the C-Suite? Organizational Structure and the Division of Labor in Top Management," Harvard Business School Working Paper 12-059, June 18, 2013 [publication forthcoming in *Management Science*].

34. Alex Taylor III, "Fixing Up Ford," CNN Money (online), May 12, 2009.

Deliver Performance

35. Chris McChesney and Sean Covey, *The 4 Disciplines of Execution* (New York: Free Press, 2012), 24.

36. Ira Sager, "Boards: CEOs Not Good at Managing People," The Management Blog *Bloomberg Businessweek* (online), May 28, 2013.

37. Michael D. Schultz, "Setting Expectations in Molecular Optimizations: Strengths and Limitations of Commonly Used Composite Parameters," *Bioorganic and Medicinal Chemistry Letters*, 23 (21; November 1, 2013), 5980–5991.

38. Geoff Smart, *Leadocracy* (Austin, TX: Greenleaf, 2012), 37.

39. Katy McLaughlin, "Frank Talk from Whole Foods' John Mackey," *Wall Street Journal* (online), August 4, 2009.

40. Nick Paumgarten, "Food Fighter," *The New Yorker* (online), January 4, 2010.

41. Charles Riley, "Reclusive Huawei CEO Breaks Media Silence," CNN Money (online), May 9, 2013.

42. Chris Anderson, "Elon Musk's Mission to Mars," *Wired* (online), October 21, 2012.

43. Paul DeJoe, "What It's Like to Be the CEO," OnStartups (online; adapted from an answer on Quora), June 5, 2012.

INDEX

acquisitions, 87, 88, 116, 151–52, 156, 187, 188, 269–70

adaptability of CEO, 67–68

Advanced Micro Devices (AMD), 22, 83–86, 91, 137–38, 205–6

Aflac, 20

A-level employees, 80–81, 109–12, 116, 129–30, 144–45, 156, 169, 242–43

alignment within the company, 48–51, 53–55, 88–89, 167–70, 171, 227–28

amateur CEOs, 52–53

AMD (Advanced Micro Devices), 22, 83–86, 91, 137–38, 205–6

Amos, Dan, 20

analytical approaches to problems, 37

anarchist CEOs, 166–67

Anderson, Chris, 254

annual reviews, 143

Apotheker, Léo, 24–25, 88

Apple, 28–29

architect role of CEO, 36. *See also* strategy

Art of Action, The (Bungay), 54, 232

Attila the Hun CEOs, 178

auditor CEOs, 238–39

authoritarianism, 16–17

autonomy, 157, 231–32

Bakke, Dennis, 195

balance, 5, 8, 9–11, 13, 16–18, 39, 176–82

Balsillie, Jim, 69

Bankable Leadership (Eurich), 181

Barbarians at the Gate (movie), 12, 212

battle-picking, 191–93

behavioral interviewing, 133–34

best friend CEOs, 176, 177

big picture. *See* decision nexus

birthday party for Tyco CEO's wife, 27

black hole CEOs, 194

black-swan CEOs, 106–8

Blanchard, Ken, 168
B-level employees/B players, 81
board of directors, 215–16, 233–35
Bock, Laszlo, 133–34
body-count CEOs, 105–6
bonding events, 158
Branson, Richard, 63
Broughton, Philip Delves, 131–32
Buckingham, Marcus, 53, 160
budgets
   budget-driven companies, 85,
      92–93
   CEO failure modes, 86–88
   cost/benefit trade-offs, 92
   dispersing control, 90–91
   funding requests from two
      executives, 95–97, 102
   and goals, 90–92, 94
   overview, 83–86, 94
   rolling forecast vs., 89–90
Bungay, Stephen, 54, 232
bureaucrat CEOs, 165–66
Business Insider, 115

capital, 9–10, 43–44, 78, 89, 213
caring of CEO, 25–28, 38–39,
   53–54, 234–35, 248–49, 258
carpet bomber CEOs, 193
celebrity CEOs, 248–49
CEO Project, 34
CEO responsibilities
   balance, 12–13, 262
   board of directors' grading CEO
     for, 235

   department vs. department issues,
     220–23
   difficult and significant decisions,
     199–201
   direct reports, 35–36, 154–55,
     220, 223
   firing, 138, 139, 140–41, 148
   hiring and firing, 169
   overview, 4, 11–12, 13, 23–24,
     254–55
   prioritizing, 8–9
   providing resources, 9–10
   retaining A players, 80–81,
     242–43
   values, 167–70
   See also culture; decision making;
     performance delivery; resources;
     vision
CEO roles
   architect, 36
   coach, 35–36, 195–96, 227
   engineer, 37
   firefighter, 33
   learner, 37–38
   overview, 8, 31–33, 39, 247–48
   player, 34–35
   priest, 38–39, 53–54
   shock absorber for highs and
     lows, 62–63
certainty and reward/threat
   response, 156–57
Chainsaw Al CEOs, 140–41
challenges, 4–5, 266, 271
Charan, Ram, 50
charitable contributions, 262

cheerleader CEOs, 57, 58–61
CIO Magazine, 46
Clausewitz, Carl von, 50
C-level employees, 81, 143, 145–48
coach role, 35–36, 195–96, 227
Coffman, Curt, 53, 160
Colvin, Geoffrey, 50
communication
  culture, 151
  and decision making, 194–95,
    201–2
  good communicators, 46
  growth goals, 100–101
  infrastructure within the
    company, 58
  mission, strategy, and vision, 9, 43,
    44–45, 53–55, 158
  with shareholders, 213–14
  strategy, 9, 44, 54–55
  and transparency, 58, 64, 156–57
companies, reasons for working at,
  111
competence, 23–25, 214, 234–35,
  248–49
competitive advantage of individual
  employees, 80–81, 118, 134–35
competitors, 71, 86, 126, 210, 231,
  240
Conant, Douglas, 160
confidence of CEOs, 87, 200,
  247–48
confirmation bias, 187
consensus, 192
continuous improvement, 37–38,
  232–33, 265–68

contributor role, 24, 34–35
control
  autonomy of employees, 157
  of budgets, 90–91
  CEO failure modes, 16–17,
    32–33, 165–66
  lack of, 17–18
  line between responsibility and,
    39
  need-to-know principle as, 51–52
  and rules, 171
  See also influence
corporate jets, 26, 155, 259–60
Covey, Sean, 229–30
"Creating the Best Workplace on
  Earth" (Goffee and Jones),
  170–71
creative initiative, 131–34
credibility, 19–22, 57–58, 139, 140,
  148, 200, 234–35, 248–49
Csikszentmihalyi, Mihaly, 172
cubicle debacle, 269–70
cult leader CEOs, 67, 68–69
culture, 149–82
  creating and applying specific
    values, 167–70
  effect of Eeyores, 60–61
  and job candidates, 130–31
  metrics for, 160–61
  monkey conditioning, 163–64
  and opportunities for A players,
    111, 129–30, 145, 156
  overview, 10, 151–52
  and reward/threat responses, 154

values-based vs. rule-based,
164–65, 170–71
See also SCARF model
customers
CEO paying attention to, 251–52
customer satisfaction
representative, 210–11
engaging with vision, 45
for outside intelligence, 71–72
as priority in decision making,
206, 208, 209–10
and profitability, 211–12
regular interaction with, 37
customer service, 210–12

Daniels, Mitch, 244
data and data collection, 238–39
death-by-growth, 98
Decision Maker, The (Bakke), 195
decision making, 183–223
across departments, 220–23
battle-picking, 191–93
CEO failure modes, 193–94
communicating after decision is
made, 201–2
company life span considerations,
206–8
confirmation bias, 187
denial of results, 188
department vs. department issues,
186, 219–23
devil's advocate for, 200
emotional investment in
decisions, 187–88, 200–201
four villains, 186–89

framing decisions, 187, 205–6
over centralization of, 220–21
overruling others, 198–99
overview, 10–11, 185–86, 203
perspective of others, 200–201
pondering while others wait, 17
postmortem, 202–3, 265
process for, 192–93, 239
reevaluating and changing bad
decisions, 199–200, 202
triage, 194–201
and values, 46, 167–70, 168
See also department vs.
department issues
decision nexus
and corporate contributions, 262
customers, 209–12
employees, 209
overview, 208–9, 216
shareholders, 212–16
Decisive (Heath and Heath),
186–87
DeJoe, Paul, 262
department vs. department issues,
186, 219–23
devil's advocate for decision
making, 200
difficult and significant decisions,
195, 199–201
directed opportunism, 54
direct reports, 35–36, 154–55,
220–21, 223
disciplined approach, 39
disruptive events and recruiting,
110, 115–16

Dorsey, Jack, 39
dress code, 165
Drive (Pink), 51–52, 153
dual sales process, recruiting as,
  110–12
Dunlap, Al "Chainsaw Al," 140
Dykes, Spike, 103

Eeyore CEOs, 60–61
emotional investment in decisions,
  187–88, 200–201
emotional needs of CEOs, 262–63
employees
  alignment with company vision,
    48–51, 53–55
  allocation of, 9–10
  benefits package, 253
  calibrating performance, 230–31
  commitment to objectives, 19
  and competence of CEO, 23–24, 26
  decision making by, 159, 185,
    191–93, 195–97, 208
  engagement of, 45, 141–42, 154,
    160–61
  Gallup Q12 survey, 53, 131, 142,
    160–61, 179, 242
  and goal tracking system, 228–29,
    230–32
  integrating new employees,
    126–27, 131, 158, 169, 230–31
  pay scale, 93, 111–12, 144–45,
    156–57
  performance reviews, 143, 156–57
  as priority in decision making,
    206, 209

rating competitive advantage,
    80–81, 118, 134–35
  and rules, 170–71
  saving poor performers, 137–38,
    139–40, 141, 148
  saving the best, 143–45
  and spendthrift CEOs, 261–62
  termination of, 138, 139, 140–41,
    145–48, 169
  and understanding of instructions
    vs. vision, 47–49
  See also recruiting
engineer role of CEO, 37
England, 258
entrepreneurs, 6, 99, 166, 254, 260,
  262–63
Eurich, Tasha, 165, 181
exceptional job candidates, 128–29
executive pay and shareholders, 207
executives. *See* management
expectations for performance, 11
experience, 126–27, 134, 265,
  266–67
expertise. See CEO roles
external relationships, 251–52

failure modes, 13. *See also specific
    CEO failure modes (for example,
    firefighter CEO)*
fairness and reward/threat response,
    159–61
favoritism, 217, 218–19, 221–22
feedback, 91, 143, 169, 233, 235,
    267. *See also* Gallup Q12
    employee survey

Finding Your Balance, 13

Fiorina, Carly, 7

firefighter CEO, 32–33

First, Break All the Rules
(Buckingham and Coffman),
53, 160

Five Dysfunctions of a Team, The
(Lencioni), 218

flexibility of leaders, 67–68, 88–89

flexibility of organizations, 165

flow, 172

football teams, 103, 109, 119

For Better or for Work (Hirshberg),
260

forecasting, 89–90, 241

Fortune 500 companies, 69

40/70 rule, 188

4 Disciplines of Execution, The
(McChesney and Covey),
229–30

framing decisions, 187

friction, 50–51, 53

Friedes, Peter E., 178–80

Fulton, Cathy, 63

Gallup Q12 employee survey, 53,
131, 142, 160–61, 179–80, 242

game theory, 188

goals
alignment in company, 49–50, 54
and budgets, 90–92, 94
clear understanding of, 43–45,
48–49
departmental goals, 228
employee goals, 228–29

engineering process, 37

growth goals, 100–101

intercompany tracking of, 228–29

priority goals, 228

setting achievable goals, 229–30

sustaining goals, 228

team accomplishment of, 34

Goffee, Rob, 170–71

Goldberg, Bryan, 191–93, 197–98

Goode, Earl, 244–45

Google, 133–34

government performance, 244–45

grandparent CEOs, 238

Greig, Tom, 213

Groupon, 98

growth, 11, 97–102, 132–33, 197,
209

Harvard Business Review, 117, 210

hats. *See* CEO roles

Hawkins, Mike, 265–68

Heath, Chip, 186–87

Heath, Dan, 186–87

Hellfighters (movie), 43

Hewlett-Packard (HP), 7, 24–25,
88, 196–97

hiring freezes, 92–93

hiring process, 105–8, 112–13,
122–25. *See also* recruiting

Hirshberg, Meg Cadoux, 260

honesty, 20

housekeeping functions, 52

Howard Hughes CEOs, 250–51

Huawei, 250

human resources (HR), 221, 253.
    See also employees; recruiting
Human Side of Enterprise, The
    (McGregor), 16–17
Hurd, Mark, 7

idea generation, 72, 197
Indiana, 244–45
influence, 18–19, 23–29, 214. *See*
    also credibility
Inman, Stu, 121–22
integrity, 25–28
interviews of job candidates, 104–5,
    113–14, 115, 130, 132, 133–34

Jeffries, Michael, 259–60
job candidate attributes, 127–34.
    See also recruiting
Jobs, Steve, 28–29
joint projects with other companies,
    252–53
Jones, Gareth, 170–71
Jordan, Michael, 8, 121–22

Keeping the Republic (Daniels), 244
Khorus software, 228–29, 230
Kimes, Mina, 219–20
Knight, Bob, 62, 121–22
knowledge, applying, 268
knowledge workers, 167
Koch, Charles, 80
Kozlowski, Dennis, 27

Lampert, Eddie, 219–20
Las Vegas, 47–49, 257–58

layoffs, 64, 138, 139–40, 141–42
leaders, 4, 12, 13, 17, 67
leadership, 20, 156–57, 234–35. *See*
    also CEO roles; influence
Leadocracy (Smart), 244–45
learner role of CEO, 37–38,
    232–33, 265–68
Legere, John, 72–73
Lehman Brothers bankruptcy, effect
    of, 77–78
Lencioni, Patrick, 218
Loeb, Dan, 21

Mackey, John, 249
Malmendier, Ulrike, 87
management, 38, 72, 109, 169,
    197–99, 207
management styles
    and budget, 85–88, 90–91
    chief operations officer, 37
    command and control, 185
    disciplined approach, 39
    fear-based, 28, 61, 99
    flexibility related to business
        conditions, 67–68
    growth junkies, 97–99
    micromanagement, 16–17,
        165–66
    paranoid optimism, 61–65
    Theory X and Theory Y, 16–17,
        19
    traditional approach, 165–66
    walking around, 39
    *See also specific CEO failure modes
        (for example,* cult leader CEO)

managers and employee rankings,
81
Marmot, Michael, 154
martyr CEOs, 260–61
Mason, Andrew, 98
master strategist CEOs, 17–18, 176
material needs of CEOs, 261–62
Mayer, Marissa, 114–15
McChesney, Chris, 229–30
McGregor, Douglas, 16–17, 19
meetings, 35–36, 144, 172–73, 222,
266–67
mentors, 267–68
metrics
    characteristics of, 239–40
    culture, 160–61
    customer satisfaction, 210
    departments, 233–34
    employee retention, 242–43
    Gallup Q12 employee survey, 53,
        131, 142, 160–61, 179–80, 242
    goals and budgets, 91–92
    government performance, 244–45
    overview, 243–44
    performance delivery, 239–44
    product success, 230
    recruiting, 117–19
    sales and marketing, 242
micromanagement, 16–17, 165–66
Mikitarian, George, 141–42
military operations, 15–16, 50, 51
military service record, 117
mission, communicating, 9
monkey conditioning, 163–64
morale of the organization, 38–39,

51–52, 53–54, 59–60, 138,
    139–40
Mother Teresa, 138–39
motivation, 154, 160, 172–73, 212.
    See also SCARF model
Mr. Mayhem CEOs, 70
Musk, Elon, 254

Naval Nuclear Power School, 15,
    51, 267
NBA basketball team metaphor, 80
NBA draft, 121–22
need-to-know principle of control,
    51–52
negative outlook CEOs, 60–61
Net Promoter Score (NPS), 210
NetQoS
    benefits package, 253
    decorating fund for new
        employees, 171
    forecasting, 89, 241
    funding requests from two
        executives, 95–97, 102
    hiring executives, 176–77
    idea generation technique, 72
    mission, vision, and values, 43–46,
        169
    and recession of 2008, 77–79
    recruiting, 109, 110–14, 116–17,
        118, 123–24, 129, 131–32
    recruiting coordinator position,
        198–99
    sale of, 200–201
    and September 11, 2001, terrorist
        attacks, 63–64, 213

starting up, 175, 191–92
and venture capital, 43–44, 78–79, 213
vision adjustment, 71
Northern Quest Resort and Casino, 90
NPS (Net Promoter Score), 210

onboarding, 117
One Minute Manager, The (Blanchard), 168
"One Number You Need to Grow, The" (Reichheld), 210
On War (Clausewitz), 50
operations role of CEO, 37
opportunism, directed, 54
opportunities for A players, 111, 129–30, 145, 156
overconfidence, 87, 200, 247–48

paranoid optimism, 61–65
Parrish Medical Center (PMC), 141–42
pay scale, 93, 111–12, 144–45, 156–57
peer groups, 34, 38, 139–40
penny-pincher CEOs, 99–100
people resources. *See* employees; recruiting
performance delivery, 225–64
and board of directors, 233–35
calibrating performance, 230–31
CEO responsibility, 11
continuous improvement, 37–38, 232–33, 265–68

and goal setting and tracking, 228–30
and improving as a CEO, 265–68
internal and external roles of CEO, 251–55
overview, 227–28, 245, 255
performance reviews, 143, 156–57
personal needs of CEOs, 261–64
perspective and rules, 171
perspectives, sources for, 71–72
Pfeffer, Jeffrey, 214–15
Pink, Daniel, 51–52, 153
Pinocchio, 21–22
planning, 47, 49–51, 55, 62. *See also* budgets; strategy
playboy king CEOs, 258–60
player role of CEO, 24, 34–35
postmortem for decisions, 202–3, 265
Powell, Colin, 188
Power of Negative Thinking, The (Knight), 62
preparation for CEO position, 5–8
priest role of CEO, 38–39, 53–54
priority goals, 228, 229
processes, value of, 166–67
productivity, 154, 156, 166, 176–77, 178–82, 185
professional development, 156
profitability, 95–102

Quinn, Tim, 90

rating employee contributions, 80–81, 118, 134–35, 143. *See also* A-level employees

Reagan, Ronald, 237
recession of 2008, 77–78
recruiting
  A players, 80–81, 109–12, 116,
    129–30, 144–45, 156, 169,
    242–43
  for emergency replacement,
    104–5
  experience vs. talent, 126–27
  hiring failure, 107–8
  hiring freezes vs., 92–93
  hiring process, 105–8, 112–13,
    122–25
  interviews, 104–5, 113–14, 115,
    130, 132, 133–34
  job candidate attributes, 127–34
  overview, 79, 81, 103–4, 119
  pay scale, 93, 111–12
recruiting coordinator, 112, 116,
    198–99
recruiting tips
  A-level recruiters, 112, 116
  cultivate unique sources, 116–17
  disruptive events as source, 110,
    115–16
  hire A-level talent, 109–10
  overview, 108–9
  recruiting as a continuous process,
    109
  sell your company, 110–12
  setting the bar, 113–15
  timeliness, 112–13
  tracking your recruiting
    performance, 117–19
  training plans, 117

Reichheld, Fred, 210
relatedness and reward/threat
    response, 157–59
relationships and results, 176–77,
    178–82
Research in Motion (BlackBerry),
    69
resources, 75–148
  allocation of, 9–10, 186, 242
  books, 266
  and budgets, 85–88
  capital, 9–10, 43–44, 78, 89, 213
  overview, 77–82
  unplanned expenses, 95–97
  See also employees
responsibility, 15–16, 39
results and relationships, 176–77,
    178–82
resume-snob CEOs, 122–24
returns, timing for measuring,
    214–15
revenue predictions, 89
reward/threat response. See SCARF
    model
Riley, Pat, 62–63
risks and rewards, 3–4, 199–200. See
    also SCARF model
Rock, David, 153
rolling forecasts, 89–90
Rule of 45, 101–2
rules-based vs. values-based culture,
    164–65, 170–71

saint CEOs, 138, 139–40

sales executive's career progression, 6–7

Salesforce.com, 191–92

salespeople and customers, 211

sales process and forecasting, 89–90, 241

Sandberg, Sheryl, 45

"SCARF" (Rock), 153

SCARF model
autonomy, 157
certainty, 156–57
fairness, 159–61
overview, 153–54, 205–6
relatedness, 157–59
status, 154–56, 173

Schleckser, Jim, 34

Schultz, Michael, 239

Science of Success, The (Koch), 80

Scott, Byron, 63

Sears Holding, 219–20

secret agent CEOs, 51–52, 172

self-assessments, 267

self-awareness, 12

September 11, 2001, terrorist attacks, 63–64, 213, 241

shareholders
and board of directors, 215–16
CEO paying attention to, 251–52
communicating with, 213–14
engaging with vision, 45
motivation of, 212
as priority in decision making, 206–7, 208
revolt by, 207

and timing for measuring returns, 214–15

"Shareholders First? Not So Fast..." (Pfeffer), 214–15

silos, 208

social experience and reward/threat response. *See* SCARF model

social status, 154–56, 173

spiritual advisor role, 38–39, 53–54

sports, 80, 103, 109, 119, 227

staffing vs. recruiting, 105

stakeholders, 168–69, 206–8, 216, 251–53. *See also* customers; decision nexus; employees; shareholders

Stanford Graduate School of Business, 12

status and reward/threat response, 154–56, 173

Status Syndrome, The (Marmot), 154

strategic partners, 252–53

strategic priorities, 54

strategist or chief technologist, 221

strategy
architect role of CEO, 36
communicating, 9, 44, 54–55
and decision making, 185–86
master strategist CEOs, 17–18, 176
mission, vision, and, 46, 72–73
planning, 47, 49–51, 55, 62
See also budgets

strategy consultants, 72

successes, credit for, 26

super VP CEO, 33

sustaining goals, 228

talent acquisition, 109–12, 122, 125, 169. *See also* recruiting
talent development (coaching), 35–36, 195–96, 227
Tate, Geoffrey, 87
teaching to clarify understanding, 267
team building, 126, 138, 155, 157, 158, 217–18
technologist or strategist, 221
telecom business model, 72–73
temp-addict CEOs, 124–25
Theory X and Theory Y management styles, 16–17, 19
Thompson, Scott, 21–22
threat/reward response. *See* SCARF model
titles and reward/threat responses, 155
top-down management approach, 165–66
total-control CEOs, 16–17
trade-offs, 46, 92–93, 222–23
trade shows, 37, 47
training
  for CEO position, 5–8, 37–38, 266
  for executives, 197
  experience and, 126–27
  for new employees, 117, 126–27, 131, 158, 169, 230–31
  taking time for, 123–24
Trammell, Joel

and AMD, 22, 83–86, 91, 137–38, 205–6
check bounced, 3
in England, 258
hotel in Las Vegas, 47–49
interviewing technique, 130, 132, 133
and Mother Teresa, 138–39
at Naval Nuclear Power School, 15, 51, 267
observing other CEOs, 31–32, 67–68, 218
and U.S. presidents, 58–59
See also NetQoS
transparency, 58, 64, 156–57, 172–73, 185–86, 228–29, 243–44
travel bans, 92, 93, 155
triage for decisions, 194–201
Truman, Harry, 26
"Trust, but verify" concept, 70–73, 233, 237. *See also* metrics
Twitter, 97
2R Manager, The (Friedes), 178–80
Tyco, 27
tyrant CEOs, budget, 86, 88

uncertainty, threat response to, 156–57
U.S. Navy, 15–16, 51
U.S. presidents, 58–59

value of job candidates, 134
value-performance grid, 169
values

alignment with corporate level
  policies, 171
creating and applying specific
  values, 167–70
and culture, 10, 45
of job candidates, 130–31
misalignment with, 146
overview, 173
prioritizing living the values,
  146–47
values-based vs. rule-based
  culture, 164–65, 170–71
vendors, managing relationships
  with, 84–85, 253
venture capital, 43–44, 78, 213
vision, 41–73
  adjusting, 71, 73
  alignment within the company,
    48–51, 53–55

  creating, 46
  owning, 9, 43–46
  planning, 47
Welch, Jack, 146–47
Whitman, Meg, 196–97
Whole Foods, 249
"Who Lives in the C-Suite?"
  (Harvard Business School), 220
"Why CEOs Fail" (Charan and
  Colvin), 50
Winning (Welch), 146–47
Winters, Dean, 70
Woods, Tiger, 128
writing to clarify thoughts, 266

Yahoo, 21–22, 114–15

Zhengfei, Ren, 250

ABOUT THE AUTHOR

Some boys dream of being a doctor or a fireman or an astronaut, but Joel Trammell always wanted to be a CEO. He's lived out that dream for more than 20 years as a successful entrepreneur and CEO of software companies. He is currently CEO of Khorus, which provides a business management system for CEOs. Joel is also chairman of the Austin Technology Council and cofounder and managing partner of the private equity firm Lone Rock Technology Group. In addition, he serves on the boards of several public, private, and nonprofit companies. Joel blogs at The American CEO.

Joel's leadership as a CEO has resulted in successful nine-figure acquisitions by two Fortune 500 companies. As CEO of the network management software firm NetQoS, he delivered 31 consecutive quarters of double-digit revenue growth and nearly $60 million in revenue. CA Technologies acquired the company in 2009, generating more than a 10x return on capital to its private equity investors. In 2010, Joel cofounded Cache IQ, a storage software company that NetApp acquired two years later.

Joel holds a bachelor's degree in electrical engineering from Louisiana Tech University and is a former instructor at the Naval Nuclear Power School. He lives in Austin, Texas, with his wife, Cathy, and has three children.